More Praise for *Depression, War, and Cold War*

"No American knows more about the link between the growth of Big Government and war than Higgs. . . . [I]n *Depression, War, and Cold War*, economic historian Higgs asks—and answers—such questions as why the Great Depression lasted so long, how the Cold War altered relations between government and big business and how Congress abetted the growth of the military-industrial complex."
  —*Pittsburgh Tribune-Review*

"A reading of the distressingly true facts and arguments in *Depression, War, and Cold War* raises fundamental questions as to what can be done: how to find and apply the necessary correctives to the popular and scholarly willingness to remain emotionally invested in erroneous explanations, and how to avoid responding to social and economic problems by waging destructive war. This most recent addition to Robert Higgs's body of work is an invaluable guide in that further quest."
  —*Journal of American Studies*

"*Depression, War, and Cold War* presents very interesting and important reinterpretations of the role of government in the economy since 1930."
  —**Stanley L. Engerman,** Munro Professor of Economics, University of Rochester

"*Depression, War, and Cold War* questions some of the traditional (Keynesian) assumptions, . . . Recommendable . . . convincing . . . ."
  —*Economics of Peace and Security Journal*

"*Depression, War, and Cold War* marks Higgs as one of the most important and original political analysts of our time. An intellectual tour de force!"
  —**Jonathan Bean,** Professor of History, Southern Illinois University

"Higgs's interpretive framework presents key challenges to both the macromonetary and Keynesian explanations of the American experience in the era of depression and world war."
  —*Journal of Markets & Morality*

"Higgs's book is a great anti-state tonic that is a direct challenge to government propaganda where history is shown to conform nicely to economic logic."
  —*Quarterly Journal of Austrian Economics*

"*Depression, War, and Cold War*. . . is one of those rare offerings that explicates the truth of things related to the inimical conflation of government, the military, and our congressional banditti these past seventy years or so."
  —*Human Events*

Depression, War, and Cold War

Challenging the Myths of Conflict and Prosperity

Robert Higgs

The INDEPENDENT INSTITUTE

Oakland, California

The Independent Institute
100 Swan Way, Oakland, CA 94621-1428
Telephone: 510-632-1366 · Fax: 510-568-6040
Email: info@independent.org
Website: www.independent.org

Cover Design: Christopher Chambers
Text Design and Composition: Leigh McLellan Design
Cover Art: © Gerrit Greve / Corbis

Library of Congress Cataloging-in-Publication Data

Higgs, Robert.
  Depression, war, and cold war : challenging the myths of conflict and prosperity /
Robert Higgs.
      p. cm.
  Originally published: Oxford University Press, c2006.
  Includes bibliographical references and index.
  ISBN-13: 978-1-59813-029-4 (alk. paper)
  ISBN-10: 1-59813-029-3 (alk. paper)
  1. United States--Economic conditions--20th century. 2. War--Economic aspects--
United States. 3. Depressions--1929--United States. I. Title.
  HC106.H535 2009
  330.973'092--dc22
                              2009011485

10 9 8 7 6 5 4 3 2 1   05 06 07 08 09

Contents

For Elizabeth,
who wouldn't let me give up on it.

Love is patient, love is kind.

Introduction

WARFARE IS THE QUINTESSENTIAL government activity. As a rule, a national government that is unprepared to defend itself against armed attackers cannot expect to retain control of its territory, resident population, and other resources. Hence, nearly all governments devote substantial efforts to maintaining effective armed forces. Military preparedness requires that resources be diverted from civilian uses. The organizing and financing of that reallocation, normally effected by some combination of market and nonmarket means, have important consequences for the performance of the entire economy, especially when the reallocation takes place on a large scale. With huge costs and benefits at stake, the nation's political and governmental systems invariably become actively and pervasively engaged in the process.

The political economy of actual warfare or "defense" (preparation for warfare) in modern times calls to mind the so-called military-industrial complex. In the United States, since World War II, a more illuminating concept is the "military-industrial-congressional complex" (MICC) [Higgs, 1990]. A closely related idea is that of the "iron triangle," which when applied to defense issues, denotes an arrangement composed of at least a military purchasing agency, a private supplier, and the congressional committees with oversight and appropriations authority (Adams, 1982). Around this institutional triad, other actors often congregate: consulting firms, trade and veterans' associations, scientific organizations, universities, think tanks, labor unions, "public interest" groups, and representatives of local governments, among others. From the pulling and hauling of all of these interest groups emerges the policies and actions that constitute the operation of the MICC. The general public's role is to bear the costs of the vast operation and to enjoy, so to speak, the benefits of "national security" in the event that the MICC succeeds in producing any of that hard-to-define output.

The workings of the MICC may be viewed usefully as a process in which the various actors, each relying on his own knowledge, opinions, and ideology, create the policies and take the actions that establish, maintain, and modify the military establishment. Conceptually, the analyst can understand better the connection between the actors and their ideas, on the one hand, and their actions, on the other hand, by analyzing the institutional context within which the actors take their actions. The prevailing institutions establish the actors' incentives and constraints, and they condition the expectations on which the actors rely as they make their decisions. Once established, institutional arrangements tend to persist; in the now familiar terminology, institutional "path dependency" prevails.

Scholars have devoted much effort to understanding the operation of the MICC and its consequences for the economy, polity, and society in which it is embedded. My own work along these lines began in the early 1980s and found substantial expression first in my book *Crisis and Leviathan: Critical Episodes in the Growth of Government* (1987, pp. 123–58, 196–236, 238, 241, 244–6, 250–1), which contains two long chapters on the political economy of the world wars, as well as some discussion of the Cold War. In that work, I was concerned with relating the nation's military experience to the long-term growth of the federal government's size, scope, and power and, in particular, with showing how various wartime actions and events had significant long-term consequences, ideological as well as institutional.

In the years since the publication of *Crisis and Leviathan,* I have continued to study and to write about a variety of related research topics. Ten of my more substantial recent essays are included in the present collection. Together, they extend and refine the ideas expressed in the 1987 book. These essays present new interpretations of familiar data, new evidence, and new statistical analyses. Most of them appeared originally in peer-reviewed journals. One (chapter 8) is published here for the first time in its present form (that is, with documentation).

In this introduction, I place the essays into a wider scholarly context by calling attention to the approaches, findings, and interpretations that others have presented. In some cases, my own views have changed somewhat as I have continued to study certain issues, such as the relation between World War II and the prosperity that resumed in 1946 after a decade and a half of depression and war. I also take this occasion to indicate how other research, which I either disregarded or did not know about when I made my own studies, bears on the reports gathered in the present volume.

The Great Depression and the New Deal continue to receive much attention from economists, economic and political historians, and other scholars.[1] In my own research, I focused first on the initial New Deal response to the Depression and on the enduring consequences of the New Deal policies for the growth of government (Higgs, 1987, pp. 159–95). Later, in the 1997 article reproduced as chapter 1 of this volume, I considered how the New Deal policies prolonged the Depression by creating "regime uncertainty" and how a number of related political changes brought about or hastened by the war diminished that uncertainty enough to permit a resumption of genuine prosperity (as opposed to the spurious "wartime prosperity") after the war ended.

Since writing the 1997 essay, I have become aware of a major body of evidence bearing on my "regime uncertainty" hypothesis: Gary Dean Best's *Pride, Prejudice, and Politics: Roosevelt versus Recovery, 1933–1938* (1991). The evidence that Best has compiled and organized adds significant weight to the views that I previously documented with regard to how business people and investors perceived the New Deal and the seriousness of its threat to the security of private property rights during the latter 1930s.

How does my interpretation relate to other interpretations of the duration of the Depression, especially to those that characterize the recovery as, like the preceding Great Contraction, little more than a macro-monetary phenomenon?[2] In brief, my interpretation complements, rather than substitutes for, those that focus on macro-monetary relations. I do not claim that the latter are wrong, only that, even if they are correct as far as they go, they are insufficient. If property rights are seriously up for grabs, no amount of pumping money into a depressed economy can bring about genuine complete economic recovery. From 1935 to 1940, such "up for grabs" conditions were precisely the ones that prevailed in the United States; hence, the unevenness and incompleteness of the recovery, even as late as 1940, more than ten years after the onset of the Great Contraction.

Moreover, my interpretation proves its value decisively when one approaches the task, not merely as one of explaining the slow recovery between 1933 and 1941, but as one of explaining several related aspects of a longer span of economic events (e.g., private output, long-term civilian investment, and unemployment) between 1935 and 1948. My interpretation shows how we can incorporate a defensible view of the wartime economy into our understanding of both the incomplete late-1930s recovery *and* the enormously successful reconversion to civilian production between 1945 and 1947. In this more ambitious endeavor, the first five chapters of this volume constitute essential pieces of one big puzzle, offering at once a new view of the prolongation of the Depression, a new view of the nature of the war production "boom" and a new view of the transition from wartime command economy to postwar civilian prosperity—all within a single interpretive framework. In the light of these chapters, the old (and still widely accepted) view of how "the war got the economy out of the depression" must be abandoned.

Hugh Rockoff has long been a major contributor to the economic analysis of World War II.[3] In his recent work, Rockoff takes into account the 1992 article (reprinted here as chapter 3) in which I first made a serious effort to challenge the concept of "wartime prosperity" and to link my interpretation of the war economy to an exploratory interpretation of why the postwar transition took place so smoothly. (The essays that appear here as chapters 1 and 5 give a much more complete and coherent account of that smooth postwar transition.) Rockoff, however, most notably in his important 1998 essay, continues to resist a complete acceptance of my interpretation and to criticize certain aspects of it. Readers who want to hear "both sides of the story" will need to consult Rockoff's work. Ultimately, that work and my own, I believe, will be seen far more as complements than as substitutes. Our major difference pertains to our interpretation of real output changes during the war. Whereas I believe that the conventional measures of those changes, as given by the standard National Income and Product Accounts figures, are well-nigh worthless, Rockoff seems much more inclined to credit the picture that those figures paint.

Another new aspect of my interpretation is that, even though the economy had returned to its secular trend of potential output in 1948, the events of the Depression and the war had the effect of reducing the trend rate of growth between the business cycle peaks of 1929 and 1948. Therefore, the economy in 1948, though operating near its maximum capacity to produce, was producing considerably less than it might have produced had it been spared the preceding policy-induced distortions, especially to the magnitude and structure of capital accumulation, occasioned by the Depression and the war. Additional analysis of the wartime distortions of the capital structure, a neglected aspect of the government's wartime "socialization of investment," appears in my most recent work, included here as chapter 4.

My 1994 article reprinted as chapter 6 of this collection provides an analytical survey of the Cold War political economy, as seen in a macroeconomic perspective. A recently published volume, *Atomic Audit: The Costs and Consequences of U.S. Nuclear Weapons since 1940,* edited by Stephen I. Schwartz (1998) makes a major contribution to the related literature, and readers will do well to use the findings of the ambitious collaborative research reported in the Schwartz volume to supplement my own survey. Other notable recent contributions to this literature include the collaborative volume on *The Political Economy of Military Spending in the United States,* edited by Alex Mintz (1992); Derek Leebaert's fact-filled interpretive history of the Cold War, *The Fifty-Year Wound: The True Price of America's Cold War Victory* (2002); and Aaron L. Friedberg's extended argument that, in spite of the voracious demands that the MICC made on the U.S. economy during the Cold War, things might have been even worse, but for the remnants of resistance in the civil society (Friedberg, 2000).

Some readers of the 1994 article have complained that, because of the emphasis I placed on the official control and manipulation of relevant information and the exploitation of both real and purported crises, I gave short shrift to the "actual threats" that the United States faced during the Cold War. To clarify my position in this regard, I affirm that I do not now, and never did before, suppose the Soviet regime to have been a benign one in any respect. Ronald Reagan spoke a simple truth when he called it an "evil empire." To recognize the nasty character of the Soviet regime, however, hardly settles where responsibility lay for the various dimensions of the Cold War, especially for the arms races that formed its core process, creating grave threats to humanity and causing technological and economic distortions that severely damaged the U.S. economy and utterly doomed the backward, inherently ill-fated Soviet command economy. Moreover, if the Soviet government did the devil's work, so, on many occasions, did the U.S. government and its allies. Not the least of the self-damage was the transformation of the executive branch of the federal government into a secretive, highly discretionary, often ill-advised, and badly informed organization that was far too dedicated to attempting the futile task of running the whole world. The best thing one can say about U.S. involvement in the Cold War is that one can easily imagine how it might have turned out even worse, indeed, catastrophically worse. Its termination has allowed people the world over to breathe easier, although its legacies, including vast stocks of nuclear weapons and materials—potential "loose nukes" and accidents waiting to happen—continue to pose a grave threat to humanity.

Chapters 7 and 8 focus on the role of Congress in the MICC. Since those essays were written, a number of related books and articles have been published. Especially important are the books by James M. Lindsay, *Congress and Nuclear Weapons* (1991), and Kenneth R. Mayer, *The Political Economy of Defense Contracting* (1991). These works add much detail to the views expressed earlier by Lindsay and Mayer at a conference I organized in 1987.[4]

The essay that appears as chapter 9 of this collection, on the extraordinary profits of defense contractors in the 1970s and 1980s, apparently has gone unchallenged. These findings can now be placed in a larger context, however, by drawing on a recently published book by Stuart D. Brandes, *Warhogs: A History of War Profits in America* (1997).

Chapter 10 pertains to the relation between the actual change of defense spending, on the one hand, and public opinion about the desired change, on the other hand. This chapter compresses into testable econometric form some of the ideas about ideology and information expressed in my 1987 book and in the 1994 essay that appears as chapter 6 in the present collection. In the public opinion chapter, I show that my index of the "public opinion balance" can explain statistically nearly all of the annual variance in the rate of change of defense spending during the latter half of the Cold War. The inclusion of this work in this collection serves to clarify and expand my previous work on the relations between public opinion and defense spending during the Cold War, especially that reported in my 1994 essay.

The topics dealt with in the essays included in this collection continue to attract much research effort, and no doubt we shall continue to learn more about these subjects with the passage of time and the completion of other research now in progress. I myself continue to work in this area from time to time, as opportunities permit. In my dreams, I see myself writing a fresh, coherent treatise in which the materials contained in the present collection, along with many other materials, would serve as inputs. Recognizing that this dream may never be realized, however, it seems to me that an interim report of the sort this collection composes might well serve a useful purpose for students and researchers in political economy and history. With regard to the political economy of war and defense, synthetic works are few, and those that do appear are often eccentric or tendentious. Researchers who delve into the details often disdain writing works of broad interpretation, and writers who do paint with a broad brush often fail to appreciate adequately the various devils that reside in the details. My hope is that by bringing together these essays, each of which involved a considerable amount of getting my hands dirty, readers will begin to see that these trees do add up to a forest, that the individual studies, laid back to back, do tell a coherent overarching tale.

Notes

1. See Bordo, Goldin, and White (1998); "Symposium: The Great Depression" (1993); Hall and Ferguson (1998); Couch and Shughart II (1998); Wheeler (1998); Kennedy (1999); and Smiley (2002).
2. See Friedman and Schwartz (1963)—but see pp. 495–6, where Friedman and Schwartz argue along lines very similar to my own. See also Romer (1992).
3. For example, *Drastic Measures: A History of Wage and Price Controls in the United States* (1984); "The Paradox of Planning in World War II" (1996); and "The United States: From Ploughshares to Swords" (1998).
4. Essays by Lindsay and Mayer appear in my edited volume *Arms, Politics, and the Economy* (Higgs, 1990).

References

Adams, Gordon. (1982) *The Politics of Defense Contracting: The Iron Triangle.* New Brunswick: Transaction Books.

Atomic Audit: The Costs and Consequences of U.S. Nuclear Weapons since 1940, edited by Stephen I. Schwartz. (1998) Washington: Brookings Institution Press.

Best, Gary Dean. (1991) *Pride, Prejudice, and Politics: Roosevelt versus Recovery, 1933–1938.* New York: Praeger.

Bordo, Michael D., Claudia Goldin, and Eugene N. White, eds. (1998) *The Defining Moment: The Great Depression and the American Economy in the Twentieth Century.* Chicago: University of Chicago Press.

Brandes, Stuart D. (1997) *Warhogs: A History of War Profits in America.* Lexington: University Press of Kentucky.

Couch Jim F., and William F. Shughart II. (1998) *The Political Economy of the New Deal* Northampton, Mass.: Edward Elgar, 1998.

Friedberg, Aaron L. (2000) *In the Shadow of the Garrison State: America's Anti-Statism and Its Cold War Grand Strategy.* Princeton: Princeton University Press.

Friedman, Milton, and Anna J. Schwartz. (1963) *A Monetary History of the United States, 1867–1960.* Princeton: Princeton University Press, pp. 493–545.

Hall, Thomas E., and J. David Ferguson. (1998) *The Great Depression: An International Disaster of Perverse Economic Policies.* Ann Arbor: University of Michigan Press.

Higgs, Robert. (1987) *Crisis and Leviathan: Critical Episodes in the Growth of Government.* New York: Oxford University Press.

Higgs, Robert. (1990) Introduction: Fifty Years of Arms, Politics, and the Economy. In *Arms, Politics, and the Economy: Historical and Contemporary Perspectives,* edited by Robert Higgs. New York: Holmes & Meier for the Independent Institute, pp. xv–xxxii.

Kennedy, David M. (1999) *Freedom from Fear: The American People in Depression and War, 1929–1945.* New York: Oxford University Press.

Leebaert, Derek. (2002) *The Fifty-Year Wound: The True Price of America's Cold War Victory.* Boston: Little, Brown.

Lindsay, James M. (1991) *Congress and Nuclear Weapons.* Baltimore: Johns Hopkins Press.

Mayer, Kenneth R. (1991) *The Political Economy of Defense Contracting.* New Haven: Yale University Press.

The Political Economy of Military Spending in the United States, edited by Alex Mintz.(1992) New York: Routledge.

Rockoff, Hugh. (1984) *Drastic Measures: A History of Wage and Price Controls in the United States.* New York: Cambridge University Press.

Rockoff, Hugh. (1996) The Paradox of Planning in World War II. NBER Working Paper Series on Historical Factors in Long Run Growth. Historical Paper 83. Cambridge, Mass.: National Bureau of Economic Research.

Rockoff, Hugh. (1998) The United States: From Ploughshares to Swords. In *The Economics of World War II: Six Great Powers in International Comparison.* Cambridge, England: Cambridge University Press, pp. 81–121.

Romer, Christina D. (1992) What Ended the Great Depression? *Journal of Economic History* 52 (December): 757–84.

Smiley, Gene. (2002) *Rethinking the Great Depression.* Chicago: Ivan R. Dee.

Symposium: The Great Depression [with essays by Christina D. Romer, Robert A. Margo, Charles W. Calomiris, and Peter Temin]. (1993) *Journal of Economic Perspectives* 7 (Spring): 19–102.

Wheeler, Mark, ed. (1998) *The Economics of the Great Depression.* Kalamazoo, Mich.: W. E. Upjohn Institute for Employment Research.

1

Regime Uncertainty

Why the Great Depression Lasted So Long
and Why Prosperity Resumed after the War

> There have been endless analyses of individual
> economic policies; there has been little attention
> to changes in policy regimes.   *Peter Temin*

THE GREAT DEPRESSION is one of the most studied
topics in American economic history, and one about which scholars remain
in serious disagreement. Perhaps the topic is too big, and its study would
be more fruitful if it were broken down into subtopics. Thus, one might
consider separately the causes of the Great Contraction, the unparalleled
macroeconomic collapse between 1929 and 1933; the Great Duration, the
twelve successive years during which the economy operated substantially
below its capacity to produce; and the Great Escape, generally understood
to have been brought about, directly or indirectly, by American participation in World War II. The Great Contraction has received the most
attention, and its investigators show no signs of reaching a consensus.
The Great Duration has received somewhat less study, though still a good
deal, and the range of views among students of this aspect of the Great
Depression is perhaps slightly narrower. Regarding the Great Escape, until
recently, there seemed to be hardly any disagreement.

In an essay published in 1992, however, I called into question the prevailing understanding of the Great Escape by challenging the reality of
"wartime prosperity" during World War II. In this chapter, I extend that
argument, attempting to shed new light on the Great Duration and the

Great Escape. For present purposes, I make no attempt to explain the Great Contraction, merely recognizing that it occurred and that it had certain aspects, including, most notably, a collapse of private investment.

In the earlier essay, I argued that a return to genuine prosperity—the true Great Escape—occurred only after World War II ended, not during the war, as suggested by the idea of wartime prosperity. During the war years, the economy operated essentially as a command system, and as a result, the normal measures of macroeconomic performance (e.g., gross domestic product [GDP], the price level, and the rate of unemployment) were either conceptually or statistically incomparable with corresponding measures before and after the period subject to the wartime distortions.

In my understanding, one simply cannot speak with confidence about such matters as, for example, the rate of growth of real GDP or the rate of inflation from year to year during the period 1941–47. During this time, vast quantities of munitions were produced, along with a restricted set of price-controlled civilian goods, some of which were physically rationed (Krug, 1945; Harris, 1945). Comprehensive price controls, gradually imposed in 1941 and 1942, were not abandoned for good until late in 1946 (U.S. Bureau of the Budget, 1946, pp. 235–73; Rockoff, 1984, pp. 85–176). Because the actual wartime prices could not even have approximated the prices of an economy in full competitive equilibrium, they cannot serve as appropriate weights for the construction of a meaningful national product aggregate. Unemployment virtually disappeared as conscription, directly and indirectly, pulled more than 12 million potential workers into the armed forces and millions of others into draft-exempt employment, but under the prevailing conditions, the disappearance of unemployment can hardly be interpreted as a valid index of economic prosperity (Higgs, 1992, pp. 42–44).

Given the institutional discontinuity created by the wartime command economy, our understanding of the period from the late 1930s to the late 1940s, so far as it depends on the usual macroeconomic measures, must necessarily contain a huge gap. To insist on using the standard measures, notwithstanding the complete evaporation of their institutional underpinnings, would mislead us far more than frankly facing up to the fact that, for the war years, the usual measures have no real substance. One can compute them, of course, by making a great many assumptions and swallowing hard. But the wartime numbers that look so solid and comparable sitting there in the middle of a long time series are essentially arbitrary.

What we can say with confidence is that, as of 1940, the economy had not yet recovered fully from the Great Depression; when the meaningfulness of the macroeconomic indexes began to fade, in the second half of 1940, the Great Escape had not yet been completed. For the next five years the war-command system foreclosed conventional comparable measurements of the performance of the macro economy. Then, from mid-1945 until perhaps as late as the first quarter of 1947, the demobilization, reconversion, and decontrol of the economy continued to muddy the macroeconomic waters. Finally, certainly by 1948, and probably by 1947, economic conditions were sufficiently free of wartime distortions and their postwar carry-overs that we can confidently make comparisons with, say, 1940 or earlier years. What we see then, of course, is that the postwar economy enjoyed a high degree of prosperity, whether judged by its low unemployment rate or by its high real GDP, relative to the corresponding index for any prewar year.

We know, then, that sometime during the period 1941–47, the economy made its Great Escape. In my 1992 essay, I argued that the war years themselves witnessed a deterioration of economic well-being, in the sense of consumer satisfaction, either present (via private consumption) or prospective (via accumulation of capital with the potential to enhance future civilian consumption), and that the Great Escape actually occurred during the demobilization period, especially during its first year, when most of the wartime controls were eliminated and most of the resources used for munitions production and military activities were returned to civilian production.

In light of the foregoing observations, we may justifiably adopt the following chronology: Great Depression, 1930–40; transition to the war economy, 1940–41; war-command economy, 1942–45; demobilization, reconversion, and decontrol (the true Great Escape), 1945–46; and postwar prosperity, 1946 and beyond.

I shall argue here that the economy remained in the depression as late as 1940 because private investment had never recovered sufficiently after its collapse during the Great Contraction. During the war, private investment fell to much lower levels, and the federal government itself became the chief investor, directing investment into building up the nation's capacity to produce munitions. After the war ended, private investment, for the first time since the 1920s, rose to, and remained at, levels sufficient to create a prosperous and normally growing economy.

I shall argue further that the insufficiency of private investment from 1935 through 1940 reflected a pervasive uncertainty among investors about the security of their property rights in their capital and its prospective returns. This uncertainty arose, especially, though not exclusively, from the character of the actions of the federal government and the nature of the Roosevelt administration during the so-called Second New Deal, from 1935 to 1940. Starting in 1940, the makeup of FDR's administration changed substantially as pro-business men began to replace dedicated New Dealers in many positions, including most of the offices of high authority in the war-command economy. Congressional changes in the elections from 1938 onward reinforced the movement away from the New Deal, strengthening the so-called Conservative Coalition. From 1941 through 1945, however, the less hostile character of the administration expressed itself in decisions about how to manage the war-command economy; therefore, with private investment replaced by direct government investment, the diminished fears of investors could not give rise to a revival of private investment spending. In 1945, the death of Roosevelt and the succession of Truman and his administration completed the shift from a political regime that investors perceived as full of uncertainty to one in which they felt much more confident about the security of their private property rights. Sufficiently sanguine for the first time since 1929, and finally freed from government restraints on private investment for civilian purposes, investors set in motion the postwar investment boom that powered the economy's return to sustained prosperity, notwithstanding the drastic reduction of federal government spending from its extraordinarily elevated wartime levels.

What Happened to Investment?

As economic historian Alexander Field (1992) has written, "no coherent account of the depth and duration of the Depression can ignore the causes of fluctuations in investment spending" (p. 786). Figure 1-1 shows both real GDP and real gross private investment (GPI) from 1929 to 1950.[1] As Figure 1-1 shows, both real GDP *(bars, left-side scale)* and real GPI *(thin line, right-side scale)* plunged from 1929 to a trough in either 1932 or 1933, the former by 29 percent and the latter by 84 percent. Both variables recovered rapidly after 1933: by 1937, real national product had regained 96 percent of its loss in the Great Contraction, and investment had recouped 64 percent of its loss. The "Roosevelt recession" of 1937–38 cut short the recovery: real GDP fell by 4 percent in 1938, and gross investment fell by 34 percent. Real national product recovered quickly after 1938, and in 1939, it finally exceeded the previous peak value, which occurred in 1929. (Of course, this level of GDP was no longer a "full-employment" level; the rate

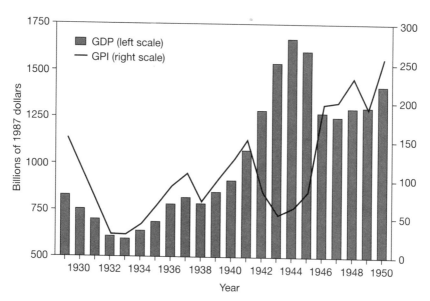

Figure 1-1. Gross domestic product (billions of 1987 dollars) and gross private investment (billions of 1987 dollars), 1929–50.

of unemployment [Darby variant] was 11.3 percent.)[2] Investment recovered more slowly. Even in 1941, when stimulus from the defense mobilization had become substantial, real GPI had not quite regained its 1929 level. For what the data are worth, they show that private investment plunged to very low levels during the years when the United States was a declared belligerent. After the war ended, however, real GPI exceeded its previous (1929) peak substantially; it stood 23 percent higher, even during the recession year 1949. Both real GDP and real GPI data show that during the period 1946–50, the Great Escape had been made.

Figure 1-2 shows an alternative depiction of the course of private investment spending (along with government spending, for comparison).[3] This approach, using current-dollar investment as a proportion of current-dollar GDP, avoids the distortions potentially affecting the data shown in figure 1-1 because of the index number problem or because of measurement errors

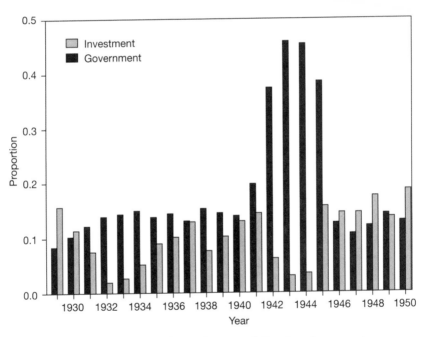

Figure 1-2. Government purchases (current dollars) and gross private investment (current dollars) relative to gross domestic product, 1929–50.

in the deflators. As figure 1-2 shows, GPI plunged from almost 16 percent of GDP in 1929 to less than 2 percent in 1932; it recovered to 13 percent in 1937, before falling again in the recession of 1938; and as late as 1941, it stood at only 14 percent. During the war years, private investment ratios ranged from 3 to 6 percent. From 1946 through 1950, they ranged from 14 to 19 percent and averaged 16 percent—the same as in 1929.

One appreciates even better the deficiency of investment in the 1930s by considering net, rather than gross, investment. From 1929 to 1941, the capital consumption allowance amounted to 8 to 10 percent of GNP (U.S. Bureau of the Census, 1975, p. 234, Series F144–145). In 1929, when GPI was $16.2 billion, net investment was $8.3 billion. Net investment fell precipitously to $2.3 billion in 1930, and then became negative during each of the following five years. In the period 1931–35, net investment totaled *minus* $18.3 billion. After reviving to positive levels in 1936 and 1937, net investment again fell into the negative range in 1938 (–$0.8 billion) before resuming its recovery. For the eleven years from 1930 to 1940, net private investment totaled *minus* $3.1 billion. Only in 1941 did net private investment ($9.7 billion) exceed the 1929 amount.[4]

The data leave little doubt. During the 1930s, private investment remained at depths never plumbed in any other decade for which data exist. Stimulus from the defense buildup increased it in 1940 and 1941; then wartime controls curtailed it from 1942 through 1945. Only in 1946 and the following years did private investment reach and remain at levels consistent with a prosperous and growing economy.

A Hypothesis about Why Investment Remained Depressed

Eleven years is an extraordinarily long time for investment to remain drastically subpar, so it is plausible that the long doldrums had some extraordinary cause—in any event, that is the idea explored here. Nothing in this investigation is meant to test, refute, or otherwise shed light directly on any of the many macroeconomic models that have been advanced over the years to explain business fluctuations in general or the Great Depression in particular. Rather, my inquiry may be viewed as complementary to any analysis that holds the failure of private investment to revive fully to have been at least partially responsible for the Great Duration.

Many such explanations have been advanced. For example, economist Lester Chandler (1970) concluded in a widely cited book: "The failure of the New Deal to bring about an adequate revival of private investment is the key to its failure to achieve a complete and self-sustaining recovery of output and employment" (p. 132). In very similar language, economic historian Peter Fearon (1987) observed: "Perhaps the New Deal's greatest failure lay in its inability to generate the revival in private investment that would have led to greater output and more jobs" (p. 208). Obviously, regardless of what else might have been happening, no one could expect a resumption of prosperity when the economy—its labor force continuing to grow—went more than a decade without any increase of the capital stock.

My hypothesis supplements my previous argument to the effect that the Great Escape did not occur until after the end of the war. Indeed, the argument I shall make ties together events during the latter half of the Depression and events during the war years to arrive at an explanation of why investment finally recovered fully only after VJ-Day, creating sustained prosperity and normal economic growth thereafter.

The hypothesis is a variant of an old idea: The willingness of business people to invest requires a sufficiently healthy state of "business confidence," and the Second New Deal ravaged the requisite confidence (Krooss, 1970, pp. 199–201; Collins, 1981, pp. 23–52; Fearon, 1987, pp. 209–11; Brinkley, 1995, pp. 31–34). Of course, one difficulty with the hypothesis is that business confidence is a vague notion, and one for which no conventional empirical measure has been developed. I shall try to narrow the concept somewhat and to show that one can shed empirical light on it by using the findings of systematic opinion surveys and evidence on the behavior of investors in the financial markets.

To narrow the concept of business confidence, I adopt the interpretation that business people may be more or less "uncertain about the regime" by which I mean the likelihood that investors' private property rights in their capital and the income it yields will be attenuated further by government action. Such attenuations can arise from many sources, ranging from simple tax-rate increases, to the imposition of new kinds of taxes, to outright confiscation of private property. Many intermediate threats can arise from various sorts of regulation, for instance, of securities markets, labor markets, and product markets. In any event, the security of private property rights rests not so much on the letter of the law as on the character of the government that enforces, or threatens, presumptive rights.

> What does provide some degree of protection . . . is the political system, together with the economic pressure groups that ensure that the state does not go "too far" in interfering with the owner's control over assets. This politically determined thin line may be understood as the real definition of property rights conferred by the state, as distinct from the somewhat fictitious legal notion of property rights. How broadly property rights are defined in this real sense and how effective states' (largely nonlegal) commitment is to their security is a more serious problem than the issue of legal protections against the more traditional form of takings. (Rapaczynski, 1996, p. 93)

As Lee J. Alston, Thrainn Eggertsson, and Douglass C. North (1996) have recently observed, echoing venerable wisdom, "In an economy where entrepreneurship is decentralized, economic actors will hold back on long-term investments unless the state makes credible commitments to honor its contracts and respect individual ownership rights" (p. 4).

It would be easy to dismiss an investigation of, first, increased regime uncertainty as a cause of the investment drought that contributed to the Great Duration and, second, reduced regime uncertainty as a cause of the investment surge that propelled the Great Escape. In retrospect, it seems hyperbolic to put much weight on the fears of investors in the latter half of the 1930s that the regime might soon undergo changes that would seriously jeopardize their private property rights—after all, we know quite well that the U.S. economy did not fall into outright fascism, socialism, or some other variant of government takeover. Roosevelt, we now know, never became a dictator along the lines of his contemporaries Stalin, Mussolini, and Hitler; the New Dealers were no Brown Shirts. But what seems so obvious to us in retrospect had a quite different appearance to many contemporaries (Flynn, 1944, pp. 166–258; Roose, 1954, pp. 209–31, 250; Krooss, 1970, pp. 159–209; Garraty, 1973). No one knew for sure what the future held. According to economic historian Herman Krooss (1970), "Business leaders sincerely believed that the government was in evil hands . . . and preparing the way for socialism, communism, or some other variety of anti-Americanism" (p. 197). As I shall demonstrate shortly, the possibility that the United States might undergo an extreme regime shift seemed to many investors in the late 1930s and early 1940s not only possible, but likely.

In recent years, economists have developed a number of models incorporating uncertainty more explicitly into the analysis of investment. This new approach recognizes that much investment not only entails irreversibilities or sunk costs, but can be delayed. Given these attributes, economist Robert Pindyck (1991) reports, "investment spending on an aggregate level may be highly sensitive to risk in various forms . . . [including] uncertainty over future tax and regulatory policy." One implication is that "a major cost of political and economic instability may be its depressing effect on investment" (p. 1141; see also pp. 1110–12). As Pindyck notes, "[m]ost econometric models of aggregate economic activity ignore the role of risk, or deal with it only implicitly. A more explicit treatment of risk may help to better explain economic fluctuations, and especially investment spending" (p. 1142). Although I make no attempt here to estimate an econometric model incorporating uncertainty, the approach of my analysis is, in its substance, compatible with the approach of the new investment models.

At the same time, it is also compatible with the views expressed by many economists of an earlier generation, including Joseph A. Schumpeter (1939), who noted "how unrealistic any theory of investment opportunity is which leaves the political factor out of account" (p. 1043), and Kenneth D. Roose (1954), who argued that the relations of business and government during the latter half of the 1930s were "infected with such hatreds and distrusts" that "the risks and uncertainties of investment decision were seriously increased" (p. 224). Roose concluded that "the uncertainties created by government policies as to the nature of the economic system which was evolving undoubtedly reduced the number of long-term investment commitments" (p. 232). In their monumental monetary history, Milton Friedman and Anna Jacobson Schwartz (1963) endorsed Roose's assessment (pp. 495–96).

The Sources of Regime Uncertainty

Despite the encroachments of taxation, regulation, and other government action at all levels that had been occurring for half a century or more (Hughes, 1991, pp. 92–135; Higgs, 1987, pp. 77–167; Keller, 1990), as late as 1932, business people in general and investors in particular remained— certainly in retrospect—relatively free of major threats to the prevailing regime of private property rights.

Then, during the next two presidential terms, the Roosevelt administration proposed and Congress enacted an unparalleled outpouring of laws significantly attenuating private property rights (Leuchtenburg, 1963; Badger, 1989). State legislatures followed suit with their "little New Deals" (Leuchtenburg, 1963, pp. 198–88; Badger, 1989, pp. 283–84) and relentless increases in taxes (Brownlee, 1996, pp. 83, 85). Table 1-1 lists only some of the more important federal enactments attenuating or threatening private property rights. As financial economist Benjamin Anderson ([1949]1979), an astute contemporary observer, remarked, "The impact of these multitudinous measures—industrial, agricultural, financial, monetary, and other—upon a bewildered industrial and financial community was extraordinarily heavy" (p. 357).

Anderson was hardly the only contemporary economist convinced that the New Deal measures caused the Great Duration. Schumpeter, one of the world's leading authorities on business cycles, wrote in the first edition of his *Capitalism, Socialism and Democracy,* published in 1942:

Table 1-1. Selected acts of Congress substantially attenuating
or threatening private property rights, 1933–1940

1933

Agricultural Adjustment Act
National Industrial Recovery Act
Emergency Banking Relief Act
Banking Act of 1933
Federal Securities Act
Tennessee Valley Authority Act
Gold Repeal Joint Resolution
Farm Credit Act
Emergency Railroad Transportation Act
Emergency Farm Mortgage Act
Home Owners Loan Corporation Act

1934

Securities Exchange Act
Gold Reserve Act
Communications Act
Railway Labor Act

1935

Bituminous Coal Stabilization Act
Connally ("hot oil") Act
Revenue Act of 1935
National Labor Relations Act
Social Security Act
Public Utilities Holding Company Act
Banking Act of 1935
Emergency Relief Appropriations Act
Farm Mortgage Moratorium Act

1936

Soil Conservation & Domestic
    Allotment Act
Federal Anti-Price Discrimination Act
Revenue Act of 1936

1937

Bituminous Coal Act
Revenue Act of 1937
National Housing Act
Enabling (Miller-Tydings) Act

1938

Agricultural Adjustment Act
Fair Labor Standards Act
Civil Aeronautics Act
Food, Drug & Cosmetic Act

1939

Administrative Reorganization Act

1940

Investment Company Act
Revenue Act of 1940
Second Revenue Act of 1940

The subnormal recovery to 1935, the subnormal prosperity to 1937 and the slump after that are easily accounted for by the difficulties incident to the adaptation to a new fiscal policy, new labor legislation and a general change in the attitude of government to private enterprise all of which can . . . be distinguished from the working of the productive apparatus as such. . . . [S]o extensive and rapid a change of the social scene naturally affects productive performance for a time, and so much the most ardent New Dealer must *and also can* admit. I for one do not see how it would otherwise be possible to account for the fact that this country which had the best chance of recovering quickly was precisely the one to experience the most unsatisfactory recovery. (Schumpeter, 1962, pp. 64–5, emphasis in original)

Schumpeter had elaborated on this interpretation three years earlier in his treatise *Business Cycles* (1939, pp. 1037–50), insisting that "the individual measures obviously tended to reinforce each other" (p. 1045) in their discouraging effect on investors.

Taken together, the many menacing New Deal measures, especially those from 1935 onward, gave business people and investors good reason to fear that the market economy might not survive in anything like its traditional form and that even more drastic developments, perhaps even some kind of collectivist dictatorship, could not be ruled out entirely (Roose 1954, pp. 65–69). As Schumpeter (1939) remarked of businessmen in the late 1930s, "They *are* not only, but they *feel* threatened. They realize that they are on trial before judges who have the verdict in their pocket beforehand, that an increasing part of public opinion is impervious to their point of view, and that any particular indictment will, if successfully met, at once be replaced by another" (p. 1046).

One of the chief ironies of the Roosevelt administration's policies is that "for the most part the New Deal relied on private investment to stimulate recovery yet its rhetoric precluded the private confidence to invest" (Badger, 1989, p. 116). Early in his presidency, Roosevelt took seriously "the risk of worsening the economic depression by undermining business confidence and investment," but by 1935, he "had gained confidence in the prospects for economic recovery and was less worried about a business backlash" (Brownlee, 1996, pp. 71–72). Under political pressure from radical challengers, such as Huey Long, Francis Townsend, Father Charles Coughlin, and others, FDR had begun to voice heightened hostility to investors as early as 1934 (Leuchtenburg, 1963, pp. 95–117). In 1935, Roosevelt "lost patience with corporation leaders, and younger New Dealers came to the fore who shared his reluctance to make concessions to conservative business opinion. . . . The men around Roosevelt were now highly skeptical of the ability of business to act in the national interest" (Badger, 1989, pp. 96–97). Ignoring the opposition of business groups, such as the U.S. Chamber of Commerce and the National Association of Manufacturers, in 1935, FDR supported the Social Security Act, the National Labor Relations Act, the Banking Act, and the Public Utilities Holding Company Act, as well as a host of other laws, including soak-the-rich taxes, opposed by most business groups.

Accepting his party's nomination for the presidency in 1936, Roosevelt railed against the "economic royalists" who were allegedly seeking a "new industrial dictatorship" (quoted by Leuchtenburg, 1963, pp. 183–84). Privately, he opined that "businessmen as a class were stupid, that newspapers were just as bad; nothing would win more votes than to have the press and the business community aligned against him" (Leuchtenburg, 1963, p. 183). Just before the election of 1936, in an address at Madison Square Garden, he fulminated against the magnates of "organized money . . . [who were] unanimous in their hate for me," and declared, "I welcome their hatred." To uproarious applause, he threatened: "I should like to have it said of my second Administration that in it these forces met their master" (quoted by Leuchtenburg, 1963, p. 184).

In 1935, 1936, and 1937, the Roosevelt administration requested tax legislation aimed at punishing the wealthy. The so-called Wealth Tax of 1935 ultimately included a graduated corporation income tax, a tax on intercorporate dividends, increases of estate and gift taxes, and increases of surtaxes on incomes greater than $50,000 that ranged up to a top rate of 75 percent. In 1936, FDR sought to tax retained corporate earnings in lieu of all other corporate income taxes. Congress approved a graduated surtax on corporate earnings, based on the percentage of earnings retained, and increased the tax rate on intercorporate dividends. The overall effect was to raise corporate income taxes. The 1937 tax act closed a variety of "loopholes," including the use of personal holding companies to avoid taxes.[5] These soak-the-rich efforts left little doubt that the president and his administration intended to push through Congress everything they could to extract wealth from the high-income earners who were responsible for making the bulk of the nation's decisions about private investment. According to economic historian Elliot Brownlee (1985, p. 417), "the tax reform of 1935–37, more than any other aspect of the New Deal, . . . stimulated business hostility to Roosevelt. . . . [B]usiness opponents of New Deal tax reform charged that Roosevelt's taxes, particularly the undistributed profits tax, had caused the recession [of 1937–38] by discouraging investment" (p. 417).[6]

Although Congress reversed some of the tax provisions that were most offensive to investors in 1938 and 1939, Roosevelt continued to rail against businessmen, who, as he said in a 1938 speech, "will fight to the last ditch to retain such autocratic control over the industry and finances of the country as they now possess" (quoted by Brownlee, 1996, p. 81). Although historians emphasize the president's defeats with respect to taxation in the late 1930s, contemporary businessmen must have appreciated the reality of increased taxation: In fiscal 1940, with the Depression still lingering, the federal government collected 57 percent more total revenue than it had in the prosperous year 1927 (U.S. Bureau of the Census, 1975, p. 1122, Series Y568).

Meanwhile, other developments heightened the perceived threat to established private property rights. Early in 1937, FDR brought forth his plan to pack the Supreme Court. Although he failed to gain congressional support for this scheme, which many perceived as "a naked bid for dictatorship" (Anderson [1949] 1979, p. 430), the intimidated justices, weary of public contempt and worried that their constitutional power might be undercut, finally capitulated. Beginning in 1937, the court abandoned its employment of the doctrine of substantive due process, under which, since the 1890s, it had struck down state and federal government interferences with private contracting. Subsequently, the court, increasingly composed of FDR's appointees, upheld state minimum wage laws, the Social Security Act, the National Labor Relations Act—indeed, the entire panoply of New Deal regulatory measures—under an interpretation of the Interstate Commerce Clause so sweeping that it embraced virtually all economic activity (Siegan, 1980, pp. 184–204; Ely, 1992, pp. 119–34). In the face of this "monumental change in the Court's attitude toward property rights and entrepreneurial liberty" (Ely, 1992, p. 132), investors correctly perceived that the strongest bulwark against the government juggernaut had evaporated, exposing them to whatever legislative and executive incursions the political process might generate.

Simultaneously, wielding the new powers granted them by the National Labor Relations Act, labor unions carried out their most rapid surge of organizing. Membership rose from 3.8 million in 1935 to between 8.7 and 10.2 million (sources differ) in 1941—the latter representing 28 percent of non-agricultural employment (U.S. Bureau of the Census, 1975, pp. 177–78). As union power increased, unions became a major force in the New Deal coalition, and Democratic politicians and office-holders across the country increasingly deferred to them. In the starkest demonstration of their new power, unionists began sit-down strikes, occupying employers' facilities and refusing either to work or to leave until their demands were met. President Roosevelt declined to use force to eject the sit-down strikers; likewise, many state and local officials would not enforce the law against this willful trespassing on private property. As historian William E. Leuchtenburg (1963) observed, "Property-minded citizens were scared by the seizure of factories, incensed when strikers interfered with the mails, vexed by the intimidation of nonunionists, and alarmed by flying squadrons of workers who marched, or threatened to march, from city to city" (p. 242).

In 1937 and 1938, Roosevelt's attempt to reorganize the executive branch of government seemed to many of his opponents to be still another attempt by a would-be dictator "to subvert democratic institutions" by "importing European totalitarianism into the United States" (Leuchtenburg, 1963, pp. 277, 279). As described by historian Charles Schilke (1985), "the capstone of the reorganization was to be the transformation of the advisory National Resources Board into a vigorous statutory National Resources Planning Board to engage in continuous central planning and program coordination" (p. 356). Not surprisingly, business leaders "argued that reorganization legislation would erode business confidence and impede recovery." After the House of Representatives defeated the president's reorganization bill in 1938, FDR introduced a watered-down replacement in 1939, which gained quick enactment (Brinkley, 1995, pp. 21–23). This law, "the last major New Deal measure before the Second World War," nonetheless "represented a significant shift in power from Congress to the presidency," and Roosevelt used it skillfully to create the Executive Office of the President and an Office of Emergency Management (Schilke, 1985, p. 355), both of which proved instrumental in the president's maneuvering to bring the United States into World War II (U.S. Bureau of the Budget, 1946, pp. 14–16, 22).

Further disturbing business confidence, in June 1938, the federal government created the Temporary National Economic Committee (TNEC). A product of the misguided idea that "monopolies" had brought about or sustained the Depression (Roose, 1954, pp. 142–43), the TNEC interrogated 552 witnesses between December 1, 1938, and March 11, 1941, and ultimately published a report of 43 volumes. The main accomplishments of the committee were to showcase the rudimentary Keynesian ideas of economists such as Alvin Hansen and Lauchlin Currie and to heighten business suspicions that the government intended to launch an antitrust jihad (May, 1985, pp. 419–20). At the time, critics of the TNEC investigation regarded it as "an important, if ominous, event" (Brinkley, 1995, p. 123). Raymond Moley, a member of FDR's Brains Trust who had become estranged from the New Deal, described the TNEC in 1940 as a "time bomb"—in the words of historian Alan Brinkley, "sputtering along misleadingly but certain to produce unwelcome, radical results" (Brinkley, 1995, p. 123).

The fear seemed well justified, given the frenetic activities of Thurman Arnold, who took charge of the Antitrust Division of the Department of Justice in 1938. Despite having written a book mocking the antitrust laws, Arnold proceeded to lead an unprecedented attack on business concentration and trade practices, enormously expanding the number of prosecutions (Brinkley, 1995, p. 111). In retrospect, one may be tempted to view this crusade as little more than an insignificant spasm of a bewildered administration seeking to shift the blame for the recession of 1937–38. But contemporaries could not know, as we do, that the crusade would peter out in 1941 and 1942, when the managers of the wartime economy used their prerogatives to shield companies from antitrust actions on grounds of military necessity (Brinkley, 1995, pp. 120–21).

In contemplating the state of mind of investors between 1935 and 1940, one ought to recall just how radically the government's policies with respect to industrial structure and business practices had shifted. As late as 1935, the National Recovery Administration was still enforcing the comprehensive cartelization of all American industry. Just three years later, an unprecedented hurricane of antitrust enforcement swept over business shores.

In a recent evaluation of the New Deal's effects on the recovery, economic historian Gene Smiley (1994) notes that businesses "were further discouraged from investing by the new capital market regulations generated by the Securities and Exchange Act, the government's entry into the utility industry through the TVA, the continued tax increases (particularly the undistributed corporate profits tax) and rhetoric about the need to equalize incomes." By these and a multitude of other policy changes, the Roosevelt administration "abruptly and dramatically altered the institutional framework within which private business decisions were made, not just once but several times" (p. 136), with the result that regime uncertainty was heightened and recovery substantially retarded. Fearon (1987) concurs that the "shifts in government policy and the bitterness of the exchanges between business and Roosevelt were not likely to encourage an expansion in investment" (p. 210).

In these conclusions, economic historians only echo the observations of one of America's leading investors, Lammot du Pont, in 1937 (quoted by Krooss, 1970, p. 200):

> Uncertainty rules the tax situation, the labor situation, the monetary situation, and practically every legal condition under which industry must operate. Are taxes to go higher, lower or stay where they are? We don't know. Is labor to be union or non-union? . . .

Are we to have inflation or deflation, more government spending or less? . . . Are new restrictions to be placed on capital, new limits on profits?

. . . It is impossible to even guess at the answers.

Poll Data, 1939–41

The evidence summarized in the preceding section establishes, at least, that a variety of political and legal developments in the latter half of the 1930s gave investors ample reason to fear that their private property rights were at great risk of further attenuation and might conceivably be destroyed completely. But such evidence, by its very nature, is somewhat selective and bears only indirectly on the question at issue—whether regime uncertainty truly troubled investors. Can we somehow gain direct access to the actual expectations of more than a handful of select or fortuitous testifiers?

To the extent that public opinion surveys succeed in their objectives, we can. Modern polling, based on scientific sampling, dates from the mid-1930s. By 1939, the polling organizations had begun to ask questions that bear more or less directly on the state of business confidence and business people's expectations regarding the property rights regime. Of course, poll data present a variety of well-known difficulties (Bennett, 1980, pp. 64–93); they can never settle a question conclusively. Still, they offer some definite advantages over alternative sorts of evidence, and one would be cavalier to dismiss them peremptorily, as economists usually do. On other occasions, poll data have demonstrated remarkable explanatory power (Higgs and Kilduff, 1993), and I propose to give them another hearing here.

Although most of the poll data I shall cite rest on the responses of business people alone, some polls of the general public merit attention as well, if only to establish that the views of business people were not wildly aberrant. In the spring of 1939, a nationally representative poll by the American Institute of Public Opinion (AIPO) asked: "Do you think the attitude of the Roosevelt administration toward business is delaying business recovery?"

In March, 54 percent said yes, 26 percent said no, and the rest had no opinion. In May, 53 percent said yes, 31 percent said no, and the rest had no opinion (Cantril, 1951, p. 64).

Also in May 1939, a nationally representative AIPO poll asked: "Do you think that ten years from now there will be more government control of business than there is now or less government control of business?" Of the respondents, 56 percent expected more government control, 22 percent expected less, 8 percent expected neither more nor less, and 14 percent didn't venture an opinion (Cantril, 1951, p. 345).

Clearly, a majority of the general public believed that the Roosevelt administration's stance vis-à-vis business was delaying recovery, and expected government control of business to increase over the next decade, which presumably would further impede recovery.

In May 1939, *Fortune* pollsters asked a national sample of business executives: "With which of these two statements do you come closest to agreeing? (1) The policies of the administration have so affected the confidence of businessmen that recovery has been seriously held back; (2) businessmen generally have been unjustly blaming the administration for their troubles." Of the executives responding, 64.8 percent agreed with the first statement, 25.6 percent agreed with the second, and 9.6 percent said that they didn't know (Cantril, 1951, p. 64).

When the government began to mobilize the economy for war in the second half of 1940, many business managers were reluctant to become contractors for the War and Navy Departments. In an October 1940 *Fortune* poll, the 58.8 percent of responding business executives who reported that they knew others who had "any reservations about rearmament work" were singled out for a follow-up question and presented with seven alternative reasons for such reservations. Of the seven options, the following reason received the most assent (77.3 percent chose it): "Belief that the present administration in Washington is strongly antibusiness and a consequent discouragement over the practicability of cooperation with this administration on rearmament" (Cantril, 1951, p. 346). Evidently, many business executives so distrusted the Roosevelt administration that they would rather forgo potentially lucrative munitions contracts than deal with the administration.

In December 1940, the *Fortune* pollsters asked a related question of business executives: "Do you think that present conditions are such that business as a whole is now justified in making constructive commitments for expansion?" Of the respondents, 13 percent said yes, 26 percent said no, and 61 percent said "only in war industries" (Cantril, 1951, p. 337). Even at an advanced stage of the recovery, business people who viewed civilian investment as unjustified outnumbered those regarding it as justified by a 2-to-1 margin.

In May 1941, the *Fortune* pollsters asked a national sample of business executives: "If you consider lack of mutual confidence between government and business a major or secondary factor [in the slow pace of rearmament], do you feel that the government is more to blame, business is more to blame, both equally to blame?" Of the respondents, 77.8 percent put the greater blame on government, 1.9 percent put it on business; 14.3 percent blamed government and business equally; and 6 percent gave another answer or no answer at all (Cantril, 1951, p. 347).

In the same sample, respondents who were "critical of defense progress" were asked to rate eleven specified "factors . . . contributing to the trouble." One of the factors was "long-standing lack of mutual confidence between government and business" which was rated as a "major cause" by 41.8 percent of the respondents, was rated as "secondary" by 21.1 percent, and was rated as "unimportant" by just 7.7 percent (0.9 percent said "don't know," and 28.5 percent did not answer). The only factor selected by more of the respondents as a major cause—43.5 percent picked it—was "methods of placing government orders, red tape, delays" which itself was another form of blaming the government (Cantril, 1951, p. 347).

In November 1941, just before the Japanese attack on Pearl Harbor propelled the United States into total war, the *Fortune* pollsters asked a sample of business executives a question that bears quite directly on the regime uncertainty at issue in this chapter. The question was: "Which of the following comes closest to being your prediction of the kind of economic structure with which this country will emerge after the war?" The respondents were presented with four options, as follows (the percentage of respondents selecting that option as the closest to their own prediction is shown in brackets):

(1) A system of free enterprise restored very much along the prewar lines, with modifications to take care of conditions then current [7.2 percent]

(2) An economic system in which government will take over many public services formerly under private management but still leave many opportunities for private enterprise [52.4 percent]

(3) A semi-socialized society in which there will be very little room for the profit system to operate [36.7 percent]

(4) A complete economic dictatorship along fascist or communist lines [3.7 percent] (Cantril, 1951, p. 175)

These responses constitute an extraordinary testimony to the fears of business executives on the eve of the war. Almost 93 percent of them expected the postwar regime to be one that would further attenuate private property rights to a greater or lesser degree. More than 40 percent expected a regime in which government would dominate the economy—options (3) and (4). If these poll data are even approximately indicative of the true expectations of American investors, then it is astonishing that the recovery of investment had proceeded as far as it had.

The Changing of the Guard, 1940–45

After the outbreak of war in Europe in 1939, if not before, President Roosevelt focused his time and energy on foreign and military affairs. Effective U.S. rearmament, even if only to serve as the "arsenal of democracy," required the cooperation of business people, especially those in control of the nation's biggest corporations. As Henry Stimson, a pillar of the eastern Republican establishment, observed in 1940, "If you are going to try to go to war, or to prepare for war, in a capitalist country, you have got to let business make money out of the process or business won't work" (Stimson and Bundy, 1947, p. 166).

To accommodate the business titans, FDR enlisted their leadership in a succession of mobilization committees, boards, and agencies (Higgs, 1993; Hooks, 1991, pp. 165–77; Riddell, 1990; Brinkley, 1995, pp. 175–200). In June 1940, Roosevelt put a firm foundation under his coalition with big business by naming Stimson as Secretary of War and publisher Frank Knox, who had been the Republican candidate for vice-president in 1936, as Secretary of the Navy. Just below these men, top operational authority would be exercised by Under Secretary of War Robert P. Patterson, formerly a corporate lawyer and federal judge, and Under Secretary of the Navy James V. Forrestal, formerly a Wall Street investment banker. Under such leadership, the armed services, which quickly became the greatest buyers in industrial history, were not likely to manage their procurements in a fashion hostile to business, and they did not do so (Smith, 1959; Higgs, 1993). By the middle of 1942, more than 10,000 business executives had taken positions in federal war agencies. Roosevelt, who created many of the mobilization agencies by executive order, "believed that businessmen would respond more readily to direction from other businessmen than to orders from what they considered a hostile federal government" (Brinkley, 1995, p. 190). Besides, only business managers had the practical knowledge required to run the war economy—politicians, lawyers, and economists have rather severe limitations when it comes to organizing the production of battleships, bombers, and tanks.

Leading New Dealers correctly perceived that as FDR transformed himself from Dr. New Deal to Dr. Win the War, he was not only "ceding power to the corporate world," but "freezing out those within the government who had been struggling to expand the role of the state in managing the economy" (Brinkley, 1995, p. 180). From 1940 on, the ranks of the most stalwart New Dealers grew thinner and thinner. As described by historian Alan Brinkley (1995, p. 145), "[v]irtually none of them moved into important positions in the war bureaucracies; many of them lost their positions in the civilian agencies in which they had been serving. By the end of 1943, the liberal diaspora was nearly complete. Almost no real 'New Dealers' remained." Here Brinkley exaggerates—the extreme left liberals did not disappear from the government—but his description of the overall change is surely correct. To the extent that "personnel is policy" the administration became much less threatening to investors as the war years passed.

Simultaneously, support for business-threatening policies was dwindling in Congress. After the election of 1936, the Democrats held 76 seats in the Senate. After each of the next four elections, however, the number declined, and after the election of 1944, only 56 senators were Democrats. Despite some reversals, the trend was similar in the House of Representatives. The Democrats held 331 seats after the election of 1936, but only 242 after the election of 1944. The margin in the House had been even narrower after the election of 1942, when victories in just six more districts would have given the Republicans a majority. After 1938, the Conservative Coalition, composed of Republicans and conservative Southern Democrats, held sufficient power in Congress to stymie most efforts to extend the New Deal domestically (Porter, 1985, p. 73). In the elections of 1946, the Republicans finally regained control of both houses of Congress.

Roosevelt's death, on April 12, 1945, removed from the presidency an enormously shrewd and resourceful leader who had for the past decade expressed a hostility bordering on hatred for investors as a class. Many business people, among others, had feared that FDR harbored dictatorial ambition; some believed that he ultimately did exercise arbitrary power in some, if not all, areas—for instance, in his unconstitutional "destroyer deal" of 1940, without congressional approval, he gave away 50 warships of the U.S. Navy to a foreign power. His demise must have enhanced the confidence that many investors felt in the future security of their remaining private property rights.

Harry S Truman, who became president when FDR died, was a New Dealer himself, but hardly one of Roosevelt's stripe or stature. Hence, he posed much less threat to investors. Truman looked askance at the type of New Dealers who had devised much of the administration's program during the heyday of the Second New Deal, in the mid-1930s—the intellectual wheeler-dealers variously known as "the liberal crowd," "the long-haired boys,"[7] or "the Harvard crowd" whose leading lights included Tom Corcoran, Ben Cohen, William O. Douglas, Thurman Arnold, Jerome Frank, James Landis, Leon Henderson, Mordecai Ezekiel, Alvin Hansen and, above all, Felix Frankfurter. As president, Truman "lent intermittent support to reform, but never to the centralized and professionalized administration central to the New Deal." In 1945 and 1946, he "fired or accepted resignations from a host of New Dealers, including Henry Wallace and Harold Ickes" and he "filled the spots vacated by crusading New Dealers with cronies from Missouri, centrists, and businessmen" (Hooks, 1991, pp. 200–1). Just before the war, in discussing the New Deal, Schumpeter had pointed out that "the personnel and methods by which and the spirit in which a measure or set of measures is administrated, are much more important than anything contained in any enactment" (1939, p. 1045). Much of the New Deal legislation remained on the statute books, but under Truman's leadership, top federal officials posed a much reduced threat to investors in comparison to that perceived from 1935 through 1940. Investors might not like the Truman administration, but they could live with it. As Roose (1954) observed, in the postwar years, there were still uncertainties, "but one of these uncertainties is not the type of economy in which business decisions are to be made" (p. 256).

Poll Data, 1944–45

Unfortunately, the poll data relevant to the question of regime uncertainty are far fewer for the late war and postwar years than they are for the years immediately preceding the war. That disparity may itself testify to the diminished salience of the issue. Pollsters are not likely to ask questions about people's expectations concerning future changes of regime when hardly anybody expects such changes to occur. Nevertheless, a few questions that bear on the issue were posed.

The *Fortune* pollsters put one somewhat ambiguous question to a sample of business executives in May 1944, after the war-command economy had been operating in its full-fledged form for more than two years.

The question was: "In general, does it seem to you that after the war the prospects of your company will be better, or worse, or about the same as they were before?" In reply, 51.2 percent said better, 8.5 percent said worse, 36.8 percent said about the same, and 3.5 percent didn't know what to say (Cantril, 1951, p. 1121). Obviously, the respondents might have had different interpretations of the phrase "prospects of your company," and even if they all understood it as referring to, say, profitability, their responses do not necessarily bear a tight relation to their regime expectations. Still, it is difficult to believe that such responses would have been made if the respondents had still held the gloomy regime expectations that they expressed in polls taken just before the U.S. declaration of war.

Two other questions, asked shortly after Roosevelt's death, bear more directly on regime expectations. In May 1945, AIPO pollsters asked: "Do you think Truman will be more favorable or less favorable toward business than Roosevelt was?" Of the business and professional respondents, 60 percent expected Truman to be more favorable, 7 percent expected him to be less favorable, 18 percent expected him to be the same, and 15 percent had no opinion (Cantril, 1951, p. 887).

In the same poll, respondents were asked: "Do you think Truman will be more favorable or less favorable toward labor unions than Roosevelt was?" Of the business and professional respondents, 5 percent expected Truman to be more favorable, 55 percent expected him to be less favorable, 20 percent expected him to be the same, and 20 percent had no opinion (Cantril, 1951, pp. 887–88). Not surprisingly, the responses to this question form the mirror image of the responses to the previous question. Taken together, these responses indicate that business and professional people felt much less threatened by Truman than they had by Roosevelt.

Evidence from these polls matches the conclusions that Herman Krooss (1970) reached on the basis of his less systematic survey of the opinions expressed by business leaders: "For most business leaders, the mood during the first couple of years after V-J Day was one of cautious confidence and optimism" (p. 219)—a far different mood from that of business leaders between 1935 and 1941.

Evidence from Financial Markets

If investors truly feared for the future security of their private property rights, they should have met the Great American Challenge: Put your money where your mouth is. Did investors manifest their fears by their actions in the financial markets?

The stock market provides some evidence. After plunging from a peak in 1929 to a trough in 1932, stock prices climbed substantially during Roosevelt's first term as president. Between 1932 and 1936, the annual average real value of the S&P Index of Common Stock Prices increased by 110 percent.[7] Still, the real value of the S&P index in 1936 remained substantially below its value in either 1928 or 1930, not to speak of its peak value in 1929. With the onset of the recession in 1937, stock prices fell. Except for a slight reversal in 1939, they continued to fall for five years. The real S&P index for 1941 was only 57 percent as high as its value for 1936. These stock price movements are broadly consistent with the concurrent political events described earlier, although the little crest in 1936–37 seems somewhat incongruent. It is noteworthy that even after the economy's recovery from the recession of 1937–38 had become obvious to everyone, the stock market continued to slide, which suggests that longer-term pessimism was outweighing the brighter near-term prospect for profits.

Unfortunately, a change in stock prices, in itself, tells us nothing about whether the change reflects altered expectations with respect to profits at one point in the future or another. Obviously, if the profits expected in the near term were to increase sufficiently, investors would bid up stock prices even though they had simultaneously revised downward somewhat their expectations of later profits. Evidently, such expectations motivated investors from 1935 to 1937, when, in economist Alvin Hansen's words, "Business men avoided as much as possible long-term capital commitments"[7] (quoted by Roose, 1954, p. 174; see also Friedman and Schwartz, 1963, p. 495).

The investment data confirm Hansen's assessment. We can divide gross private domestic investment into three components that correspond to differing lengths of the newly created capital's expected economic life: gross private new construction (the longest lived); gross private producers durables (intermediate); and additions to business inventories (the shortest lived). During the last five years of the 1920s, on average, these components constituted the following proportions of private investment: 0.62, 0.32, and 0.06, respectively.[8] During the business recovery that was in progress during the first three years of the Second New Deal (1935–37), however, the proportions were 0.38, 0.44, and 0.18, respectively, showing a marked shift away from the longest-term investments. The proportions remained much the same during the second business recovery of the Second New Deal (1939–41), when they were 0.45, 0.40, and 0.15, respectively. Clearly, the real investments made during the first and second Roosevelt administrations remained far more concentrated in short-term assets than the investments made during the latter half of the 1920s.

In contrast to the stock market data, evidence from the corporate bond market permits a more discriminating assessment of changes in expectations. By examining changes in the yield of bonds of various terms to maturity, we can identify how investors changed the discount rate that they applied to contracted interest payments that were payable at different points in the future.

In the late 1920s and early 1930s, the first-quarter nominal yields of high-grade corporate bonds of various terms to maturity differed little and fluctuated in a narrow range. After 1932, nominal yields began to fall and—most significant for present purposes—a wide spread opened between the yields of bonds with short terms to maturity and those with longer terms to maturity. By 1935, the yield of a bond with one year to maturity was only 1.05 percent, and such yields remained below 1 percent from 1936 through 1942 (U.S. Bureau of the Census, 1975, p. 1004). Yields of bonds with longer terms to maturity did not fall nearly so much.

Figure 1-3 permits a visual assessment of the effective risk premium on bond payoffs in the more remote future. As the figure shows, virtually no such premium existed from 1926 through 1934. All observations are for the first quarter of the year.[9] Between 1934 and 1936, yields of longer-term bonds increased sharply, relative to the yield of a bond with one year to

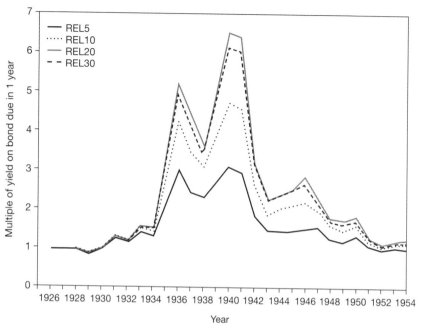

Figure 1-3. Relative yield on high-grade corporate bonds,
by term to maturity, first quarter, 1926–54.

maturity. In 1936, bonds with five years to maturity had a yield that was *three times* that of a bond with one year to maturity. The yield multiple was more than four for a bond with ten years to maturity, five for a bond with twenty years to maturity, and more than five for a bond with thirty years to maturity. Although the yield multiples of longer-term bonds fluctuated from year to year, they remained at extraordinarily high levels from 1936 through the first quarter of 1941. By the first quarter of 1942, however, the yield multiples had dropped precipitously. By 1943, they had returned to their 1934 levels and, despite rising slightly between 1943 and 1946, tended downward thereafter. By the early 1950s, the yield multiples were about the same as they had been in the early 1930s.

The bond yield data displayed in figure 1-3 tell a dramatic story. Investors' confidence in their ability to appropriate the longer-term interest payments and principal repayments promised by the country's most secure corporations plummeted between early 1934 and early 1936. Confidence remained at an extremely depressed level from 1936 through the first quarter of 1941. It then improved rapidly, despite the country's becoming a declared belligerent in the greatest war of all time. The correspondence between these financial data and the political events and opinion data described earlier is truly striking.[10]

Conclusion

It is time for economists and historians to take seriously the hypothesis that the New Deal prolonged the Great Depression by creating an extraordinarily high degree of regime uncertainty in the minds of investors.

Of course, scholars have had their reasons for not taking the idea seriously. For a long time, historians have viewed the statements of contemporary business people about "lack of business confidence" as little more than routine grumbling—sure, sure, what else would one expect Republican tycoons to have said? Historians generally report such statements as if they were either attempts to sway public opinion or unreflective whining.

Since World War II, economists, with only a few exceptions, have overlooked regime uncertainty as a cause of the Great Duration for other reasons, such as the availability of standard macroeconomic models whose variables do not include the degree of regime uncertainty and, even if one wanted to incorporate it into an existing model, the absence of any conventional quantitative index of such uncertainty. Somewhat inexplicably, most economists regard evidence about expectations drawn from public opinion surveys as scientifically contemptible. Moreover, economists crave general models that are equally applicable to all times and places, and so they resist explanations that emphasize the unique aspects of a specific episode, such as the Great Depression.

In opposition to these professional inclinations, one can offer several good reasons to take seriously the idea that the regime uncertainty created by the Second New Deal contributed significantly to the Great Duration. First, the Great Depression was not just another economic slump. In depth and duration, it stands far apart from the next most severe depression in U.S. history, that of the 1890s. We are talking about history, not physics; unique events may have unique causes. Second, the hypothesis about regime uncertainty makes perfectly good economic sense. Nothing in the logic of the explanation warrants its dismissal or disparagement. Third, given the unparalleled outpouring of business-threatening laws, regulations, and court decisions, the oft-stated hostility of President Roosevelt and his lieutenants toward investors as a class, and the character of the anti-business zealots who composed the strategists and administrators of the New Deal from 1935 to 1941, the political climate could hardly have failed to discourage some investors from making fresh long-term commitments. Fourth, there exists a great deal of direct evidence that investors did feel extraordinarily uncertain about the future of the property rights regime between 1935 and 1941. Historians have recorded countless statements by contemporaries to that effect; and the poll data presented earlier confirm that in the years just before the war, most business executives expected substantial attenuations of private property rights, ranging up to "complete economic dictatorship." Fifth, investors' behavior in the bond market attests in a striking way that their confidence in the longer-term future took a beating that coincides exactly with the Second New Deal.

Finally, this way of understanding the Great Duration meshes nicely with a proper understanding of the Great Escape after the war. The Keynesians all expected a reversion to depression when the war ended. Most business people, in sharp contrast, "did not think that there was any threat of a serious depression" after the war (Krooss, 1970, p. 217). The business people forecasted far more accurately than the Keynesian economists: The private economy blossomed as never before or since. Official data, which understate the true increase because of mismeasurement of the price level, show an increase of real nongovernment domestic product of 29.5 percent from 1945 to 1946 (U.S. Council of Economic Advisers, 1995, p. 406). Private investment boomed and corporate share prices soared in 1945 and 1946 (Higgs, 1992, pp. 57–58). None of the standard explanations can account for this astonishing postwar leap, but an explanation that incorporates the improvement in the outlook for the private property regime can account for it.

From 1935 through 1940, with Roosevelt and the ardent New Dealers who surrounded him in full cry, private investors dared not risk their funds in the amounts typical of the late 1920s. In 1945 and 1946, with Roosevelt dead, the New Deal in retreat, and most of the wartime controls being removed, investors came out in force. To be sure, the federal government had become, and would remain, a much more powerful force to be reckoned with (Higgs, 1987; Hughes, 1991). But the government no longer seemed to possess the terrifying potential that business people had perceived before the war. For investors, the nightmare was over. For the economy, once more, prosperity was possible.

Notes

1. As indicated earlier, the data plotted for 1941 to 1946, especially those for 1942 to 1945, are unsuitable for analysis. I show them in this and the succeeding figure to reveal what would be at stake if one were to proceed in a conventional manner, treating these observations as comparable with the preceding and succeeding ones. Data source is U.S. Council of Economic Advisers (1995, p. 406).

2. Darby's measure of unemployment counts persons employed in government emergency work-relief programs as employed, whereas the official measure of unemployment counts these persons as unemployed. See Darby (1976).

3. Data source is U.S. Council of Economic Advisers (1970, p. 77).

4. The 1929 benchmark was quite representative of the latter 1920s: gross private investment averaged $15.7 billion per year from 1925 through 1929 (Swanson and Williamson, 1972, p. 55).

5. On the tax laws, see Witte (1985, p. 100–108), Brownlee (1985, pp. 415–18), and Brownlee (1996, pp. 74–82).

6. For evidence that the undistributed profits tax did have harmful effects on resource allocation, with costs "borne disproportionately by young, growing firms," see Calomiris and Hubbard (1995, quotation at p. 477). For the effect of the tax on business expectations, see Roose (1954, pp. 212–16).

7. Data source is U.S. Bureau of the Census (1975, p. 224, Series F5, and p. 1004, Series X495). My price index is the GNP deflator.

8. These and the following proportions are computed from data in Swanson and Williamson (1972, p. 70).

9. Data source is U.S. Bureau of the Census (1975, p. 1004, Series X487–491).

10. Some critics have insisted that the yield spreads shown in figure 1-3 reflect nothing more than a "flight to liquidity" that drove the prices of short-term bonds up (and therefore their yields down) relative to the prices of longer-term bonds. They point to the fact

that the drop in short-term yields accounts for most of the spread that appeared after early 1934. I am not persuaded by this explanation, because (1) a flight to liquidity should have expressed itself much sooner, especially as the financial system was crumbling from 1930 through the first quarter of 1933; (2) a flight to liquidity cannot account for the large spread that opened between, say, the yield on bonds with five years to maturity and the yield on bonds with ten years to maturity (the former being hardly "liquid"); and (3) the drastic narrowing of the spreads between early 1941 and early 1942 seems very difficult to attribute to a sudden disappearance of the alleged flight to liquidity.

References

Alston, Lee J., Thrainn Eggertsson, and Douglass C. North. (1996) Introduction. In *Empirical Studies in Institutional Change,* edited by L. J. Alston, T. Eggertsson, and D. C. North. New York: Cambridge University Press.

Anderson, Benjamin M. ([1949]1979) *Economics and the Public Welfare: A Financial and Economic History of the United States, 1914–46.* Indianapolis: Liberty Press.

Badger, Anthony J. (1989) *The New Deal: The Depression Years, 1933–40.* New York: Noonday Press.

Bennett, W. Lance. (1980) *Public Opinion in American Politics.* New York: Harcourt Brace Jovanovich.

Brinkley, Alan. (1995) *The End of Reform: New Deal Liberalism in Recession and War.* New York: Knopf.

Brownlee, W. Elliot. (1985) Taxation. In *Franklin D. Roosevelt, His Life and Times: An Encyclopedic View,* edited by O. L. Graham, Jr., and M. R. Wander. Boston: G. K. Hall & Co., pp. 415–18.

Brownlee, W. Elliot. (1996) *Federal Taxation in America: A Short History.* Washington and New York: Woodrow Wilson Center Press and Cambridge University Press.

Calomiris, Charles W., and R. Glenn Hubbard. (1995) Internal Finance and Investment: Evidence from the Undistributed Profits Tax of 1936–37. *Journal of Business* 68 (October): 443–82.

Chandler, Lester V. (1970) *America's Greatest Depression, 1929–1941.* New York: Harper & Row.

Collins, Robert M. (1981) *The Business Response to Keynes, 1929–1964.* New York: Columbia University Press.

Darby, Michael R. (1976) Three-and-a-Half Million U.S. Employees Have Been Mislaid: Or, an Explanation of Unemployment, 1934–1941. *Journal of Political Economy* 84 (February): 1–16.

Ely, James W., Jr. (1992.) *The Guardian of Every Other Right: A Constitutional History of Property Rights.* New York: Oxford University Press.

Fearon, Peter. (1987) *War, Prosperity and Depression: The U.S. Economy 1917–45.* Lawrence: University Press of Kansas.

Field, Alexander James. (1992) Uncontrolled Land Development and the Duration of the Depression in the United States. *Journal of Economic History* 52 (December): 785–805.

Flynn, John T. (1944) *As We Go Marching.* Garden City, N.Y.: Doubleday, Doran and Co.

Friedman, Milton, and Anna Jacobson Schwartz. (1963) *A Monetary History of the United States, 1867–1960.* Princeton: Princeton University Press.

Garraty, John A. (1973) The New Deal, National Socialism, and the Great Depression. *American Historical Review* 78 (October): 907–44.

Harris, Seymour. (1945) *Price and Related Controls in the United States.* New York: McGraw-Hill.

Higgs, Robert. (1987) *Crisis and Leviathan: Critical Episodes in the Growth of American Government.* New York: Oxford University Press.

Higgs, Robert. (1992) Wartime Prosperity? A Reassessment of the U.S. Economy in the 1940s. *Journal of Economic History* 52 (March): 41–60.

Higgs, Robert. (1993) Private Profit, Public Risk: Institutional Antecedents of the Modern Military Procurement System in the Rearmament Program of 1940–1941. In *The Sinews of War: Essays on the Economic History of World War II,* edited by G. T. Mills and H. Rockoff. Ames: Iowa State University Press, pp. 166–98.

Higgs, Robert, and Anthony Kilduff. (1993) Public Opinion: A Powerful Predictor of U.S. Defense Spending. *Defence Economics* 4: 227–38.

Hooks, Gregory. (1991) *Forging the Military-Industrial Complex: World War II's Battle of the Potomac.* Urbana: University of Illinois Press.

Hughes, Jonathan R. T. (1991) *The Governmental Habit Redux: Economic Controls from Colonial Times to the Present.* Princeton: Princeton University Press.

Keller, Morton. (1990) *Regulating a New Economy: Public Policy and Economic Change in America, 1900–1933.* Cambridge, Mass.: Harvard University Press.

Krooss, Herman E. (1970) *Executive Opinion: What Business Leaders Said and Thought on Economic Issues, 1920s–1960s.* Garden City, N.Y.: Doubleday and Co.

Krug, J. A. (1945) *Production: Wartime Achievements and the Reconversion Outlook.* War Production Board Document No. 334, October 9.

Leuchtenburg, William E. (1963) *Franklin D. Roosevelt and the New Deal, 1932–1940.* New York: Harper & Row.

May, Dean L. (1985) Temporary National Economic Committee. In *Franklin D. Roosevelt, His Life and Times: An Encyclopedic View,* edited by O. L. Graham, Jr., and M. R. Wander. Boston: G. K. Hall & Co., pp. 419–20.

Pindyck, Robert S. (1991) Irreversibility, Uncertainty, and Investment. *Journal of Economic Literature* 29 (September): 1110–48.

Porter, David L. (1985) Congress, United States. In *Franklin D. Roosevelt, His Life and Times: An Encyclopedic View,* edited by O. L. Graham, Jr., and M. R. Wander. Boston: G. K. Hall & Co., pp. 72–76.

Public Opinion, 1935–1946, edited by Hadley Cantril. (1951) Princeton: Princeton University Press.

Rapaczynski, Andrzej. (1996) The Roles of the State and the Market in Establishing Property Rights. *Journal of Economic Perspectives* 10 (Spring): 87–103.

Riddell, Kelly. (1990) The State, Capitalism, and World War II: The U.S. Case. *Armed Forces & Society* 17 (Fall): 53–79.

Rockoff, Hugh. (1984) *Drastic Measures: A History of Wage and Price Controls in the United States.* Cambridge, England: Cambridge University Press.

Roose, Kenneth D. (1954) *The Economics of Recession and Revival: An Interpretation of 1937–38.* New Haven: Yale University Press.

Schilke, Charles. (1985) Reorganization Act. In *Franklin D. Roosevelt, His Life and Times: An Encyclopedic View,* edited by O. L. Graham, Jr., and M. R. Wander. Boston: G. K. Hall & Co., pp. 355–57.

Schumpeter, Joseph A. (1939) *Business Cycles: A Theoretical, Historical, and Statistical Analysis of the Capitalist Process.* New York: McGraw-Hill.

Schumpeter, Joseph A. (1962) *Capitalism, Socialism and Democracy.* New York: Harper Torchbooks.

Siegan, Bernard H. (1980) *Economic Liberties and the Constitution.* Chicago: University of Chicago Press.

Smiley, Gene. (1994) *The American Economy in the Twentieth Century.* Cincinnati: South-Western Publishing.

Smith, R. Elberton. (1959) *The Army and Economic Mobilization.* Washington, D.C.: U.S. Government Printing Office.

Stimson, Henry L., and McGeorge Bundy. (1947) *On Active Service in Peace and War.* London: Hutchinson & Co.

Swanson, J. A., and S. H. Williamson. (1972) Estimates of National Product and Income for the United States Economy, 1919–1941. *Explorations in Economic History* 10 (Fall): 53–73.

Temin, Peter. (1989) *Lessons from the Great Depression.* Cambridge, Mass.: MIT Press.

U.S. Bureau of the Budget. (1946) *The United States at War: Development and Administration of the War Program by the Federal Government.* Washington, D.C.: U.S. Government Printing Office.

U.S. Bureau of the Census. (1975) *Historical Statistics of the United States, Colonial Times to 1970.* Washington, D.C.: U.S. Government Printing Office.

U.S. Council of Economic Advisers. (1970) *Annual Report.* Washington, D.C.: U.S. Government Printing Office.

U.S. Council of Economic Advisers. (1995) *Annual Report.* Washington, D.C.: U.S. Government Printing Office.

Witte, John F. (1985) *The Politics and Development of the Federal Income Tax.* Madison: University of Wisconsin Press.

Acknowledgments   For helpful comments on a previous draft, I am grateful to Dan Klein, Charlotte Twight, Lee Alston, Hugh Rockoff, and Donald Boudreaux. For their reactions to the ideas expressed here, I thank those attending my presentations at the University of California at Irvine, the Public Choice Society meetings, Seattle University, the Cato Institute, the Eris Society meetings, the "Mises University" at Auburn University, and the *Liberty Magazine* Editors' Conference.

2

Private Profit, Public Risk

*Institutional Antecedents of the Modern
Military Procurement System in the
Rearmament Program of 1940–41*

> If you are going to try to go to war, or to prepare for war,
> in a capitalist country, you have got to let business make
> money out of the process or business won't work. . . .
> *Henry L. Stimson, 1940*

> Business likes its wars without risk.   *I. F. Stone, 1941*

AFTER WORLD WAR II, the United States did not fully
demobilize its armed forces. It continued to maintain a military establishment that, by historical standards, can only be called immense. Keeping
large numbers of men heavily armed with ever more sophisticated weapons has created a tremendous demand for munitions. Most of the munitions have been produced by privately owned corporations, many of which
rely on the Pentagon for the bulk of their sales. The dealings between the
armed forces and the major defense contractors form the heart of what is
known as the military-industrial complex.

This chapter deals primarily with one aspect of the military procurement program, namely, the arrangements by which economic risks are
shifted from the private contractors to the government—that is, to the
taxpayers—thereby allowing the companies to "function in a world of
socialized risks and private profit" (Adams and Adams, 1972, p. 284).
Also examined are two related matters: the high degree to which prime
defense contracting is confined to a small fraternity of large companies,
whose managers, along with their counterparts in the Department of

Defense and the armed services, form a sort of "old boy network"; and how such concentration and the privileges associated with it make possible the realization of rates of return that are, given the low risk actually borne, exceptionally high. At issue here are the origins of these aspects of the modern military supply business.

Hallmarks of the Modern Military Procurement System

Only a small proportion of all defense procurement spending is transacted by means of sealed-bid competitive contracting, in which the contractor submitting the lowest bid automatically gets the sale. Instead, the military purchaser typically negotiates a deal with a selected supplier, sometimes after a preliminary (but limited) design or research competition, to set the conditions under which a sole corporate supplier will provide the goods or services desired. Often, no firm price is fixed for the product; rather, the military buyer promises to reimburse the full costs of production and to pay the supplier a fixed fee, commonly described as profit. Having entered into such a contract, the company cannot lose. More likely, its gains will turn out to be greater than originally stipulated, because the contract is not binding—that is, the military buyer either initiates or acquiesces in contractual changes, many of which result in enhanced returns to the supplier.[1]

Because of the great attraction of low-risk, high-return deals with the Pentagon, firms engage in "fierce oligopoly rivalry" to acquire the contracts (Gansler, 1980, p. 101). Usually, the firm that gets the research and development (R&D) contract to develop a new weapon can count on, first, having the government pay all of its R&D costs and, second, receiving a sole-source contract to produce the weapon it has begun to develop, the "follow-on" business. Contractors go to great lengths—financial, technical, political, and even legal and ethical—to get the big contracts (Adams, 1982, p. 185; Rasor, 1985, pp. 237–53; Proxmire, 1970, p. 162; Gansler, 1980, pp. 101, 297). But the intensity of their highly politicized struggles for the business should not be confused with traditional procurement competition (i.e., publicly advertised, sealed-bid competition in which the contractual terms are definite and the lowest bidder automatically wins). Military officials are free to choose higher-priced bidders on the grounds of technical, organizational, or other perceived superiority, and they often do so. Hence, nothing prevents established personal and corporate intimacies between the military buyers and the corporate suppliers from swaying decisions about the award of contracts. Moreover, although the rivalry to get the big R&D contracts may sometimes be fierce, it is hardly a free-for-all, because only "qualified" contractors, those certified by the government purchaser, may compete.

To shield the chosen contractors from risking their own assets, in many cases, the government provides them with plants, equipment, and materials. It provides working capital in the form of advance and progress payments, as well as deferrals of tax payments. Therefore, the contractors accrue profits, even though they have placed little or nothing at risk (Kaufman, 1972, p. 289; Dumas, 1976, p. 458; Dumas, 1986, pp. 331–42; Gansler, 1980, pp. 3–6, 47–9, 54–62, 89, 138, 149, 171–2, 201, 288, 292). A more exacting classification would categorize such "profits" as transfer payments.

Should a major contractor, notwithstanding the government's arrangements to shield it from risk, still fall into financial difficulty, the government stands ready to bail it out. Contractual adjustments, loans or loan guarantees, and strategic placement of new contracts may be used to ensure that the contractor stays in business. Although the Lockheed bailout of the early 1970s is the best-known episode, scholars have identified an extensive pattern of rotating major contracts that has been dubbed a "bailout imperative," a virtual guarantee against bankruptcy, regardless of mismanagement or other corporate ineptitude (Nieburg, 1966, pp. 201, 269; Kurth, 1973, pp. 142–4; Kaufman, 1972, pp. 289; Dumas, 1977, p. 458; Gansler, 1980, pp. 49, 172, 227).

The defense business is highly concentrated. Typically, the leading one hundred contractors get 65 to 75 percent of the total value of prime procurement contracts. Within well-defined product classes (e.g., ballistic missile submarines or surveillance satellites), only one or two producers may have the "market" to themselves. Furthermore, as Bernard Udis and Murray Weidenbaum have observed, "the procurement of sophisticated weapons systems takes place in a rarified atmosphere in which the distinction between the buyer and seller becomes blurred due to the interdependence of the organizations, the growing commonality of goals, and the daily intermingling of personnel from both groups over extended periods of time. . . . [This is] an environment far removed from the presumed 'arm's length' dealings of the market" (Udis and Weidenbaum, 1973, p. 33 [also pp. 31–2]; Gansler, 1980, pp. 3, 11, 30, 34, 36–50, 100). Senator William Roth has complained that "one cannot do business in some Army procurements unless one is part of the 'old boy network'" and Senator William Proxmire has pointed to "an active, ever-working, fast-moving, revolving door between the Pentagon and its big suppliers." Thousands of high-ranking military officers retire and find immediate executive employment in the defense industry, while industry officials routinely occupy high-ranking positions in the Pentagon bureaucracy.[2]

Defense profits are a hotly disputed topic (partly because of the opaque accounting practices of the companies), but it seems fairly clear that, in view of the small risk borne, the major contractors generally realize extraordinarily high rates of return on their investment. As Jacques Gansler has emphasized, many large contractors "achieve a high return on investment through the unique advantage of having a great deal of government plant space, equipment, and money, which means that they must invest very little."[3] Procurement officers pay attention to limiting a contractor's rate of returns on sales, but they virtually ignore the more significant rate of return, namely, that on the contractor's investment.

In sum, the military-industrial complex of the post-World War II era presents a clear case of private profit and public risk. Buyer and seller blur; revolving doors spin; costs escalate and are duly reimbursed. The taxpayers pick up the entire bill, while the big contractors pocket the billions in fees. Profits—properly a return for betting one's own resources on uncertain prospects in the market—go to parties who have borne little or no risk and have already been fully, or more than fully, reimbursed at third-party expense, often in advance of performance, for every conceivable cost they have borne.

It was not always thus. The roots of the modern system can be found in the rearmament program of 1940–41.

Military Procurement and Planning before 1940

Before 1940, everything about military procurement was different. The scale of the business was, by later standards, minuscule. The armed forces—army, navy, and marines together—never exceeded 335,000 officers and men on active duty during 1922–39, and until the late 1930s, usually numbered about 250,000. Congress appropriated meager sums for munitions, too little even to equip the existing personnel to fight effectively. During the fiscal years 1922–39, federal outlays for national security averaged just $744 million per year, only a portion of which could be spent for procurement. What little purchasing the armed forces did they transacted according to rigidly specified legal procedures. Normally, the military purchaser publicly advertised its demand for a definite quantity of a specific item, accepted bids, and automatically awarded the contract to the lowest bidder. During the fiscal years 1937–40, for example, the War Department placed about 84 percent of its procurement business by means of invitations to bid. The Navy Department operated similarly. Elberton Smith observed that "contracting officers were ill-prepared to meet the Pandora's box of problems suddenly released in the summer of 1940 by the deluge of appropriations exceeding, within three short months, the total for the previous nineteen years" (U.S. Bureau of the Census, 1975, pp. 1141, 1115; Beaumont, 1977, p. 120; Smith, 1959, pp. 216, 218; Connery, 1951, p. 64).

Disillusioned by World War I and its aftermath, during the interwar years, the American public remained overwhelmingly hostile toward war and militarism in general, and toward arms manufacturers in particular. Stigmatized as "merchants of death," military suppliers and financiers were subjected to prolonged investigation before the Nye Committee of the

Senate during 1934–36, and they were widely blamed for U.S. participation in the Great War. In a public opinion survey in 1936, 82 percent of the respondents agreed that the manufacture and sale of munitions for private profit should be prohibited. To preclude foreign entanglements that might drag the nation into war, Congress passed Neutrality Acts in 1935, 1936, 1937, and 1939. According to public opinion polls taken in 1939, business executives opposed war even more than the general public. They feared especially the "regimentation" that war would probably bring, anticipating that wartime governmental controls, especially if implemented by the antibusiness Roosevelt administration, would destroy their property rights and perhaps usher in dictatorship (Cantril, 1951, p. 491; Stromberg, 1953, pp. 3, 69). Offering scant profits and considerable opprobrium, military business held few attractions for American businessmen in the twenty years before the outbreak of World War II.

No matter how unpopular war might be, the government still had to attend to national security affairs. Under the National Defense Act of 1920, the War Department, in cooperation with the navy, had a responsibility to make plans for economic mobilization, so called M-Day Plans, to be implemented in the event of war. Accordingly, with the encouragement and advice of Bernard Baruch, head of the War Industries Board during World War I and the recognized expert on the economics of war, plans were drawn up in 1931, 1933, 1936, and 1939. In formulating the plans, the military authorities routinely consulted with representatives of big business, but with few others. In 1939, at the instigation of Assistant Secretary of War Louis Johnson, the president appointed a War Resources Board (WRB), headed by U.S. Steel's chairman Edward R. Stettinius, Jr., and for the most part composed of big businessmen, to review the latest M-Day Plan. The WRB endorsed, with few qualifications, the army's plan to place the wartime economy under the direction of a powerful emergency superagency to be directed by patriotic businessmen, a War Resources Administration, to be patterned after the War Industries Board of World War I, only stronger. Reports of the WRB's proceedings ignited an explosion of protest. New Dealers, farm representatives, and labor unionists hastened to attack the WRB and its proposals.

Chastened by the reaction and jealous of his own powers over a mobilized economy, Roosevelt disbanded the WRB and suppressed its report. (Nevertheless, the army's and the WRB's plans and recommendations were, in part, ultimately implemented. The War Production Board [1942–45], for example, made a reality of much of the prewar vision.) [Huston, 1966, pp. 403–10; Blum, 1962; Blum, 1972; Rutherford, 1939.]

Parallel to the interwar plans for economic mobilization, the purchasing agencies of the army and navy devised plans for wartime alterations in procurement practices and sources of supply. According to an official army history, "a basic assumption and recommendation of army procurement planning long before World War II was prompt suspension, at the beginning of an emergency, of the peacetime restrictions on contract placement." The procurement agencies envisioned, especially for the acquisition of novel or complex products, the use of negotiated, cost-plus types of contracts (Smith, 1959, pp. 71, 243 [quotation], 246; U.S. Civilian Production Administration, 1947, p. 57). In addition, military planners "anticipated that government corporations may be formed to take business war risks not reasonable to expect of private corporations," perhaps by offering subsidized loans and war risk insurance to munitions makers.[4] In April 1939, Congress authorized the navy to negotiate cost-plus-fixed-fee (CPFF) contracts for the construction of bases outside the continental United States. The navy had requested the authority on the grounds that under the usual bidding system the risks involved in such projects would cause the navy's costs to be exorbitant (Connery, 1951, p. 66; Miller, 1949, p. 86). Clearly, the idea of shifting the risks from the military suppliers to the taxpayers had gained a following among military planners and their business associates well before the United States began to rearm in earnest in 1940.

The Great Scare and the Commitment to Rearm

Attitudes toward U.S. rearmament changed radically in 1940 in reaction to events in Europe. Americans had been shocked and dismayed when Germany overran Poland, prompting France and Britain to declare war in

September 1939, but the following winter saw little action, and the situation in Europe came to be characterized as a "phony war" or "sitzkrieg." The quiet was violently shattered during April–June 1940, when Germany invaded and occupied Denmark and Norway; captured Luxembourg, Belgium, and Holland; compelled the French to capitulate; and almost destroyed the British army at Dunkirk. In May, only 36 percent of Americans polled in a public opinion survey favored aiding Britain at the risk of war; in December, 60 percent did. Commentary in the business press indicated that businessmen also were "pretty thoroughly converted" from isolationism to favoring aid to the British (U.S. Bureau of the Budget, 1946, pp. 17–21; Stromberg, 1953, pp. 72–73; Smith, 1959, pp. 128–29).

Suddenly, Congress gained an appreciation of the country's precarious military condition and made unprecedented appropriations for rearmament. Funds were provided to speed the construction of a "two-ocean Navy." Between June 1940 and December 1941, about $36 billion was made available to the War Department alone—more than the army and navy combined had spent during World War I. As Secretary of War Henry L. Stimson remarked, however, "the pinch came in getting money turned into weapons." The United States possessed enormous potential to produce munitions, but early in 1940, its munitions industry was, in Donald Nelson's words, "only a token industry," and by comparison with the munitions industries of Europe and Japan, "a pigmy." The rearmament program somehow had to "enable American industry to make the heavy capital commitments, plant expansion, and organizational changes essential to large scale armament production" (Huston, 1966, p. 412; Stimson and Bundy, 1947, p. 166; Nelson, 1946, pp. 34–35; Smith, 1959, pp. 129, 219).

Having rejected the plan endorsed by the WRB, the president chose to organize the rearmament program by reviving, under authority of a 1916 statute, the Advisory Commission to the Council of National Defense (NDAC). On May 28, Roosevelt announced its establishment and its membership. The key positions went to U.S. Steel's chairman Stettinius (industrial materials) and General Motors' president William S. Knudsen (industrial production). Nelson, a Sears executive, was designated coordinator of national defense purchases and thereby became a de facto commissioner of the NDAC. Businessmen's fears that the rearmament program would lead to a New Deal takeover of industry began to subside. With the appointment of leading businessmen to direct the NDAC, "the great bugaboo of iron dictatorship [by Roosevelt] had been laid to rest" (U.S. Bureau of the Budget, 1946, pp. 21–25; Stromberg, 1953, pp. 74–75).

In January 1941, Roosevelt, again by executive order, created a new agency to oversee the rearmament program, the Office of Production Management (OPM), headed by Knudsen and well staffed by dollar-a-year men drawn predominantly from big business. These men occupied positions in the rearmament program for the token salary of a dollar a year or, more commonly, for no compensation at all. Clearly, after years of acrimony, the president was striving to make his peace with the capitalists. Under both the NDAC and the OPM, big business was visibly in the driver's seat. Roosevelt hoped that this arrangement would reassure businessmen and thereby prompt their participation in the rearmament program. They were somewhat reassured, no doubt; but evidently, that reassurance was not enough to make them clamor for defense contracts. Indeed, a striking aspect of the "defense period" from mid-1940 to the end of 1941 was the reluctance of many businessmen to seek or accept war-related business. Oddly, as an official history of the war expressed it, "It was necessary to induce manufacturers to accept defense contracts" (U.S. Bureau of the Budget, 1946, pp. 53–63 [quotation p. 25]; Stone, 1941; Catton, 1948, pp. 22, 29–30; Janeway, 1951, pp. 162–65). Why?

Businessmen's Reluctance to Accept Defense Contracts

Even after fears had subsided that a Rooseveltian dictatorship might be ushered in by the rearmament program, businessmen had numerous worries and reservations about participation in the military buildup. After all, the United States might never actually go to war. Even if it were to do so, the war might not be very big or last very long. Many businessmen, plagued by excess capacity throughout the 1930s (e.g., steel, aluminum), hesitated to add even more capacity that would be unremunerative in the postwar economy. During a war, returns on investment might be legally limited or captured by excess-profits taxes. Who would finance the new plants? Private financial institutions might consider them too risky. But if the government financed the new facilities, the result might be that after the war the government would use its financial leverage to restructure the competitive situation or go into business itself. Might the government again, as it had after World War I, file suits after the war for recovery of funds advanced to stimulate investment in war facilities? In any event, it made little economic sense to forgo production for current civilian markets, which were becoming robust again after the long depression (e.g., automobiles), in order to convert facilities for uncertain employment in the rearmament program. In sum, the widely noted reluctance of businessmen to seek or accept war-related business during the defense period reflected the existence of substantial risks, some with regard to world events and some with regard to public policies, and the businessmen's judgment that, in the circumstances, they would rather not bear those risks (Yntema, 1941, pp. 375–77) Stone, 1941, pp. 144, 157, 163, 186–90; U.S. Bureau of the Budget, 1946, 25–27, 60, 82; White, 1949, pp. 159–60, 163, 183; "The War Goes to Mr. Jesse Jones," 1941, 190; Nelson, 1946, pp. 80, 94, 106, 126, 163, 217–24; Janeway, 1951, pp. 163–65, 181; U.S. Civilian Production Administration, 1947, pp. 25, 49, 56, 79, 153–54, 187, 189, 193–97; Stromberg, 1953, p. 77; Stimson and Bundy, 1947, 166–67; Bernstein, 1966; Mitchell, 1940; Henderson and Nelson, 1941, pp. 391, 402–3; Jones, 1951, pp. 317, 320, 331).

Hence arose what critics of business, especially in the summer of 1940, styled a "strike of capital." I. F. Stone, who wrote a book titled *Business As Usual* in 1941, charged that "industry, with the connivance of the Defense Commission, was carrying on a sitdown strike for special tax privileges." Even as sympathetic a source as *Barron's Financial Weekly* (July 29, 1940) spoke of an "attitude of some defense industries that they must be assured of a profit." The president had conceded in his "fireside chat" radio broadcast of May 26 that industry could not be expected to bear all of the risks of the rearmament program.[5]

Both sides were engaged in active political maneuvering and bargaining. The government had committed itself, and the taxpayers' money, to a massive rearmament. The effort to get the goods—and get them fast—required the participation of businessmen to convert and expand production facilities. No one of political importance ever considered seriously that the government itself might produce a large proportion of the desired weapons in its own arsenals. Prewar military planning and politically potent business sentiment both upheld the desirability of privately managed production of munitions. Government production of essential raw materials, such as steel, copper, and aluminum, was even less thinkable in the prevailing ideological and political context. As Bruce Catton observed, the government faced "the necessity to bring into the defense effort, as active co-operators, the proprietors of the nations' chief physical assets. . . . For the duration of the prewar defense period, therefore, the game had to be played their way." Yet, even as late as October 1940, 59 percent of the executives polled in the *Fortune* survey reported that businessmen of their acquaintance had reservations about rearmament work. Table 2-1 lists the reasons given for this reluctance, which were diverse but generally reflected a continued distrust of the Roosevelt administration. By that time, however, the situation had been fundamentally altered. Big business had established its indispensability. The government had taken major steps to relieve defense producers of risks, to allay their fears, and in Carton's words, to "give them a piece of the performance" (Cantril, 1951, p. 346; Catton, 1948, p. 22). In a while, business opinion would catch up with the institutional changes set in motion during June–October 1940.

Negotiated Contracts, Cost-Plus, and Advance Payments

According to John Perry Miller, a careful analyst of wartime procurement, "adoption of the negotiated contract in place of the contract awarded by formal competitive bidding represented the greatest single step in the

Table 2-1. Reasons for businessmen's reservations
about rearmament work, October 1940

Reason	Percent with reservations who indicated this reason
Belief that the present administration in Washingtonis strongly antibusiness and a consequent discouragement over the practicability of cooperation with this administration on rearmament	77.3
Government's delay over letting them charge off the cost of their new plants for rearmament within five years for tax purposes	64.6
Fear that acceptance of rearmament orders will subject their plants to added interference with their labor policies	45.2
Belief that profits allowed on rearmament contracts are too small to justify the investment of the risks involved	38.4
Fear that an excess-profits tax will wipe out most of their profits on the rearmament orders	36.6
Feeling that the emergency is not so acute as the president should have them feel	35.0
Public sentiment against war profits, as a result of which businessmen would rather not handle war orders	20.1

Source: Fortune survey of a national cross-section of business executives, conducted by Elmo Roper, as reported in Cantril, Hadley. 1951. *Public Opinion, 1935–1946.* Princeton: Princeton University Press, p. 346.

development of procurement policies during the war." Impetus for the change came from Nelson, the government's chief purchasing expert, and his fellow dollar-a-year men. The businesslike practice of negotiating deals gained the approval of the NDAC, which favored it "because of its greater effectiveness in mobilizing industry." The army and later the president gave their approval, and in late June and early July of 1940, Congress enacted important legislation to authorize the use of negotiated contracts. An act of June 28 authorized the navy and the coast guard "to negotiate contracts for the acquisition, construction, repair, or alteration of complete naval vessels or aircraft, or any portion thereof, including plans, spare parts, and equipment therefor, that have been or may be authorized, and also for machine tools and other similar equipment, with or without advertising or competitive bidding. . . ." An act of July 2 gave even broader authority to the Secretary of War to purchase military supplies, land, and construction services "with or without advertising." The act also conveyed to the president the essentially open-ended power, "with or without advertising, through the appropriate agencies of the Government . . . to provide for emergencies affecting the national security and defense" (Miller, 1949, pp. 84, 87; Nelson, 1946, pp. 102–4, 149; 54 Stat 676 [28 June 1940]; 54 Stat 712 [2 July 1940], at 712, 714).

Under this authority, the military departments immediately changed their purchasing practices. In the fiscal year ending on June 30, 1940, the War Department had made 87 percent of its purchases through advertising and invitations to bid. During the following eight months, in stark contrast, the department spent ten times as much and placed 74 percent of the contracts, by value, through negotiation. Although many small contracts continued to be placed by competitive bidding, the big contracts were thereafter almost all negotiated. As a contemporary writer stressed, procurement officers could now base their decisions on "factors other than low prices," such as managerial reliability and cooperativeness, ability to deliver high-quality goods quickly, and possession of effective R&D facilities (Smith, 1959, p. 247 [also pp. 72, 223, 243, 246]; Gragg, 1941, p. 227). Henceforth, only rarely would large defense contractors have to bear the burden of submitting the lowest bid in order to get the business.

In lieu of advertised contracts and competitive bidding, the expediting acts of June 28 and July 2 authorized the use of negotiated, CPFF contracts. The fee was limited to 7 percent of the estimated cost. According to an official army history, the fixed fee "represented the contractor's compensation for undertaking and performing the contracts. . . . [It] constituted a guaranteed clear profit. . . . Thus all major risks under CPFF contracts were transferred to the government." The expediting acts outlawed the use of contracts guaranteeing suppliers their costs plus a percentage of costs (CPPC), which had produced scandalous results during World War I; but in practice, the CPFF contracts of World War II (and since) amounted to something similar. As Smith observed, "the fee was determined by the application of a standard or reasonable percentage figure to the estimated costs." Furthermore, the contracts were not made binding. Significant changes in the contractor's circumstances or in the scope of the contract during its term could result in "appropriate increases" of the supposedly fixed fee. The expediting act of June 28 explicitly authorized such changes in existing contracts (54 Stat. at 677, 680, 713; Smith, 1959, pp. 282–83, 312).

Cost-plus-fixed-fee contracts received much criticism from the public and members of Congress. Harry Truman, chairman during 1941–44 of the Senate's Special Committee to Investigate the National Defense Program, wrote in his memoirs, "Huge fixed fees were offered by the government in much the same way that Santa Claus passes out gifts at a church Christmas party. . . . [T]he fees allowed to contractors by the government sometimes made it possible for them to earn, on a three-month job at government risk, three or four times as much as they had formerly been able to make at their own risk in an entire year of work." Truman discovered that the navy's CPFF contracts with private shipbuilders were "extremely liberal"; the government's payments of fees and bonuses "bore no relation whatever to the average net profits of the companies during the period from 1936–1940." Despite the official and unofficial criticism of CPFF contracts, not much was done to reduce their use during the war (or since). They accounted for 46 percent of the value of all army, navy, and Maritime Commission supply contracts of more than $10,000 (excluding awards for foodstuffs, construction, and production facilities) during 1940–41; by the second half of 1944, they had been reduced only to 40 percent.[6]

Although the procurement officers had an official rationale for their extensive use of CPFF contracts—they claimed, inter alia, that it was cheaper for the government to use CPFF contracts than to pay the risk premiums that contractors would demand on fixed-price contracts—a chief reason, in fact, was that "some contractors themselves seemed happy with their relatively riskless contracts." Miller explained:

> Many contractors sought a contract which approached as closely as possible the CPFF contract in its risklessness but carried the higher profit associated with risk-taking. While the services were willing to assume many of those risks over which the contractor had no control, they sought a fixed-price contract which had sufficient pricing risk to provide incentive to efficiency and at the same time would not yield profits which were too excessive when viewed at the completion of the contract. The result of this conflict of interest was a wide variety of contractual forms in which risks, rewards, and incentives were mixed in various ways. It is not an exaggeration to say that as a result we came closer than is generally realized to financing this war on a disguised CPPC basis.

Often, the contractor's actual costs turned out to be far lower than the initially estimated costs, especially when high-volume production permitted significant economies of learning from experience. Hence the fixed fee, relative to actual costs, gave the contractor far more than a 7 percent profit margin (the maximum, relative to estimated costs, allowed by the law) [Smith, 1959, p. 283; Miller, 1949, pp. 120, 130, 132–33].

Finally, besides providing for negotiated and CPFF contracts, the expediting acts of the summer of 1940 authorized the army and navy to make advance payments of up to 30 percent of the contract price, as well as progress payments during the performance of the work. Also, the president was authorized to provide government property for use in privately owned plants—a gift of the services of fixed capital. Smith described the availability of working capital in the form of advance and progress payments as "a most important consideration underlying the decision of many producers to accept contracts and undertake cash outlays for conversion to war production." Miller recognized that advance and progress payments were "another facet to the program for facilitating production with minimum

risk to the contractor. . . ." From mid-1940 to September 1945, the War De-
partment made advance payments of more than $7 billion and the Navy
Department made payments of about $2 billion (54 Stat. at 676, 713, 714;
Smith, 1959, p. 220; Miller, 1949, pp. 118–19; U.S. Civilian Production
Administration, 1947, p. 60; Connery, 1951, pp. 367–68.)

Changes in Tax Laws

Even if the contract ensured a profit to the private contractor, the possibility remained that what the government had given in the form of contractual fees it might reclaim in large part by prohibiting or taxing away
"excess profits." Under the Vinson-Trammel Act of 1934 and the Merchant
Marine Act of 1936, both as amended, profit margins on government contracts for aircraft and ships were already subject to limits that ranged from
8 to 12 percent. In the event of war, the government would raise corporate income-tax rates and impose an excess-profits tax—the experience of
World War I left little doubt about these matters. Firms therefore faced
the prospect that investments in expanded or new facilities would yield
scant aftertax returns during the war, then leave them saddled with excess
capacity after the war. No wonder that "private enterprise showed considerable reluctance to begin the task" (Smith, 1959, p. 457; Stone, 1941, pp.
165–66).

At the military departments and the NDAC, in mid-1940, the government's economic mobilizers found themselves in what Nelson called
a "stalemate" and critics of business called a "strike of capital." Commissioner Stettinius complained that the navy's construction program was
being held up by armor-plate producers who would not increase their capacities until Congress produced a "definite ruling" on accelerated depreciation allowances for tax purposes. Congress had appropriated funds for
some 4,000 aircraft and the War Department had awarded the contracts,
but as late as August 9, Secretary Stimson told a congressional committee
that the aircraft companies had signed the contracts for only thirty-three
planes. In a section of his 1941 book titled *Treason,* Stone charged that

"the aviation industry was used as front for the rest of business in its fight for special tax privileges on defense contracts." Six major aircraft companies, headed by Douglas, were reportedly producing under a temporary agreement, awaiting congressional passage of a tax bill. Stimson, blunt as ever, observed that businessmen "were not going to sign contracts until they had a bill protecting them against large losses. . . ." (Nelson, 1946, p. 106; Connery, 1951, p. 91; Mitchell, 1940, p. 66; Stone, 1941, pp. 160, 168; Stimson and Bundy, 1947, p. 166).

At the NDAC, Nelson and a fellow commissioner, the economist and New Dealer Leon Henderson, took the initiative in formulating a tax provision to move the defense contractors "off dead center." In collaboration with the financier William C. Potter of the Guaranty Trust Co. and the big businessman Floyd B. Odium of the Atlas Corporation, they devised a plan to permit businessmen to depreciate certified emergency facilities in five years, instead of the usual twenty, or in a shorter period if the emergency should end sooner or if the facilities should cease to be necessary for the war program. The Treasury was persuaded "not to oppose" the measure. Knudsen gave it a stirring defense before the Senate Finance Committee, which finally approved it, but just barely, by a vote of 11–10. On October 8, it was enacted into law as Title III of the Second Revenue Act of 1940 (Nelson, 1946, pp. 106–7; Janeway, 163–65; 54 Stat. 974 [8 October 1940] at 998–1003; Blakey and Blakey, 1940, pp. 729–33; Brown and Patterson, 1943, 636–40).

The act also abolished the profit limitations of the Vinson-Trammel Act and the Merchant Marine Act, but at the insistence of the president and his fellow New Dealers, it raised corporate income taxes (to a top bracket of 24 percent) and imposed an excess-profits tax (to a top bracket of 50 percent). Loopholes allowed escape from much of the apparent burden. Corporations were allowed a choice of methods for computing their excess-profits tax liability, so no one was denied an opportunity to earn a substantial after-tax rate of return. Eighteen leading aircraft companies, for example, managed to earn profits of almost 26 percent on their net worth in 1940; and despite booming business, only five of twelve integrated steel companies had to pay excess-profits taxes for that year. In addition, carryback provisions "were designed specifically to lessen the financial risk of concerns in expanding their facilities for war production." Under these provisions, which amounted to various forms of income averaging, firms could charge certain war-induced costs and losses after the war against wartime income, thereby reducing their total tax liabilities. Eliot Janeway explained:

> The excess-profits tax rate was very high indeed. But the excess-profits tax that business paid was not given up—as ordinary tax money is given up—irretrievably: this money was being put on wartime deposit with the Treasury. On the inevitable day of postwar readjustment, losses could be "carried back" as claims for refunds of these excess-profits tax payments. Thus was created the biggest and most resilient cushion in the history of public finance.

Again, as contemporary analysts recognized, the government—that is, the taxpayers in general—was shouldering the financial risk from which defense contractors were being relieved. (54 Stat. at 1003; Blakey and Blakey, 1940, pp. 731–33; Smaller War Plants Corporation, 1946, 46–47; Janeway, 1951, p. 165; Stone, 1941, pp. 166, 169–70.)

Passage of the Revenue Act of October 1940 provoked companies to build new facilities "with a rush." In Nelson's judgment, "probably no other factor played a greater part in breaking the log-jam." As table 2-2 shows, total applications for certification under the accelerated depreciation program amounted to about $3 billion by the end of 1941. By the end of the war, the War Department had certified almost $5 billion, the navy about $1.5 billion, and the War Production Board some $750 million. The accelerated depreciation law, said Smith, "made a frank appeal to the profit motive. . . . [I]t converted high tax rates from a liability to an asset," because "[t]he higher the rate of corporate income and excess profits taxes, the greater was the positive inducement to retain its earnings in the form of expanded plant and equipment." (Obviously, plants that would be suitable for, or easily converted to, the production of civilian goods after the war received the most encouragement under this tax scheme.) In short, as

Janeway concluded, the five-year write-off provision was "a bonanza for business" (Nelson, 1946, p. 107; Brown and Patterson, 1943, p. 640; Smith, 1959, pp. 472–73 [quotations pp. 474–75]; Janeway, 1951, p. 164).

Government Financing of Investment in Plants and Equipment

Even with a CPFF contract to guarantee the net income, advance payments to provide the working capital, and accelerated depreciation to reduce the tax liability, a military supplier might have to bear a major risk, namely, the risk of capital loss on the physical plant and equipment in which the corporation had invested. When the plant and equipment were highly specialized in the production of exclusively war-related products, the prospect of postwar capital loss loomed large. As table 2-2 indicates, corporate investment in war facilities during the defense period for the most part took the form of investment in facilities that would lend themselves to production for civilian markets after the war. Corporations invested three times more in steel and chemical plants, for example, than they did in plants for ammunition, guns, and combat vehicles combined. Of course, the risk of capital loss could itself be shifted if someone else paid for the plants. "The use of government funds to aid the expansion of manufacturing facilities was"[7] as Miller observed, "another approach to the problem of reducing contractors' investment risks" (Miller, 1949, p. 116; White, 1949, pp. 156–83; McLaughlin, 1943, pp. 108–10, 114; Connery, 1951, pp. 92, 350; Klagsbrunn, 1943, p. 121).

Of the almost $26 billion spent for new manufacturing plants and equipment during the five years ending in mid-1945, more than $17 billion, or roughly two-thirds, was financed directly by the federal government (table 2-3). Under authority of the expediting acts of mid-1940, the army, navy, and Maritime Commission spent some $9 billion out of their appropriations from the Treasury. Most of these expenditures went to build plants for making ammunition and explosives, for bomb and shell loading,

Table 2-2. Corporate investment for war facilities certified as eligible
for accelerated depreciation, through December 1941

Product to be produced	Estimated cost of facilities (millions of dollars)
Iron, steel, and products	198
Nonferrous metals and products	198
Machinery, electrical equipment	178
Chemicals, petroleum products	141
Aircraft, aircraft engines	106
Ammunition	51
Guns	36
Ships	32
Combat and motorized vehicles	27
Miscellaneous manufacturing	75
Nonmanufacturing	284
Applications received, but not yet acted on	1,657
Total	2,983

Source: War Production Board press release, March 9, 1942, as reported in Brown, E. Cary and Gardner Patterson. 1943. Accelerated Depreciation: A Neglected Chapter in War Taxation. *Quarterly Journal of Economics* 57 (August): 640.

Table 2-3. Investment in manufacturing plants and equipment,
July 1940 to June 1945 (billions of dollars)

Industrial group	Privately financed	Federally financed	Total
Iron, steel, and products	1.04	2.87	3.91
Nonferrous metals and products	0.41	1.88	2.29
Metal fabricating industries	1.62	7.41	9.04
Chemicals, allied products	0.79	2.98	3.77
Petroleum, coal products	0.90	0.54	1.44
Other manufacturing	3.46	0.39	3.85
Not classified as to industry	0.39	1.10	1.49
Total manufacturing	8.61	17.17	25.79

Source: War Production Board data as presented in Smaller War Plants Corporation. 1946. *Economic Concentration and World War II.* Washington, D.C.: U.S. Government Printing Office, p. 38.

and for shipyards, that is, for facilities traditionally encompassed within the armed forces' arsenals and naval yards. Such facilities were operated either directly by the government or by private operators, who received a management fee and exercised little independence in the operations. Some $3.6 billion of the direct investment by the armed forces and the Maritime Commission went to construct and equip facilities operated by private contractors under lease arrangements, so-called GOCO plants (government-owned, contractor-operated). The outputs of these plants included, for the most part, basic industrial goods and raw materials, rather than explosives, ammunition, and the like (54 Stat. at 680, 712; Miller, 1949, pp. 117–18; White, 1949, pp. 156–57; Smaller War Plants Corporation, 1946, p. 48; Smith, 1959, p. 496).

Besides having the armed services themselves build industrial facilities, the government experimented with various devices to shift the risk of capital loss away from the military contractors. In the summer of 1940, the NDAC held numerous conferences with representatives of high finance, including president Potter and vice-president Broderick Haskell of Guaranty Trust, and John Hancock, Baruch's close associate, of Lehman Brothers. The result was the Emergency Plant Facility (EPF) contract, also known as the "bankable" contract. Under this plan, the contractor financed a plant certified by the government as required for the national defense program, but the government promised to repay the cost of the facility fully in sixty equal monthly payments and then to assume its ownership. The contractor's risk, as Gerald White observed, "was reduced to a minimum because of his assurance that the government would ultimately assume the cost of the facilities. Since the government would acquire title to the plant at the conclusion of the emergency, there was no possibility of a direct windfall gain to the contractor." Of course, there was also no possibility of a postwar capital loss for the contractor, which, in the circumstances of 1940, seemed a more likely contingency. To make the EPF contract even more attractive to private corporations, the government gave the contractor an option to buy the plant at the end of the war; furthermore, the government promised never to use the plant "for business or commercial purposes" (White, 1949, pp. 171–73; Miller, 1949, pp. 116–17; Smith, 1959, pp. 476–84).

The provision that made EPF contracts "bankable" was that the government's monthly reimbursement payments could be assigned to a financial institution from which the contractor had obtained the funds to build the facility. Such assignments previously had been illegal and now had to be authorized by statute. Accordingly, at the behest of the NDAC, Congress enacted the Assignment of Claims Act of October 9, 1940. Financiers had demanded a legal claim to the government's payments as security for their loans to defense contractors. Indeed, they demanded even greater protection, and their additional demands resulted in the virtual stillbirth of the EPF contract (54 Stat. 1029 [9 October 1940]; White, 1949, pp. 172–74; Smith, 1959, pp. 480–81; Klagsbrunn, 1943, pp. 121–22).

The problem arose because Congress might fail to appropriate the money for the government to make the monthly payments it had agreed to make, leaving the banker unpaid, and "no bank would want to run the risk of repayment out of funds not yet appropriated." To remove this risk, the contracts provided that the government sponsor of the loan, usually the War Department or the Navy Department, would stand ready to repay the loan in full during the last quarter of each fiscal year. The effect, as White noted, "was to put the government in the position of paying interest to a bank on a loan while having on hand sufficient resources to pay off the principal"—a conspicuously disadvantageous arrangement for the government. The EPF contracts also suffered as much in implementation as in design, and ultimately, little money was spent under this scheme: some $342 million, almost all of it during 1940–41 (White, 1949, pp. 173–74; Smith, 1959, pp. 481, 483). A more workable plan was needed to get the new war plants built while relieving the capitalists of risk.

The solution took the form of GOCO plants financed by the Defense Plant Corporation (DPC), a subsidiary of the Reconstruction Finance Corporation, created on August 22, 1940. When the DPC was created, said a *Fortune* writer at the end of 1941, "[h]ardly anyone was conscious that the government had taken a momentous step toward extensive plant ownership." In the beginning, its role was generally considered that of a minor auxiliary to the armed forces' direct investment in plants. By the end of the war, however, the DPC had invested more than $7 billion in industrial plants and equipment, thereby "expanding capacity with a minimum of risk to industry." The DPC invested mainly in facilities that would still be valuable after the war in such industries as aircraft, aluminum, machine tools, magnesium, shipbuilding, synthetic rubber, and steel. Aircraft plants alone absorbed about half of the DPC's outlays. Fourteen of the fifteen largest aircraft engine plants built during the war received financing, in whole or in part, from the DPC. Besides building entire plants, the DPC invested extensively in equipment for use in existing, privately owned plants, thereby creating "scrambled" facilities. So great was its investment that by June 30, 1945, the DPC owned 10 to 13 percent of the country's industrial capacity, including 96 percent of the capacity in synthetic rubber, 90 percent in magnesium, 71 percent in aircraft, and 58 percent in aluminum (Smaller War Plants Corporation, 1946, p. 48; Miller, 1949, p. 117 [quotation]; "The War Goes," 1941, p. 189; Smith, 1959, p. 485; Jones, 1951, pp. 316, 323; White, 1949, pp. 158, 169; Klagsbrunn, 1943, pp. 123–24).

The Reconstruction Finance Corporation (RFC), the vast financial institution in which the DPC constituted one teller's window, had been created early in 1932 as a brake on the collapse of the financial system during the Great Contraction. Afterward, especially after Roosevelt took office, it received greatly expanded authority. In pursuit of its multiple missions, it became the New Deal's chief lending and spending agency. Since 1933, it had been headed by Jesse H. Jones, a rich, conservative, but Democratic Texas banker and businessman, who by 1940 occupied numerous offices in the government. He was both Secretary of Commerce and Federal Loan Administrator. The latter position gave him command of the RFC, even though he was no longer formally its head. In a December 1941 article, a writer in *Fortune* described Jones as "a powerful man—certainly the second most powerful in the government," and "a man whom a large part of the business world considers to be the sole rock of sanity in a deranged government." Holding two cabinet-level positions and controlling the RFC, a financial empire with borrowing and spending authority independent of annual congressional appropriations, he had "power, prestige, and enormous acumen." He could, in the judgment of the perhaps-too-worshipful *Fortune* writer, "exercise a type of bold and determined leadership that might galvanize the production effort in a way that no other man has yet been able to do" ("The War Goes" 1941, pp. 91, 203). In mid-1940, it was natural that many Americans looked to Jones to break the stalemate in providing expanded industrial facilities for the national defense program.

Before Jones and the RFC could act, however, their legal mandate required still further expansion. Under existing law, the RFC could make only well-secured loans that reasonably promised "retirement or repayment." It had no authority to own, lease, or operate plants. The aid to defense industries that was being contemplated in the spring of 1940 went far beyond the limits of the RFC's statutory authority. Early in the year, while the "phony war" persisted and the British desperately sought to augment their American sources of munitions, Jones had asked two RFC lawyers, Clifford J. Durr and Hans Klagsbrunn, to consider how the RFC might assist the British. (By this time, the Roosevelt administration, though still formally neutral, was committed to giving the British all possible support, short of American combat forces.) The memorandum that the lawyers drew up in April indicated several options, including government ownership and lease of facilities through an RFC subsidiary. Officials at the RFC determined the precise legal authority that they would need in order to employ their contemplated means of action, and they drew up a bill, which they sent to Congress at the end of May ("The War Goes" 1941, p. 187; Jones, 1951, pp. 340–41; White, 1949, pp. 160–61, 166–67).

Even though the bill had the president's full approval—or perhaps because it did—some members of Congress balked at granting the RFC the sweeping authority it sought. Robert A. Taft, a vigorous critic in the Senate, declared the bill "the most outrageous legislative proposal" he had seen since becoming a senator. Under the proposal, he complained, the government "could go into just any business it chooses." Another opponent said that the measure could create "the power to set up a fascist state in America." In response to the hostile congressional reaction, the bill was rephrased, mainly to foreclose the dreaded possibility of government competition with free enterprise (Jones, 1951, p. 341; "The War Goes" 1941, p. 92; White, 1949, pp. 161–62.)

Notwithstanding its amendment, the measure enacted on June 25, 1940, endowed the RFC with extraordinary authority. With characteristic modesty, Jones described it as "a grant of perhaps the broadest powers ever conferred upon a single governmental agency"; under it, the RFC could do practically anything that the defense and war-making authorities thought best for the nation's safety and the prosecution of the war. The statute authorized the RFC:

> To make loans to, or, when requested by the Federal Loan Administrator with the approval of the President, purchase the capital stock of, any corporation (a) for the purpose of producing, acquiring, and carrying strategic and critical materials as defined by the President, and (b) for plant construction, expansion, and equipment, and working capital, to be used by the corporation in the manufacture of equipment and supplies necessary to the national defense, on such terms and conditions and with such maturities as the Corporation may determine; and (2) When requested by the Federal Loan Administrator, with the approval of the President, to create or to organize a corporation or corporations with power (a) to produce, acquire, and carry strategic and critical materials as defined by the President, (b) to purchase and lease land, to purchase, lease, build, and expand plants, and to purchase and produce equipment, supplies, and machinery for the manufacture of arms, ammunition, and implements of war, (c) to lease such plants to private corporations to engage in such manufacture, and (d) if the President finds that it is necessary for a Government agency to engage in such manufacture, to engage in such manufacture itself. The Corporation may make loans to, or purchase the capital stock of, any such corporation for any purpose within the powers of the corporations as above set forth related to the national-defense

program, on such terms and conditions as the Corporation may determine. Any corporation created or organized by the Corporation under the preceding paragraph is also authorized, with the approval of the President, to make payments against the purchase price to be paid for strategic and critical materials in advance of the delivery of such materials.

As if this tremendous authority were not enough, the RFC's powers were expanded a bit further by an act of June 10, 1941 (Jones, 1951, pp. 9, 318 [also pp. 326–27, 341]; 54 Stat. 572 at 573–74; 55 Stat. 248 at 249).

The act of June 25, 1940, provided the authority under which the DPC—and many other war subsidiaries of the RFC—came into existence. Durr seems to have played the most important part in creating it, although Klagsbrunn, Emil Schram, the RFC's chairman, and Jones himself apparently also contributed. In any event, its creation was entirely a family affair within the RFC. The new agency made its first deal, an arrangement under which the Packard Motor Car Company leased a DPC-financed plant to manufacture Rolls Royce airplane engines for the British, in early September 1940. Others, many others, soon followed ("The War Goes" p. 187; White, 1949, pp. 166–70, 176–77).

Lessees of the Defense Plant Corporation's GOCO plants paid rent in one of two main forms. Contractors selling their entire output to the armed forces paid a nominal $1 per year. (Military procurement officers were supposed to ensure that such contractors received no reimbursement under their supply contracts for plant depreciation or amortization.) Contractors who also sold goods to private customers paid a rent based on a percentage of their output, sales, or profit and calculated to amortize the cost of the plant during its useful life. As Jones noted, the DPC sometimes "shared in the profits but agreed to take the losses"—another case of shifting the risk from contractor to government. Aluminum plants, in particular, enjoyed this protection. Lessees also received options to buy the plants after the emergency. The purchase option allayed the contractors' fears that the plants might ultimately fall into the hands of competitors, fears that could cause the government's negotiations with its military contractors to become, as Klagsbrunn put it, "greatly protracted" (Jones, 1951, pp. 315–16 [quotation p. 316]; Klagsbrunn, 1943, p. 125; Miller, 1949, p. 117; White, 1949, p. 176).

Investment in plants and equipment by the DPC had several advantages for the government. It simplified and, above all, expedited the expansion of essential industrial capacity for the rearmament program. The arrangement could not have succeeded, however, without its many advantages for the contractors, who occupied the plants as lessees. White, who made an excellent study of the DPC shortly after the war, clearly identified the major advantages:

> [T]he lessee was able to operate the DPC plant with far greater freedom than if he were operating a service-owned plant under a management-fee contract. . . . [T]he lessee was free to conduct his operations as if the plant were his own. The DPC lease mechanism thus largely substituted self-policing for control by government red tape. Moreover, DPC shouldered all risk associated with the fixed capital investment. Consequently, there was no danger that the private firm operating the plant would emerge from the war burdened with debt as a result of unwise plant investment. Although thus freed from the risk of fixed capital investment, the lessee was encouraged to build an efficient plant in the first instance and to maintain it well thereafter through inclusion of an explicit purchase option in most leases and an additional provision concerning negotiated purchase. Thus, if the lessee wanted the plant after the war and would pay the government a "fair" price, he might acquire it through exercise of the purchase option for all or part of the plant through negotiated purchase. (White, 1949, pp. 182–3)

Contractors who occupied a DPC plant and entered into a negotiated CPFF contract with the government had achieved the capitalist dream: With virtually no investment in the plant or the working capital to operate it, they could accrue a substantial guaranteed net income and bear no risk whatever.

Concentration of Contracting and the "Intimate Relationship"

"This defense program" declared General Motors' president Charles E. Wilson in 1941, "is big business. We might just as well make up our minds to that. It is big business and it isn't going to be handled by thousands of small businesses alone. Small plants can't make tanks, airplanes or other large complex armaments" (Janeway, 1951, pp. 256–57). Whether they could or not, they were not going to receive the opportunity to try. The business of defense contracting was highly concentrated among a relative handful of giant corporations, from the beginning of the rearmament program in 1940 to the end of the war in 1945—and has remained so ever since.

Statistics for the defense period tell a remarkable story. During June–December 1940, the armed forces awarded more than $11 billion in prime contracts. The top one hundred companies got more than 86 percent of the business; the top twenty got about 60 percent of it. Late in July 1941, the OPM announced that so far in the rearmament almost three-fourths of the defense business had been placed with just fifty-six firms; six huge corporations held almost a third of the contracts, by value; Bethlehem Steel alone had almost 10 percent of the total. Other early leaders included New York Shipbuilding Co., General Motors, Curtiss-Wright, Newport News Shipbuilding, and Du Pont. Just before the United States formally entered the war, the top one hundred contractors were reported to hold about 82 percent of the contracts, by value (U.S. Civilian Production Administration, 1947, pp. 63, 147; Nelson, 1946, p. 272).

By mid-1941, widespread complaints had arisen, as smaller manufacturing firms, lacking official priorities for critical components and raw materials, increasingly found themselves unable to carry on their businesses. "Priorities unemployment" became a perceived and resented economic problem. Small businessmen clamored for a "fair share" of the war business and put pressure on their representatives in Congress to help them get it.

Although notable political efforts and small administrative changes were made—for example, an independent Smaller War Plants Corporation was created in 1942 to help smaller firms get military contracts—the pattern of high concentration established during the defense period continued to mark the industrial mobilization program. Smaller businesses (those with no more than five hundred employees) eventually found numerous opportunities as subcontractors, but it was estimated that they accounted for only 30 percent of total war production. From June 1940 through September 1944, the top one hundred prime contractors received about two-thirds of the awards, by value; the top ten firms got about 30 percent; the leading contractor, General Motors, by itself, accounted for nearly 8 percent of all prime contracts, by value. R&D contracts with private corporations were even more concentrated. The top sixty-eight corporations got two-thirds of the R&D awards, and the top ten firms got nearly two-fifths of the total (Heath, 1972, p. 308; Smaller War Plants Corporation, 1946, pp. 29–30, 32, 52–53). Here was a harbinger of how defense R&D would be allocated during the postwar arms race driven by scientific and technological competition with the Soviet Union.

Notably, the concentration of government-financed facilities was even greater than the concentration of war production, prime contracts, or R&D awards. Virtually all of the GOCO plants were operated by big corporations. As of June 30, 1944, the twenty-six firms listed in table 2-4 enjoyed the use of exactly half the value of all existing government-financed industrial facilities leased to private contractors. The top 168 contractors using GOCO plants employed more than 83 percent of such facilities, by value (Smaller War Plants Corporation, 1946, pp. 48–49.) The implication of this high concentration for the character of the postwar industrial structure is evident when one recalls that the operator of a GOCO plant usually held an option to buy it after the war.

Military officials gave various reasons for dealing predominantly with big business. For the army and navy, dealing with a few big corporations was simply easier than dealing with many smaller ones. (One does not exaggerate to say that the armed forces' administrative capacities for

Table 2-4. Leading corporate operators of government-owned, contractor-operated (GOCO) facilities, June 30, 1944 (ranked by value of GOCO facilities employed)

Firm	Cumulative percent of all GOCO plants' value
1. General Motors Corp.	7.1
2. Aluminum Co. of America	11.5
3. Curtiss-Wright Corp.	15.8
4. U.S. Steel Corp.	19.6
5. Ford Motor Co.	22.8
6. Bethlehem Steel Corp.	25.2
7. Chrysler Corp.	27.1
8. United Aircraft Corp.	28.9
9. Henry J. Kaiser Co.	30.7
10. General Electric Co.	32.5
11. Douglas Aircraft Co.	34.2
12. Republic Steel Corp.	35.9
13. Dow Chemical Co.	37.5
14. Anaconda Copper Mining Co.	38.9
15. Union Carbide & Carbon Corp.	40.2
16. Consolidated Vultee Aircraft Corp.	41.5
17. Standard Oil Co. of N.J.	42.6
18. Bendix Aviation Corp.	43.6
19. Packard Motor Car Co.	44.5
20. Continental Motors Corp.	45.4
21. Studebaker Corp.	46.2
22. Bell Aircraft Corp.	47.1
23. Goodyear Tire & Rubber Co.	47.8
24. Todd Shipyards Corp.	48.6
25. Koppers United Co.	49.3
26. North American Aviation, Inc.	50.0

Source: Smaller War Plants Corporation. 1946. *Economic Concentration and World War II.* Washington, D.C.: U.S. Government Printing Office, p. 49.

procurement were strained beyond the breaking point by the massive scale of the rearmament effort—remember, the size of the armed forces, as measured by active-duty personnel, grew more than 36-fold between 1939 and 1945, and the annual rate of military spending grew almost 60-fold!) The military procurement officers sought huge quantities of goods, and they placed the highest priority on speed of delivery. Big corporations had the necessary plant capacity, technical and managerial expertise, and established relations with suppliers to respond readily to the military demands. Moreover, they had the quality-control systems and R&D staffs needed to meet the exacting standards for complex weapons and military equipment and to develop and test even better munitions as the war progressed. The Under Secretary of War Robert Patterson, who headed the army's vast procurement program, summed up the matter when he testified before the Truman Committee early in 1941: "We had to take industrial America as we found it."[8] Manufacturing production was found to be already highly concentrated among a few hundred big corporations, so those were the firms that the armed forces selected to produce munitions for the rearmament program.

Patterson's testimony also mentioned another factor of consequence for the distribution of the war business. Speeding the rearmament "made it necessary that orders be placed with concerns with whom preliminary arrangements for production of munitions had been made under the industrial mobilization plan in the years preceding the emergency." In preparing its M-Day Plans during the 1930s, the army had routinely consulted with big businessmen, and accordingly, its "preliminary arrangements" had assigned their firms a preeminent place in the contemplated industrial mobilization effort.[9]

No doubt the huge rearmament program simply could not have gone forward very far without the dominant participation of big business— the brute fact was that the bulk of the industrial capacity belonged to big business—but the question of concentration in the defense business went beyond merely taking industry "as we found it." The real issues were: Who would direct the industrial mobilization, how would they do so, and for what ends, other than the obvious one of rearmament? These questions came into the open first when the WRB provoked such hostile reaction in the fall of 1939. If anything, the issue grew hotter in 1940 and 1941. It focused then on the dollar-a-year men.

The businessmen who occupied these dollar-a-year positions in the rearmament program (for a token dollar a year or for no compensation at all) represented the citadels of economic preeminence in the United States: Stettinius of U.S. Steel; Knudsen, E. F. Johnson, and John L. Pratt of General Motors; Nelson of Sears; Ralph Budd of the Burlington Railroad; John D. Biggers of Libby-Owens-Ford; W. H. Harrison of AT&T; Harold Vance of Studebaker; and a host of others. Nelson did not exaggerate when he placed them "among the nation's top bracket business and industrial leaders." Surveying the NDAC in August 1940, Jonathan Mitchell pronounced it "the greatest concentration of big-business influence ever seen in Washington," with the possible exception of the National Recovery Administration. Substitution of the OPM for the NDAC in January 1941 did nothing to alter the character of the leading mobilization officials. The OPM, declared Stone, was also "dominated by representatives of Du Pont and Rockefeller companies and those dependent upon them." Throughout the defense period, their numbers increased. By January 5, 1942, almost nine hundred people were employed by the OPM without regular compensation (Nelson, 1946, pp. 92–93 [also pp. 332–33]; Mitchell, 1940, p. 267; Stone, 1941, pp. 136–37; Truman Committee Report, 1972, p. 134.) Later, even more came on board.

Hardly anyone ever questioned the ability, honesty, or patriotism of these business leaders turned temporary government officials. They were, even Stone conceded, "as decent and well-intentioned" as any other group. The point, in brief, was simply that they were big businessmen—previously, currently (usually on leave of absence from their companies), and presumably in the future—and "some of the necessary questions on which they had to decide threatened their interests and ran counter to their habits as business men." Senator Truman's investigating committee, which took a special interest in these emergency public servants, expressed the misgivings held by many others about the dollar-a-year men's "subconscious tendency":

> It is only natural that such men should believe that only companies of the size and type with which they were associated have the ability to perform defense contracts; that small and intermediate companies ought not to be given prime contracts; that the urgencies of the defense program are such that they have no time to consider small companies for defense contracts; that the large companies ought not to be required to subcontract items which they could profitably manufacture and as to which they express lack of confidence in the productive facilities of smaller concerns; that the producers of strategic materials should not be expected or required to increase their capacities, even at Government expense, where that might result in excess capacity after the war and adversely affect their postwar profits; and that large companies should not be expected or required to convert their existing facilities into defense plants, where they prefer to use their plants to make the profits from their civilian business and, at the same time, to have additional plants directly or indirectly paid for by the government, which they can operate profitably on terms dictated by themselves.

Catton, a vigorous critic of how the war mobilization program was carried out, concluded that the extensive employment of dollar-a-year men preserved "the existing corporate control of American industry" not because they purposely acted to achieve that result, but because the alternatives were either unthinkable or unacceptable to such men, and that their control of the industrial mobilization program "insured a high degree of understanding and co-operation between industry and government" (Stone, 1941, p. 123; Truman Committee Report, 1972, pp. 136; Catton, 1948, p. 120).

Nowhere did that cooperation flourish more than it did between the armed forces and big business. As a contemporary economist, Benjamin Anderson, observed, "The attitude of suspicion, of slow, meticulous negotiation, which characterized the relation of government with business at the beginning of the war, gave way very largely to an attitude of mutual confidence as the war went on" (Anderson, 1979, p. 555). Smith, the author of the army's official history of the economic mobilization for World War II, gave an exceptionally frank account of the revolution in how procurement transactions were made:

> The relationship between the government and its contractors was gradually transformed from an "arm's length" relationship between two more or less equal parties in a business transaction into an undefined but intimate relationship—partly business, partly fiduciary, and partly unilateral—in which the financial, contractual, statutory, and other instruments and assumptions of economic activity were reshaped to meet the ultimate requirements of victory in war. Under the new conditions, contracts ceased to be completely binding: fixed prices in contracts often became only tentative and provisional prices; excessive profits received by contractors were recoverable by the government; and potential losses resulting from many causes—including errors, poor judgments, and performance failures on the part of contractors—were averted by modification and amendment of contracts, with or without legal "consideration" whenever required by the exigencies of the war effort. (Smith, 1959, p. 312; see also Beaumont, 1977, p. 130)

Although Smith's description mentions the armed forces' "unilateral" actions and their recovery of "excessive" profits, as well as their arrangements to accommodate and bail out the contractors, the most remarkable aspect of the changes he described was the dissolution of the binding force of contracts between the military services and the contractors. In procurement, everything became open, fluid, subject to alteration. A transaction became less a firm "deal" than an ongoing joint enterprise among friends—as Smith put it, an "intimate relationship"—in which military officials and businessmen cooperated to achieve a common goal that was not incompatible with, and indeed was highly facilitative of, the pursuit of their separate interests.

For the contractors, of course, the bottom line was the top concern, and although no comprehensive study of contractor profits exists, no one has ever denied that the profits were substantial—the critics usually call them "excessive" or, as Truman said, "extremely liberal." Smith concluded that the contractors' profits did not indicate "unconscionable profiteering," partly because renegotiation, which Congress mandated in 1942, recaptured about a third of the initial profits. But even Smith admitted that "World War II was highly profitable for American industry despite the existence of both renegotiation and taxes." A study of 3,178 corporate refund cases renegotiated during the fiscal year 1943 found that rates of return on net worth, after taxes and renegotiated refunds, ranged from 15 percent, for the largest firms, to 30 percent, for the smallest. When only renegotiable sales (i.e., most sales to the government, but none of the sales to private customers) are considered, the after-tax rates of return ranged from about 22 percent, for the largest firms, to 49 percent, for firms with sales between $100,000 and $500,000. The difference shows that selling defense goods to the government yielded much higher rates of return than selling goods to private customers. Some people, Smith concluded, would consider such profits too high, but to him, they appeared "appropriate to the restoration of a vigorous and dynamic industrial economy after a decade of depression and stagnation" (Smith, 1959, pp. 395–96). In view of the virtual risklessness of the contractors' war business, a less partisan observer might well consider the contractors' rates of return on investment extraordinarily high.

Retrospect and Interpretation

Since World War II, the military supply business, a big business by any standard, has formed an institutionally unique sector of the American economy. Unlike ordinary capitalist entrepreneurs, the major defense contractors can shift most of the normal economic risks onto third parties, the taxpayers in general. The ordinary capitalist entrepreneur gambles his own assets on uncertain prospects; no one assures him net revenue; he faces both price risk and quantity risk. Failure to control his costs can bankrupt him, even in a robust market. If he does make a profit, the tax collector stands ready to capture a portion of it every quarter of the year. The ordinary capitalist entrepreneur lives in constant jeopardy of competition, actual and potential. No one guarantees him a share of an ongoing market, much less perpetual profit. For the big defense contractor, in stark contrast, everything is different. Cost-plus contracts assure him a substantial net income whether he controls his costs or not; indeed, his "fixed" fees often increase when he fails to control his costs, thereby encouraging his profligacy. The government, in many cases, provides much of his fixed capital, and virtually all of his working capital, thanks to advance and progress payments and tax deferrals. No matter what the form of his contract with the military, he knows that problems can probably be worked out. After all, he is dealing with old friends and future employees, and everyone appreciates the long-run personal advantages of being "reasonable." The risk of competitive entry is minimal; most buyer-seller arrangements are of long standing and promise to be well maintained. Personal, political, and bureaucratic forces all work in favor of preserving the established, mutually beneficial arrangements. Various reasons can be, and frequently are, given to justify the shielding of defense contractors from the kinds of risk borne by ordinary capitalist entrepreneurs. The validity of the proffered explanations is not at issue here. My conjecture is that for the most part the business operates as it does because it was once set up that way and no powerful force has subsequently compelled fundamental alterations.

Historians recognize that the modern military-industrial complex originated in World War II. That war, as Roger Beaumont has written, "set precedents and built linkages between the military and its suppliers stronger than ever before" (Beaumont, 1977, p. 132; Polenberg, 1972, p. 237; Cooling, 1977, p. 190). What the historians do not sufficiently appreciate, however, is the extent to which the essential foundations of the modern military-industrial complex were laid during the defense period preceding the Japanese attack on Pearl Harbor. The distinction is important. After December 7, 1941, Congress delegated to the president, and the Supreme Court let stand, extraordinarily sweeping executive powers to control the economy (Higgs, 1987, pp. 204–6, 220–25). The Roosevelt administration then exercised the powers on a wide scale, inter alia, to allocate raw materials and to control virtually all civilian prices, wages, and rents. After 1941, the administration could have simply commanded the capitalists to produce, with or without profits, the munitions ordered by the government—such command, after all, would have been no more drastic than commanding ten million conscripts to risk their lives as involuntary members of the armed forces. But the administration had already, during the defense period, built up an elaborate legal and administrative mechanism (or set of interrelated mechanisms) for procuring munitions, and participants in the established system held powerfully entrenched positions from which to defend its continuation. Big business, including its powerful friends and representatives who occupied strategic positions in the procurement agencies of the military departments and the civilian mobilization agencies, and the newly but vastly empowered military establishment together formed a potent political faction in the circumstances of World War II. By 1942, it was probably too late to change the procurement system. Nelson, who might have had the last clear chance to do so, as head of the War Production Board early in 1942, chose not to do so. (It is far from clear that he could have succeeded, had he tried.)

The critical events, then, occurred, in 1940; and at that time, conditions were far different from the conditions after the attack on Pearl Harbor. In 1940, the nation was not actually at war, and most Americans hoped that it never would be. Business conditions were rapidly reviving after more than a decade of depression. Why not leave well enough alone? The Roosevelt administration, however, had committed itself to participation in resisting the German onslaught and, above all, to aiding the British after the debacle at Dunkirk. Congress appropriated plenty of money, but the problem, as Stimson said, was turning money into guns. In the ambiguous political circumstances of 1940, in a nation not actually at war and less than enthusiastic about going to war, the administration lacked the political resources simply to command the capitalists to convert their plants to war-related production. The big companies were reluctant to bear the risks associated with conversion from civilian to military production. The future was too uncertain, and the potential losses too great, to justify the risks. Given that the government could not command, that it had to induce the businessmen to build up an industrial base for war, its only alternative was to relieve them of the risks, to make their war-related production a sure thing. Every major device adopted in the summer of 1940 had this effect: negotiated CPFF contracts; advance and progress payments; EPF and DPC financing of privately operated plants and equipment, with postwar purchase options; accelerated depreciation of privately owned plants and equipment, with provision for tax carry-backs of postwar losses—all shifted the economic risks of war production from the contractors to the taxpayers in general.

Haste, as economists know well, does make waste—or at least greater cost. Had the U.S. government not allowed its defense capabilities to become so diminished during the interwar period, had it made better plans to mobilize the economy for the next war, then the Roosevelt administration would not have found itself in such straits in 1940. Working from a better-constructed base, according to a more intelligently laid plan, the government could have carried out its rearmament plan without having to panic and give away the Treasury. Requiring a less drastic response from industry, the government would not have needed to make such sweeping concessions to the capitalists to induce their cooperation in the defense program. But these suppositions are only speculations on what might have been. In reality, the administration began its rearmament program in mid-1940 from practically nothing. To build a credible military force, and build it quickly, the government had to pay the price. The irony is that the taxpayers have been paying the price ever since, and every indication suggests that they will go on paying it indefinitely.

Notes

1. On cost-plus contracts, see Nieburg (1966), Weidenbaum (1968), Art (1973), Dumas (1976), Gansler (1980), Levin (1984), and "GAO Says Pentagon Is Increasing Use of Contracts That Led to Overcharges" (1985). On the rarity of genuine competitive bidding, see Rasor (1985), Proxmire (1970), Nieburg (1966, pp. 269–70, 362–63), Gansler (1980, pp. 2, 30, 75–82, 92–96, 184, 202), and "Competition: A Pentagon Battlefield" (1985).

2. Senator Roth as quoted in Rasor (1985, p. 204) and Proxmire (1970, pp. 152 and passim). Also Gansler (1980, pp. 36, 46, 149, 283, 304); and Nieburg (1966, pp. 188, 191–92, 272).

3. Gansler (1980, pp. 88–89; also 86–87, 138), Weidenbaum (1968, p. 436), "Defense Contracts Yield Higher Profits than Private Work, Navy Study Says" (1985), Pound (1986), and Carrington (1986). According to a 1985 report in the New York Times, the "top Pentagon contractors" realized returns of nearly 26 percent on equity over the previous five years. See "Competition: A Pentagon Battlefield," p. 1. Noting that the large contractors receive 80 percent of their billed costs as "progress payments," David Rogers stated: "To the extent that the government pays up-front costs, it reduces the real investment by contractors, and analysts estimate that such companies' return on assets is far larger than for private commercial enterprises." See "Nuclear Arms Budget Freeze Voted by Panels" (1986).

4. Rutherford (1939). Colonel Rutherford, the Secretary of the War Resources Board, served before the war in the Army's Planning Branch (Blum, 1962).

5. Stone (1941, pp. 156, 163, quoting Barron's) and R. Elberton Smith (1959, p. 459, quoting Roosevelt).

6. Harry S Truman (1955), Smith (1959, p. 289), and Miller (1949, pp. 127, 130). By enactment of legislation on May 2, 1941 *(55* Stat. 148), the Maritime Commission also received authority to negotiate cost-plus-fixed-fee contracts, to modify existing contracts, to waive performance bonds, and to negotiate the chartering of vessels.

7. Nelson (1946, p. 107), Brown and Patterson (1943), Smith (1959, pp. 472–73, quotations pp. 474–75), and Eliot Janeway (1951, p. 164).

8. U.S. Bureau of the Census (1975, pp. 1114, 1141) and Patterson as quoted in Smith (1959, p. 414). Also, Heath (1972, pp. 298–9).

9. Patterson as quoted in Smith (1959, p. 414) and Beaumont (1977, pp. 119, 127).

References

Adams, Gordon (1982) *The Politics of Defense Contracting: The Iron Triangle.* New Brunswick: Transaction Books.

Adams, Walter, and William James Adams. (1972) The Military-Industrial Complex: A Market Structure Analysis. *American Economic Review* 62 (May): 284.

Anderson, Benjamin M. (1979) *Economics and the Public Welfare: A Financial and Economic History of the United States.* Indianapolis: Liberty Press.

Art, Robert J. (1973) Why We Overspend and Underaccomplish: Weapons Procurement and the Military-Industrial Complex. In *Testing the Theory of the Military-Industrial Complex,* edited by Steven Rosen. Lexington, Mass.: Lexington Books.

Beaumont, Roger A. (1977) Quantum Increase: The MIC in the Second World War. In *War, Business and American Society: Historical Perspectives on the Military-Industrial Complex,* edited by Benjamin Franklin Cooling. Port Washington, N.Y.: Kennikat Press.

Bernstein, Barton J. (1966) The Automobile Industry and the Coming of the Second World War. *Southwestern Social Science Quarterly* 47 (June).

Blakey, Roy R., and Gladys C. Blakey. (1940) The Two Federal Revenue Acts of 1940. *American Economic Review* 30 (December): 729–33.

Blum, Albert A. (1962) Birth and Death of the M-Day Plan. In *American Civil-Military Decisions,* edited by Harold Stein. Birmingham: University of Alabama Press.

Blum, Albert A. (1972) Roosevelt, The M-Day Plans, and the Military-Industrial Complex. *Military Affairs* 35 (April).

Brown, E. Cary, and Gardner Patterson. (1943) Accelerated Depreciation: A Neglected Chapter in War Taxation. *Quarterly Journal of Economics* 57 (August): 636–40.

Cantril, Hadley. (1951) *Public Opinion, 1935–1946.* Princeton: Princeton University Press.

Carrington, Tim. (1986) Military Services Cited for Ignoring Some Price Rules. *Wall Street Journal* 24 March.

Carton, Bruce. (1948) *The War Lords of Washington.* New York: Harcourt Brace, and Co.

Competition: A Pentagon Battlefield. (1985) *New York Times* 12 May.

Connery, Robert H. (1951) *The Navy and the Industrial Mobilization in World War II.* Princeton: Princeton University Press.

Cooling, Benjamin Franklin. (1977) Suggestions for Further Research. In *War, Business, and American Society,* edited by Benjamin Franklin Cooling. Port Washington, N.Y.: Kennikat Press.

Defense Contracts Yield Higher Profits than Private Work, Navy Study Says. (1985) *Wall Street Journal* 29 November.

Dumas, Lloyd J. (1976) Payment Functions and the Productive Efficiency of the Military Industrial Firms. *Journal of Economic Issues* 10 (June).

Dumas, Lloyd J. (1986) Commanding Resources: The Military Sector and Capital Formation. In *Taxation and the Deficit Economy,* edited by Dwight R. Lee. San Francisco: Pacific Research Institute for Public Policy.

Gansler, Jacques S. (1980) *The Defense Industry.* Cambridge: MIT Press.

GAO Says Pentagon Is Increasing Use of Contracts That Led to Overcharges. (1985) *Wall Street Journal* 24 September.

Gragg, Charles I. (1941) Negotiated Contracts. *Harvard Business Review* 19 (Winter).

Heath, Jim F. (1972) American War Mobilization and the Use of Small Manufacturers, 1939–1943. *Business History Review* 46 (Autumn).

Henderson, Leon, and Donald M. Nelson. (1941) Prices, Profits, and Government. *Harvard Business Review* 19 (Summer).

Higgs, Robert. (1987) *Crisis and Leviathan: Critical Episodes in the Growth of American Government.* New York: Oxford University Press.

Huston, James A. (1966) *The Sinews of War: Army Logistics, 1775–1953.* Washington, D.C.: U.S. Army.

Janeway, Eliot. (1951) *The Struggle for Survival: A Chronicle of Economic Mobilization in World War II.* New Haven: Yale University Press.

Jones, Jesse H. (1951) *Fifty Billion Dollars: My Thirteen Years with the RFC.* New York: Macmillan. Kaufman, Richard F. (1972) MIRVing the Boondoggle: Contracts, Subsidy, and Welfare in the Aerospace Industry. *American Economic Review* 62 (May).

Klagsbrunn, Hans A. (1943) Some Aspects of War Plant Financing. *American Economic Review* 33 (March).

Koistinen, Paul A. C. (1980) *The Military-Industrial Complex: A Historical Perspective.* New York: Praeger.

Kurth, James R. (1973) Aerospace Production Lines and American Defense Spending. In *Testing the Theory of the Military-Industrial Complex,* edited by Steven Rosen. Lexington, Mass.: Lexington Books.

Levin, Doron P. (1984) Firms Enriched by Military Buildup Search for Ways to Use the Money. *Wall Street Journal* 3 January.

McLaughlin, Glenn E. (1943) Wartime Expansion in Industrial Facilities. *American Economic Review* 33 (March).

Miller, John Perry. (1949) *Pricing of Military Procurements.* New Haven: Yale University Press.

Mitchell, Jonathan. (1940) Is Our Defense Lagging? *New Republic* 103 (26 August).

Nelson, Donald M. (1946) *Arsenal of Democracy: The Story of American War Production.* New York: Harcourt, Brace, and Co.

Polenberg, Richard. (1972) *War and Society: The United States, 1941–1945.* New York: Lippincott.

Nieburg, H. L. (1966) *In the Name of Science.* Chicago: Quadrangle Books.

Nuclear Arms Budget Freeze Voted by Panels. (1986) *Wall Street Journal* 8 August.

Pound, Edward T. (1986). Defense Contractors Repeatedly Deceive U.S., Reap Windfall Profits, Panel Says. *Wall Street Journal* 7 May.

Proxmire, Senator William. (1970) *Report from Wasteland: America's Military-Industrial Complex.* New York: Praeger.

Rasor, Dina. (1985) *The Pentagon Underground*. New York: Times Books.

Rutherford, H. K. (1939) Mobilizing Industry for War. *Harvard Business Review* 18 (Autumn).

Smaller War Plants Corporation. (1946) *Economic Concentration and World War II*. Washington, D.C.: Government Printing Office.

Smith, Elberton R. (1959) *The Army and Economic Mobilization*. Washington, D.C.: U.S. Army.

Stimson, Henry L., and McGeorge Bundy. (1947) *On Active Service in Peace and War*. London: Hutchinson & Co.

Stone, I. F. (1941) *Business as Usual: The First Year of Defense*. New York: Modern Age Books.

Stromberg, Ronald N. (1953) American Business and the Approach of War, 1935–1941. *Journal of Economic History* 13 (Winter).

Truman Committee Report as reproduced in *The Military Industrial Complex*, edited by Carroll W. Pursell, Jr. (1972) New York: Harper & Row.

Truman, Harry S. (1955) *Memoirs*. New York: Signet Books.

Udis, Bernard, and Murray L. Weidenbaum. (1973) The Many Dimensions of the Military Effort. In *The Economic Consequences of Reduced Military Spending*, edited by Bernard Udis. Lexington, Mass.: Lexington Books.

U.S. Bureau of the Budget, War Records Section. (1946) *The United States at War: Development and Administration of the War Program by the Federal Government*. Washington, D.C.: Government Printing Office.

U.S. Bureau of the Census. (1975) *Historical Statistics of the United States, Colonial Times to 1970*. Washington, D.C.: Government Printing Office.

U.S. Civilian Production Administration. (1947) *Industrial Mobilization for War: History of the War Production Board and Predecessor Agencies, 1940–1945*. Washington, D.C.: Government Printing Office.

The War Goes to Mr. Jesse Jones. (1941) *Fortune* 24 (December).

Weidenbaum, Murray L. (1968) Arms and the American Economy: A Domestic Convergence Hypothesis. *American Economic Review* 63 (May).

White, Gerald T. (1949) Financing Industrial Expansion for War: The Origin of the Defense Plant Cooperation Leases. *Journal of Economic History* 9 (November).

Yntema, Theodore O. (1941) Some Economic Problems in the Expansion of Capacity to Produce Military Goods. *American Economic Review* 30 (February).

3

Wartime Prosperity?

A Reassessment of the
U.S. Economy in the 1940s

> War prosperity is like the prosperity that an earthquake
> or a plague brings.
>
> *Ludwig von Mises,* Nation, State, and Economy

EVER SINCE WORLD WAR II, historians and econo-
mists, almost without exception, have misinterpreted the performance of
the U.S. economy in the 1940s. The reigning view has two aspects: one
pertaining to the conceptualization and measurement of the economy's
performance, the other pertaining to the explanation of that performance
in macroeconomic theory. The two are encapsulated in the title of a chapter in a leading textbook: "War Prosperity: The Keynesian Message Illustrated" (Hughes, 1990, p. 493).

I shall challenge the consensus view. The accepted profile of the economy's performance during the 1940s, peak prosperity from 1943 to 1945,
followed by much worse performance from 1946 to 1949, is indefensible as
a description of economic well-being. Further, the most widely accepted
explanation of the events of the war years cannot withstand critical scru-
tiny. The prevailing misinterpretations of economic performance during
the 1940s have arisen because historians and economists have failed to appreciate that the wartime economy, a command economy, cannot be readily compared with either the prewar or the postwar economy.

The Consensus

According to the orthodox account, the war got the economy out of the Depression. Evidence for this claim usually includes the great decline in the standard measure of the unemployment rate, the large increase in the standard measure of real gross national product (GNP), and the slight increase in the standard measure of real personal consumption. The entire episode of apparent business-cycle expansion during the war years is understood by most authors as an obvious validation of the simple Keynesian model: Enormous government spending, with huge budget deficits, spurred the military economy and produced multiplier effects on the civilian economy, with the upshot being increased employment, real output, and consumption and decreased unemployment. Some analysts, recognizing the rapid increase of the money stock during the war, have blended Keynesian and monetarist explanations, treating them as complements. This consensus account, occasionally with minor qualifications or caveats, appears in the works of historians, economists, and other authors.[1]

Employment and Unemployment

The standard measure of the unemployment rate (persons officially unemployed as a percentage of the civilian labor force) fell between 1940 and 1944 from 14.6 percent to 1.2 percent (U.S. Council of Economic Advisers, 1990, p. 330). Michael Darby's measure, which does not count those in "emergency government employment" as unemployed, fell from 9.5 percent to 1.2 percent (Darby, 1976, p. 8). Either measure signals a virtual disappearance of unemployment during the war, but in these circumstances, neither measure means what it is commonly taken to mean.

The buildup of the armed forces to more than 12 million persons by 1945 made an enormous decline in the unemployment rate inevitable, but the welfare significance of the decline is hardly the usual one. Of the 16 million persons who served in the armed forces at some time during the war, 10 million were conscripted, and many of those who volunteered did so only to avoid the draft and the consequent likelihood of assignment to the infantry (U.S. Bureau of the Census, 1975, p. 1140; Higgs, 1987, p. 202). Between 1940 and 1945, the civilian labor force ranged from 54 to 56 million (U. S. Council of Economic Advisers, 1990, p. 330). Therefore, the 12 million serving in the armed forces during the last year of the war, most of them under duress, constituted about 18 percent of the total (civilian plus military) labor force, itself much enlarged during the war.

What actually happened is no mystery. In 1940, before the military mobilization, the unemployment rate (Darby concept) was 9.5 percent. During the war, the government pulled the equivalent of 22 percent of the prewar labor force into the armed forces. Voila—the unemployment rate dropped to a very low level. No one needs a macroeconomic model to understand this event. Given the facts of the draft, no plausible view of the economy is incompatible with the observed decline in the unemployment rate. Whether the government ran deficits or not, whether the money stock increased or not, massive military conscription was sure to decrease dramatically the rate of unemployment.[2]

Between 1940 and 1944, unemployment fell by either 7.45 million (official measure) or 4.62 million (Darby measure), while the armed forces increased by 10.87 million. Even if one views eliminating civilian unemployment as tantamount to producing prosperity, one must recognize that placing either 146 or 235 persons (depending on the unemployment concept used) in the armed forces to gain a reduction of 100 persons in civilian unemployment was a grotesque way to achieve prosperity, even if a job were a job.

In fact, however, military "jobs" differed categorically. Often, they entailed substantial risks of death, dismemberment, and other physical and psychological injuries. Military service yielded little pay under harsh conditions and, like it or not, lasted for the duration of the war. Sustained exposure to combat drove many men insane (Fussell, 1989; Manchester, 1980). Physical casualties included 405,399 dead and 670,846 wounded (U.S. Bureau of the Census, 1975, p. 1140). To treat military jobs as commensurate with civilian jobs during World War II, as economists do in computing the tradeoffs between them, betrays a monumental obtuseness to their realities.

To see more clearly what happened to the labor force, one can examine the percentage of the total (civilian plus military) labor force occupied in what I call the labor force "residuum." This includes unemployed civilians, members of the armed forces, civilian employees of the armed forces, and employees in the military supply industries (table 3-1). This measure rose from 17.6 percent, almost all of it being unemployment, in fiscal year 1940, to more than 40 percent, almost all of it being war-related employment, during the fiscal years from 1943 to 1945, then dropped abruptly and remained at about 10 percent during the fiscal years from 1946 to 1949. The extraordinarily high level of the labor force residuum during the war indicates that the "prosperous" condition of the labor force was spurious: Official unemployment was virtually nonexistent, but four-tenths of the total labor force was not being used to produce consumer goods or capital

Table 3-1. Employment and unemployment, fiscal years 1940–1949 (as percent of total [civilian plus military] labor force)

Fiscal year	Nondefense employment	Defense employment	Civilian unemployment (BLS concept)	Labor force residuum
1940	82.4	1.8	15.7	17.6
1941	79.4	8.5	12.0	20.6
1942	67.3	25.7	7.0	32.7
1943	57.6	39.4	3.0	42.4
1944	58.4	40.3	1.3	41.6
1945	59.5	39.2	1.3	40.5
1946	88.5	8.9	2.6	11.5
1947	90.9	5.3	3.8	9.1
1948	90.9	5.3	3.9	9.1
1949	88.4	5.2	6.4	11.6

Source: Computed from data in U.S. Department of Defense. 1987. *National Defense Budget Estimates for FY 1988–1989.* Washington, D.C.: Office of the Assistant Secretary of Defense (Comptroller), p. 126.

Notes: Defense employment includes military personnel, civilian employees of the military, and employees of defense-related industries. The labor force residuum is 100 minus nondefense employment.

capable of yielding consumer goods in the future. The sharp drop in the labor force residuum between fiscal years 1945 and 1946 marks the return of genuine prosperity.

Real Output

To find out what happened to real output during World War II, historians usually reach for *Historical Statistics,* and economists consult the most recent issue of the Council of Economic Advisers' *Annual Report.* As table 3-2 shows, which source one chooses makes a big difference. Although the two series show roughly the same profile of real GNP during the 1940s, the latest Commerce Department version indicates, in index number form (1939 equals 100), a peak value of 192.7 in 1944. In contrast, a peak value of 172.5 in 1944 is seen in the series taken from *Historical Statistics.* Both series show a large drop in real GNP from 1945 to 1946: 12 percent in the older series and 19 percent in the newer. Another series, constructed by John Kendrick, moves similarly to the first two in the table, but displays some discrepancies. Notably, in 1945–46, Kendrick's estimate drops by just 9 percent. Analysts who employ these standard series, besides ignoring the discrepancies, seem generally unaware that the figures may be conceptually problematic.

By contrast, Simon Kuznets, a pioneer in national income accounting, expressed many concerns. In *National Product in Wartime,* Kuznets noted that national income accountants must make definite assumptions about "the purpose, value, and scope of economic activity." He observed that "a major war magnifies these conceptual difficulties, raising questions concerning the ends economic activity is made to pursue" and "the distinction between intermediate and final products." Moreover, "war and peace type products . . . cannot be added into a national product total until the differences in the valuation due to differences in the institutional mechanisms that determine their respective market prices are corrected for." During the war, Kuznets constructed several alternative series, one of which appears in table 3-2, column 4. Its values for 1942 and 1943 are substantially

Table 3-2. Real gross national product, 1939–1949
(index numbers, 1939 = 100)

| Year | Estimate of Commerce | | Kendrick | Estimate of Kuznets | | | GNP* |
	1975	1990		Wartime	Revised	Variant III	
1939	100.0	100.0	100.0	100.0	100.0	100.0	100.0
1940	108.5	107.9	109.7	109.3	109.0	109.0	108.7
1941	125.9	126.9	128.7	125.9	121.8	121.7	119.4
1942	142.2	150.8	145.5	131.9	126.5	118.2	108.4
1943	161.0	178.1	160.6	148.6	132.5	117.6	102.2
1944	172.5	192.7	172.4		135.8	122.1	105.4
1945	169.6	189.1	171.3		139.4	125.6	114.3
1946	149.3	153.1	156.7		151.0	146.5	144.8
1947	148.0	148.9	153.4		154.5	148.0	147.3
1948	154.6	154.7	160.0		155.5	153.1	152.3
1949	154.8	154.8	156.9		152.6	148.5	147.5

Note: GNP* is equal to Kuznets's variant III minus gross war construction and durable munitions and was computed from data in Kendrick, John W. 1961. *Productivity Trends,* pp. 291–92.

Sources: Column 1 was computed from data in U.S. Bureau of the Census. 1975. *Historical Statistics of the United States, Colonial Times to 1970.* Washington, D.C.: U.S. Government Printing Office, p. 224 (series F-3); column 2 from data in U.S. Council of Economic Advisers. 1990. *Annual Report 1990,* Washington, D.C.: U.S. Government Printing Office, p. 296; column 3 from data in Kendrick, John W. 1961. *Productivity Trends in the United States.* Princeton: Princeton University Press, pp. 291–92 (national security variant); column 4 from data in Kuznets, Simon. 1945. *National Product in Wartime.* New York: National Bureau of Economic Research, p. 89 (variant a); column 5 from data in Kuznets, Simon. 1952. Long-Term Changes in the National Income of the United States of America since 1870. In Simon Kuznets, ed., *Income & Wealth of the United States: Trends and Structure.* Cambridge: Bowes and Bowes, p. 40; and column 6 from data in Kuznets, Simon. 1961. *Capital in the American Economy: Its Formation and Financing.* Princeton: Princeton University Press, p. 487.

lower than those in columns 1, 2, and 3, in part because Kuznets used preliminary nominal data, as well as different deflators for expenditure on munitions (Kuznets, 1945, pp. viii–ix; Mitchell, 1943, p. 13).

After the war, Kuznets refined his estimates, producing a series (see table 3-2, column 5) that differs substantially from the standard series, "partly because of the allowance for overpricing of certain types of war production, partly because of the exclusion of nondurable war output (essentially pay and subsistence of armed forces)." Contrasting his estimate with that of the Commerce Department, he found the latter "difficult to accept" because it made too little correction for actual inflation during the war years and did not deal satisfactorily with the decline in the relative prices of munitions during the war.[3] Kuznets's refined estimates follow a completely different profile for the 1940s. Most notable is that, whereas the Commerce Department's latest estimate of real GNP drops precipitously in 1946 and remains at that low level for the rest of the decade, Kuznets's estimate increases in 1946 by about 8 percent, then rises slightly higher during the next three years.

Kuznets might have made an even greater adjustment, deleting *all* war outlays. Although computing GNP in this way now seems highly unorthodox, a strong argument can be offered for it, and Kuznets considered it seriously (Kuznets, 1951, pp. 184–200; Kuznets, 1945, pp. 3–31). The crucial question is: Does war spending purchase a final good and hence belong in GNP, or an intermediate good and hence not belong?

In his studies of long-term economic growth, Kuznets always insisted on a "peacetime concept" of GNP. In this concept, government spending counts only if it pays for a flow of goods to consumers or a flow to capital formation. Military spending enters only to the extent that it finances additions to the military capital stock, the justification being that even though military durables and construction are used for military purposes, they represent capital that could be employed for nonmilitary purposes— a justification that seems far-fetched with regard to many forms of military capital. Application of this approach in estimating real GNP during the 1940s yields the series that Kuznets designated Variant III (see table 3-2, column 6).[4] This estimate reached a peak in 1941, stalled throughout the war period, and then surged with the demobilization and reconversion. It jumped by nearly 17 percent between 1945 and 1946, and remained at the higher level for the rest of the decade. No wartime prosperity here.

Kuznets himself did not accept the Variant III concept as applicable to the war years.[5] Beginning with *National Product in Wartime* and continuing through elaborations in his contributions of the early 1950s, he maintained that although ordinarily one ought to count as part of national product only goods that either contribute immediately to consumer satisfaction or add to the stock of capital from which future flows of consumer goods can be derived, the situation changes during the "life and death struggle" of a great war. Then, one must temporarily recognize "success in war and preservation of a country's social framework as a purpose at least equal in importance to welfare of individuals." Kuznets insisted that this approach was justified only "during these extraordinary and necessarily brief intervals in the life of a body social. One must particularly beware of extending this viewpoint, justified by the necessarily temporary crises in the life of a nation, to the common run of public activities" (Kuznets, 1951, pp. 184–85). But when the Cold War developed and persisted, most economists took the position that military expenditures always perform the function that Kuznets viewed them as performing only during a war for national survival.[6]

Not everyone accepted the dominant view. Among the dissenters were William Nordhaus and James Tobin, who made numerous adjustments to the standard GNP concept to transform it into what they called a measure of economic welfare. They aimed to eliminate from GNP all "activities that are evidently not direct sources of utility themselves but are regrettably necessary inputs to activities that may yield utility"—in other words, "only instrumental." Accordingly, they deleted, among other things, all national defense spending. They did not consider military spending wasteful; they merely insisted that it purchases an intermediate good. It is a "necessary regrettable" expense (Nordhaus and Tobin, 1972, pp. 7–8, 26–28).

Earlier, Kuznets had come close to adopting this position. He regarded warfare as "the central difficulty in distinguishing between final and intermediate output of government." He found it "difficult to understand why the net product of the economy should include not only the flow of goods to the ultimate consumers, but also the increased cost of government activities necessary to maintain the social fabric within which the flow is realized." Still, Kuznets did not disavow his insistence on recognizing "two end purposes" in estimating real output during World War II.[7]

Kuznets's own logic, however, required that he go all the way: Maintenance expense remains maintenance expense, even though much more maintenance is required when the weather is stormy than when it is placid. As Kuznets himself said, "there is little sense in talking of protection of life and limb [against external enemies] as an economic service to individuals—it is a pre-condition of such service, not a service in itself" (Kuznets, 1951, pp. 193–94).

When one adopts this position on the treatment of military outlays, that is, when one deducts all of them from GNP on the grounds that they purchase (at best) intermediate, rather than final, goods, one arrives at a starkly different understanding of economic performance in the 1940s. Constructing an index purged of all military spending, one obtains the measure designated here as GNP* (see table 3-2, column 7). Like Variant III, GNP* shows a peak in 1941, followed by a U-shaped profile during the war years, with a trough in 1943. However, the U is much deeper in GNP*, with real output in 1943 more than 14 percent below its value in 1941. Moreover, although Variant III exceeded its 1941 value by 1945, GNP* did not. Between 1945 and 1946, GNP* surged upward by almost 27 percent, versus less than 17 percent for Variant III. From 1946 to 1949, with military spending at a much lower level, the two indexes were virtually identical.[8]

Finally, one can make an even more unorthodox—which is not to say incorrect—argument for rejecting the conventional wisdom. One can simply argue that outside of a more or less competitive equilibrium framework, the use of prices as weights in an aggregation of physical quantities loses its essential theoretical justification. All presumption that price equals marginal cost vanishes, and therefore, no meaningful estimate of real national product is possible (Abramovitz, 1959; Vedder and Gallaway, 1990, pp. 10–11).

In fact, price was "never a factor" in the allocation of resources for war purposes. The authorities did not permit "the price-cost relationship . . . to determine either the level of output or the distribution of the final product to individual uses."[9] Clearly, all presumption of equalities between prevailing prices, consumers' marginal rates of substitution, and producers' marginal rates of technical substitution vanished. Absent those equalities, at least as approximations, national income accounting loses its moorings; it necessarily becomes more or less arbitrary.

Some economists appreciated the perils at the time. Noting that the government had displaced the price system, Wesley Mitchell observed that comparisons of the war and prewar economies, even comparisons between successive years, had become "highly dubious." Index number problems lurked around every corner. Much output during the war, especially weapons, consisted of goods that did not exist before the war. Even for physically comparable goods, price structures and output mixes changed radically. Production of many important consumer goods was outlawed. Surrounding everything were the "obvious uncertainties concerning [price] quotations in a land of price controls and evasions."[10] Kuznets declared that the "bases of valuation for the war and nonwar sectors of the economy are inherently noncomparable. . . . It is impossible to construct directly a price index of war products that would span both prewar and war years." Kuznets's own efforts to overcome these problems, however, never escaped from arbitrariness, as he himself admitted.[11]

It will not do to maintain, as some economists have, that although the standard indexes of real GNP are deficient from a welfare standpoint, they can serve as indexes of production or resource consumption. Economics is not a science of hammers and nails, or of production or consumption in the raw; it is a science of choice, and therefore of values. Valuation is inherent in all national income accounting. In a command economy, the fundamental accounting difficulty is that the authorities suppress and replace the only genuinely meaningful manifestation of people's valuations, namely, free market prices (Buchanan, 1979, p. 86).

Real Consumption

Most authors insist that real personal consumption increased during the war. In Seymour Melman's flamboyant, but otherwise representative, portrayal, "the economy [was] producing more guns and more butter . . . Americans had never had it so good" (Melman, 1985, p. 15).

This belief rests on a weak foundation. It fails to take sufficiently into account the understatement of actual wartime inflation by the official price indexes, the deterioration of quality and disappearance from the market of many consumer goods, the full effect of the nonprice rationing of many widely consumed items, and the additional transaction costs borne and other sacrifices made by consumers to get the goods that were available. When one corrects the data to provide a more defensible measure of what happened to real consumer well-being during the war, one finds that it declined.

Table 3-3 shows the standard series on real personal consumption expenditure during the 1940s. They do not differ much. The similarity is hardly surprising, because all rest on nearly the same conceptual and statistical bases. These figures have led historians and economists to conclude that the well-being of consumers improved, though not by much, during the war.

Even if one stays within the confines of the standard series, the conclusion is shaky. Notice, for example, that the data indicate that consumption in 1943 hardly differed from consumption in 1941. The change between 1941 and 1944 varies from 3.7 to 5 percent, depending on the series considered. Because the population was growing at a rate of more than 1 percent per year, the official data imply that real personal consumption per capita remained essentially unchanged between 1941 and 1944. Merely to maintain the level of 1941, a year in which the economy had yet to recover fully from the Depression, hardly signified "wartime prosperity."[12]

The more serious problem, however, is that the standard real consumption series are quotients fatally flawed by their deflators. Everyone who has looked closely at the official price indexes recognizes that they underestimate the actual inflation during the war and—an important point that is usually overlooked—overstate the actual inflation during the immediate postwar period. But investigators have not agreed on exactly how the actual price level moved or on the proper technique for finding out.

Table 3-3. Real personal consumption expenditures, 1939–1949
(index numbers, 1939 = 100)

Year	Commerce 1975	Commerce 1990	Kendrick	Kuznets
1939	100.1	100.0	100.0	100.0
1940	105.1	104.6	105.4	105.4
1941	111.6	110.5	112.2	112.5
1942	108.9	109.8	110.2	110.6
1943	111.9	112.4	113.3	113.6
1944	115.7	115.9	117.8	117.5
1945	123.5	123.4	126.4	125.4
1946	137.3	136.3	140.7	140.6
1947	139.2	138.7	142.7	143.6
1948	142.2	141.9	145.6	146.6
1949	146.1	144.7	149.6	150.2

Sources: Column 1 was computed from data in U.S. Bureau of the *Census. 1975. Historical Statistics of the United States, Colonial Times to 1970.* Washington, D.C.: U.S. Government Printing Office, p. 229 (series F-48); column 2 from data in U.S. Council of Economic Advisers. 1990. *Annual Report 1990.* Washington, D.C.: U.S. Government Printing Office, p. 296; column 3 from data in Kendrick, John W. 1961. *Productivity Trends in the United States.* Princeton: Princeton University Press, p. 295; and column 4 from data in Kuznets, Simon. 1961. *Capital in the American Economy: Its Formation and Financing.* Princeton: Princeton University Press, p. 487.

During the war, a committee headed by Wesley Mitchell investigated how far the official consumer price index had fallen short of the true price level, but the committee neither attempted to adjust nor succeeded in correcting for all of the factors creating the discrepancy. In 1978, Hugh Rockoff made additional adjustments, concluding that the official consumer price index understated the true price level by 4.8 to 7.3 percent in June 1946, just before the price controls lapsed.[13] Rockoff's adjustments remained incomplete, as he recognized. He commented that "if anything, the errors were larger than" the estimates indicated. Moreover, "evasion and black markets were probably more severe outside the group of commodities that were covered by the consumer price index" (Rockoff, 1984, pp. 169, 171).

More recently, Rockoff and Geofrey Mills, using a different (macroeconomic) approach, have estimated an alternative deflator for net national product (NNP) during the war. This shows that the official deflator understated the price level by 2.3 percent in 1943 (the first year that the price controls had a significant effect), 4.9 percent in 1944, 4.8 percent in 1945, and 1.6 percent in 1946 (Mills and Rockoff, 1987, p. 203). These discrepancies seem too small to be credible. By comparison, Kuznets's alternative (GNP) deflator, published in 1952, differed from the official deflator for the corresponding years by 11.1 percent, 13.4 percent, 11.4 percent, and 2.2 percent, respectively.[14]

Perhaps the most credible alternative deflator has been produced by Milton Friedman and Anna Jacobson Schwartz. They found the official deflator for NNP to be understated by 3.7 percent in 1943, *7.7* percent in 1944, 8.9 percent in 1945, and 3.3 percent in 1946.[15] Their deflator is for NNP, not just for the consumption component of NNP. In using it as a deflator for consumption alone, one is taking a risk. It definitely moves us in the right direction, however, because it implies larger adjustments than Rockoff's admittedly incomplete adjustments of the official consumer price index. Moreover, it is well established that munitions prices rose much less than the prices of civilian goods; hence, a deflator for official NNP, which includes munitions, most likely still understates the extent to which the prices of consumer goods rose during the war.

If one uses the Friedman-Schwartz price index to deflate personal consumption spending per capita, the results are as shown in table 3-4, column 3. The pattern shown there diverges markedly from that shown by the standard data. According to the alternative estimate, real consumption per capita reached a prewar peak in 1941 that was nearly 9 percent above the 1939 level; it declined by more than 6 percent during 1941–43, and rose during 1943–45; still, even in 1945, it had not recovered to the 1941 level. In 1946, however, the index jumped by 18 percent, and it remained at about the same level for the rest of the decade.

In fact, conditions were much worse than the data suggest for consumers during the war. Even if the price index corrections considered earlier are sufficient, which is doubtful, one must recognize that consumers had

Table 3-4. Alternative estimate of real personal consumption
per capita (index numbers 1939 = 100)

Year	Personal consumption per capita (current dollars)	Friedman and Schwartz's deflator	Real personal consumption per capita
1939	100.0	100.0	100.0
1940	105.3	101.1	104.2
1941	118.6	109.1	108.7
1942	128.6	123.4	104.2
1943	142.3	139.6	101.9
1944	153.0	150.0	102.0
1945	167.3	156.6	106.8
1946	199.2	158.0	126.1
1947	219.8	170.8	128.7
1948	233.5	182.0	128.3
1949	233.9	179.6	130.2

Sources: Column 1 was computed from data in U.S. Council of Economic Advisers.
1990. *Annual Report, 1990.* Washington, D.C.: U.S. Government Printing Office, p. 325;
and column 2 from data in Friedman, Milton, and Anna Jacobson Schwartz. 1982.
Monetary Trends in the United States and the United Kingdom. Chicago: University of Chicago Press, p. 125. Column 3 is column 1 divided by column 2 and multiplied by 100.

to contend with other extraordinary welfare-diminishing changes during
the war. To get the available goods, millions of people had to move, many
of them long distances, to centers of war production. (Of course, costly
movements to areas of greater opportunity always occur; but the rate of
migration during the war was exceptional because of the abrupt changes
in the location of employment opportunities.) [Vatter, 1985, pp. 114–15;
Polenberg, 1972, pp. 138–45; U.S. War Production Board, 1945, pp. 14, 16–
17.] After bearing substantial costs of relocation, the migrants often found
themselves crowded into poorer housing. Because of the disincentives created by rent controls, the housing got worse each year, as landlords reduced
or eliminated maintenance and repairs. Transportation, even commuting
to work, became difficult for many workers. No new cars were being pro-

duced; used cars were hard to come by because of rationing and were sold on the black market at elevated prices; gasoline and tires were rationed; public transportation was crowded and inconvenient for many, as well as frequently preempted by the military authorities. Shoppers bore substantial costs of searching for sellers willing to sell goods, including rationed goods, at controlled prices; they spent much valuable time arranging (illegal) trades of ration coupons or standing in lines. The government exhorted the public to "use it up, wear it out, make it do, or do without." In thousands of ways, consumers lost their freedom of choice.[16]

People were also working harder, longer, more inconveniently, and at greater physical risk in order to get the available goods. The ratio of civilian employment to population (age 14 and older) increased from 47.6 percent in 1940 to 57.9 percent in 1944, as many teenagers left school, women left their homes, and older people left retirement to work (U.S. Council of Economic Advisers, 1990, p. 330; Schweitzer, 1980, pp. 89–95). The average workweek in manufacturing, where most of the new jobs were, increased from 38.1 hours in 1940 to 45.2 hours in 1944. The average workweek increased in most other industries, too—in bituminous coal mining, it increased by more than 50 percent (U.S. Bureau of the Census, 1975, pp. 169–73; Anderson, 1979, p. 515). Night shifts occupied a much larger proportion of the workforce (U.S. War Production Board, 1945, pp. 7, 32). The rate of disabling injuries per hour worked in manufacturing rose by more than 30 percent between 1940 and its wartime peak in 1943 (U.S. Bureau of the Census, 1975, p. 182). It is difficult to understand how working harder, longer, more inconveniently, and more dangerously in return for a diminished flow of consumer goods comports with the description that "economically speaking, Americans had never had it so good."

Irrelevant Macro Models

None of the standard macroeconomic theories employed to account for the wartime experience provides an acceptable explanation. The models cannot do the job because they do not pertain to a command economy, and between 1942 and 1945, the United States had a command economy. Regardless of the peculiarities of their assumptions, all standard macro models presume the existence of normally functioning markets for commodities, factor services, and bonds.

The assumption fails even to approximate the conditions that prevailed during the war. Commodity markets were pervasively subject to controls, including price controls, rationing and, in some cases, outright prohibition in the consumer goods markets, and price controls, prohibitions, priorities, conservation and limitation orders, quotas, set-asides, scheduling, allocations, and other restrictions in the market for raw materials, components, and capital equipment.[17] While taxes were raised enormously, many forms of production received subsidies so that price controls would not drive suppliers from the market (Mansfield and associates, 1947, pp. 63–65; Harris, 1945, pp. 223–46). Factor markets were no freer, and in some respects (such as conscription), they were much less free (Krug, 1945, p. 5; Mansfield and associates, 1945, pp. 63–65; Harris, 1945, pp. 223–46). Credit markets came under total control, as the Federal Reserve undertook to reduce and allocate consumer credit and pegged the nominal interest rate on government bonds at a barely positive level (Friedman and Schwartz, 1963, pp. 553, 555, 561–74). Two-thirds of the investment in manufacturing plants and equipment from July 1940 through June 1945 was financed by the government, and most of the remainder came forth in response to tax concessions and other de facto subsidies authorized in 1940 to stimulate the rearmament (Higgs, 1993; Gordon, 1969).

In sum, the economy during the war was the exact opposite of a free market system. Every part of it was either directly controlled by the authorities or subject to drastic distortion by virtue of its relations with suppliers and customers who were tightly controlled (Novick, Anshen, and Truppner, 1949, p. 7). To suppose that the economy allocated resources in response to prices set by the unhampered interplay of demands and supplies in the markets for commodities, factor services, and loanable funds is to suppose a complete fiction. Clearly, the assumptions that undergird standard macro models do not correspond with the empirical reality of the wartime economy.

So What *Did* Happen?

As the 1940s began, the economy, although substantially affected by various government intrusions, remained one in which resource allocation, for the most part, reflected the operation of the price system. It was far from classic capitalism, but also far from a command economy. Beginning in the fall of 1940, proceeding slowly until the attack on Pearl Harbor and then very rapidly, the government imposed such pervasive and sufficiently effective controls that, by the beginning of 1943, the economy became a thoroughgoing command system. This regime persisted until the fall of 1945, when the controls began to come off rapidly. Although some persisted, the overwhelming mass had been removed by 1947. In the late 1940s, the economy was once again broadly market-oriented, albeit far from pure capitalism. So, within a single decade, the economy had moved from being mainly market-directed to being nearly under the complete control of central planners to being mainly market-directed again. When one views any economic measure spanning the decade, one must keep this full revolution of the institutional framework in mind, because the meaning of such measures as the unemployment rate, GNP, and consumer price index depends on the institutional setting to which they relate.

In 1940 and 1941, the economy was recovering smartly from the Depression, but in the latter year the recovery was becoming increasingly ambiguous because more and more resources were being diverted to war production. From 1942 to 1944, war production increased rapidly. Although there is no defensible way to place a value on the outpouring of munitions, its physical dimensions are awesome. From mid-1940 to mid-1945, munitions makers produced 86,338 tanks; 297,000 airplanes; 17,400,000 rifles, carbines, and side arms; 315,000 pieces of field artillery and mortars; 4,200,000 tons of artillery shells; 41,400,000,000 rounds of small arms ammunition; 64,500 landing vessels; 6,500 other navy ships; 5,400 cargo ships and transports; and vast amounts of other munitions.[18] Despite countless administrative mistakes, frustrations, and turf battles, the command economy worked.[19] But, as always, a command economy can be said to work only in the sense that it turns out what the authorities demand. The U.S. economy did so in quantities sufficient to overwhelm enemy forces.

Meanwhile, as shown earlier, real personal consumption declined, as did real private investment. From 1941 to 1943, real gross private domestic investment plunged by 64 percent; during the four years of the war, it never rose above 55 percent of its 1941 level; only in 1946 did it reach a new high (U.S. Council of Economic Advisers, 1990, p. 296). Notwithstanding the initial availability of much unemployed labor and capital, the mobilization became a classic case of guns displacing both butter and churns. So why, apart from historians and economists misled by inappropriate and inaccurate statistical constructs, did people—evidently almost everyone—think that prosperity had returned *during* the war?

The question has several plausible answers. First, everybody with a desire to work was working. After more than 10 years of persistently high unemployment and the associated insecurities (even for those who were working), full employment relieved a lot of anxieties. Although economic well-being deteriorated after 1941, civilians were probably better off, on average, during the war than they had been during the 1930s. Second, the national solidarity of the war effort, though decaying after the initial upsurge following December 7, 1941, helped to sustain the spirits of many who otherwise would have been angry about the shortages and other inconveniences. For some people, the wartime experience was exhilarating, even though, like many adventures, it entailed hardships. Third, some individuals (for example, many of the black migrants from the rural South who found employment in Northern and Western industry) were better off after 1941, although the average person was not. Wartime reduction of the variance in personal income—and hence in personal consumption—along with rationing and price controls, meant that many people at the bottom of the consumption distribution could improve their absolute position, despite a reduction of the mean (Vatter, 1985, pp. 142–44; U.S. Bureau of the Census, 1975, pp. 301–2). Fourth, even if people could not buy many of the things they wanted at the time, they were earning unprecedented amounts of money. Perhaps money illusion, fostered by price controls, made the earnings look bigger than they really were. In any event, people were building up bank accounts and bond holdings; while actually living worse than before, they were feeling wealthier.

Which brings us to an important upshot: The performance of the war economy, despite its command-and-control character, broke the back of the pessimistic expectations that almost everybody had come to hold during the seemingly endless Depression. In the long decade of the 1930s, especially its latter half, many people had come to believe that the economic machine was irreparably broken. The frenetic activity of war production—never mind that it was just a lot of guns and ammunition—dispelled the hopelessness. People began to think: If we can produce all these planes, ships, and bombs, we can also turn out prodigious quantities of cars and refrigerators (Winkler, 1986, pp. 2, 23–24, 96). When the controls began to come off and the war ended more quickly than anticipated in 1945, consumers and producers launched eagerly into carrying out plans based on rosy forecasts and, by so doing, made their expectations a reality.[20]

Probably the most solid evidence of expectations comes from the stock markets, where thousands of transactors risk their own wealth on the basis of their beliefs about future economic conditions (table 3-5). Evidently, investors took a dim view of the prospect of a war economy. After 1939, stock values dropped steadily and substantially; U.S. entry into the war in December 1941 did not arrest the decline. By 1942, the Standard & Poor's index had fallen by 28 percent, and the market value of all stocks on registered exchanges had plunged by 62 percent in nominal terms. (Adjustments for price level changes would make the declines even greater.) The declines occurred even though current corporate profits were rising steadily and substantially. In 1943, as the tide of war turned in favor of the Allies, the stock market rallied and small additional advances took place in 1944. Still, in 1944, with the war economy operating at its peak, the stock market's real value had yet to recover to its 1939 level.

By early 1945, almost everyone expected the war to end soon. The prospect of a peacetime economy electrified investors. Stock prices surged in 1945 and again in 1946. In just two years, the Standard & Poor's index

Table 3-5. Stock prices and corporate profits, 1939–1949

Year	Standard & Poor's index of common stock prices (1941–1943 = 10)	Market value of stocks on registered exchanges (billions of current dollars)	Corporate profits* (billions of current dollars)
1939	12.06	11.426	4.0
1940	11.02	8.404	5.9
1941	9.82	6.240	6.7
1942	8.67	4.309	8.3
1943	11.50	9.024	9.9
1944	12.47	9.799	11.2
1945	15.16	16.226	9.0
1946	17.08	18.814	8.0
1947	15.17	11.587	11.7
1948	15.53	12.904	17.8
1949	15.23	10.740	17.8

*After tax, with inventory valuation and capital consumption adjustments. *Sources:* Columns 1 and 2 are from U.S. Bureau of the Census. 1975. *Historical Statistics of the United States, Colonial Times to 1970.* Washington, D.C.: U.S. Government Printing Office, pp. 1004, 1007; and column 3 is from U.S. Council of Economic Advisers. 1990. *Annual Report 1990.* Washington, D.C.: U.S. Government Printing Office, p. 395.

increased by 37 percent and the value of all shares on registered exchanges increased by 92 percent, despite a decline in current-dollar, after-tax corporate profits from their peak in 1944. Did people expect the end of "wartime prosperity" to be economically deleterious? Obviously not.

To sum up, World War II got the economy out of the Great Depression, but not in the manner described by the orthodox story. The war *itself* did not get the economy out of the Depression. The economy produced neither a "carnival of consumption" nor an investment boom, however successfully it overwhelmed the nation's enemies with bombs, shells, and bullets.[21] But certain events of the war years, including the war's transformation of economic expectations—justify an interpretation that views the war as an event that recreated the possibility of genuine economic recovery. As the war ended, real prosperity returned almost overnight.

Notes

1. Hughes (1990, pp. 493, 495, 504), but compare the statement in J. R. T. Hughes (1984, pp. 154–5). Also, Puth (1988, pp. 521, 531–2), Lebergott (1984, pp. 472, 477), Niemi (1980, p. 390), Walton and Rockoff (1990, pp. 520, 523–4, 535), Polenberg (1972, p. 36), Blum (1976, pp. 90–91), Winkler (1986, pp. 19–23), Vatter (1985, pp. 14, 20), Melman (1985, pp. 15, 16, 19), Stein (1984, pp. 65–66), Offer (1987, pp. 876–77), and Cowen (1989, pp. 525–26).

2. For those who insist on a macroeconomic framework, the employment question can be considered with reference to the model estimated by Evans (1982). Evans concludes on pp. 960–61 that in an explanation of changes in civilian employment during the war years, "emphasis . . . on conscription makes sense."

3. See Kuznets (1952, pp. 39–40). The Commerce Department later admitted the validity of Kuznets's criticism, but failed to make the implied corrections. See U.S. Department of Commerce (1954, p. 157). For detailed documentation of the falling relative prices of munitions during the war, see Miller (1949, pp. 203–11, 283–86) and U.S. War Production Board (1945, pp. 11, 21–22, 38–39).

4. Differences between Kuznets's 1952 figures and the Variant III estimates reflect the incorporation of new data showing lower proportions of durables in military purchases during the war as well as a switch (justified by the need for continuity in a longer series) back to Commerce Department deflators. See Kuznets (1961, pp. 470–71).

5. Although one might infer from his later discussion in Kuznets (1961, pp. 465–84) that he ultimately did.

6. Kendrick (1961, p. 236) and Abramovitz's comment in National Bureau of Economic Research (1972, p. 86).

7. Kuznets (1951, pp. 193–94). Again, his discussion that was mentioned earlier (1961, pp. 465–84) may be read as an implicit disavowal. There he no longer defended or even mentioned the "two end purposes" argument. Referring to a comparison of his approach and the Commerce Department's approach to treating military spending *for a period that includes World War II,* he said that (p. 471) "one errs less" by using his approach, that is, the "peacetime concept" of national product.

8. Even if one accepts GNP* conceptually, one might object that my estimate of it makes too large a deduction. Some of the military durable equipment and construction purchased during the war was used after the war for the production of civilian as well as military outputs. To delete all military spending gives rise to the error exposed by Gordon (1969, pp. 221–38). If one could make a correction completely consistent with the spirit of the argument, one would arrive at an estimate somewhere between Variant III and GNP*, the exact location being determined by the distinction between military capital potentially capable of augmenting civilian output and military capital lacking this capability. Data on war durables purchases are insufficient to allow the separation to be made with precision.

9. See Novick, Anshen, and Truppner (1949, pp. 16–18). This is not to say that prices played no role; much of the planning had to do with the manipulation of prices. But market-determined prices and costs were never permitted to play a fundamental role. See Miller (1949, pp. 97–110).

10. See Mitchell (1943, pp. 7, 13). For documentation of the extent of evasions of the price controls, see Clinard (1969, pp. 28–50).

11. See Kuznets (1945, pp. 38–41). Sixteen years later, having changed his approach in several respects, Kuznets was still apologetic (1961, p. 471): "These changes in the treatment of durable military output may seem arbitrary, and there is no denying a large element of personal judgment in the procedures."

12. In a personal communication, Professor Vatter has noted that the civilian population actually fell by nearly five million between 1941 and 1944, and hence, consumption per civilian rose more rapidly than the per capita data indicate. The point is well taken, but somewhat unsettling. It suggests a civilian population enhancing its well-being by forcing millions of men into military service, where civilian goods became wholly irrelevant to them, while their more fortunate fellows enjoyed those goods exclusively. The more fundamental problem, however, is that the numerator (*total* real consumption) is overstated.

13. See Hugh Rockoff (1978, p. 417). For an analysis of the wartime consumer price controls, see Rockoff (1984, pp. 85–176). The official history is summarized in Mansfield and associates (1947). See also Friedman and Schwartz (1963, pp. 557–8) and Anderson (1979, pp. 545–46).

14. Calculated from data in Kuznets (1952, p. 40). Barro (1978, p. 572) has obtained econometric results suggesting that all of the genuine inflation occurred during the war years, none of it during the immediate postwar years, and that 1946 actually witnessed *deflation*.

15. See Friedman and Schwartz (1982, p. 107). Using a different macroeconomic procedure, Vedder and Gallaway (1991, pp. 8–10, 30) estimated a GNP deflator whose overall changes for the periods 1941–45 and 1945–48 are similar to the corresponding changes in the Friedman-Schwartz NNP deflator.

16. On wartime living conditions, see Rockoff (1984, pp. 85–176), Novick, Anshen, and Truppner (1949, pp. 18, 302), Fussell (1989, pp. 195–98), Polenberg (1972, pp. 5–37, 131–53), Blum (1976, pp. 92–105), Winkler (1986, pp. 24–47), Schweitzer (1980, pp. 91–93), and Brinkley (1988).

17. On the wartime controls, see the recent analyses of Vatter (1985), Rockoff (1984, pp. 85–176), and Higgs (1987, pp. 196–236). Contemporary official and first hand accounts include Novick, Anshen, and Truppner (1949), Harris (1945), Catton (1948), Janeway (1951), Nelson (1946), Smith (1959), U.S. Bureau of the Budget, War Records Section (1946), U.S. Civilian Production Administration (1947), and U.S. War Production Board (1945).

18. See Krug (1945, p. 11). See pp. 29–32 for a detailed statement of the physical quantities of various munitions produced during the war. For even greater detail, see Smith (1959, pp. 3–31).

19. It was hardly a well-oiled machine. Novick and colleagues made free use of such terms as "administrative chaos," "administrative anarchy," "chasm between plan and operation" and "trial-and-error fumbling." See Novick, Anshen, and Truppner (1949, pp. 110, 140, 219, 291, 394, 395, 400, 403). These well-informed insiders concluded (p. 9) that the successes of the wartime planned economy were "less a testimony to the effectiveness with which we mobilized our resources than they are to the tremendous economic wealth which this nation possessed."

20. Compare the explanation of the economy's performance just after the war in Vedder and Gallaway (1991, pp. 14–29). Their argument calls attention to, among other things, the huge swing in the federal government's fiscal position, from massive deficit to substantial surplus, between 1945 and 1946–47 (calendar years), hence, "reverse crowding out." See also some new ideas on how wartime events affected the operation of the postwar labor market, in Jensen (1989, pp. 581–82). A much fuller interpretation of the postwar reconversion appears in chap. 5 below.

21. The phrase "carnival of consumption" comes from Blum (1976, p. 90).

References

Abramovitz, Moses. (1959) The Welfare Interpretation of Secular Trends in National Income and Product. In *The Allocation of Economic Resources,* edited by Moses Abramovitz et al. Stanford: Stanford University Press, pp. 1–22.

Anderson, Benjamin M. (1979) *Economics and the Public Welfare: A Financial and Economic History of the United States, 1914–46.* Indianapolis: Liberty Fund.

Barro, Robert J. (1978) Unanticipated Money, Output, and the Price Level in the United States. *Journal of Political Economy* 86 (August): 549–80.

Blum, John Morton. (1976) *V Was for Victory: Politics and American Culture During World War II.* New York: Harcourt Brace Jovanovich.

Brinkley, David. (1988) *Washington Goes To War.* New York: Knopf.

Buchanan, James M. (1979) General Implications of Subjectivism in Economics. In James M. Buchanan. *What Should Economists Do?* Indianapolis: Liberty Fund, pp. 81–91.

Catton, Bruce. (1948) *The War Lords of Washington.* New York: Harcourt Brace and Co.

Clinard, Marshall B. (1969) *The Black Market: A Study of White Collar Crime.* Montclair, N.J.: Patterson Smith.

Cowen, Tyler. (1989) Why Keynesianism Triumphed or, Could So Many Keynesians Have Been Wrong? *Critical Review* 3 (Summer/Fall): 518–30.

Darby, Michael R. (1976) Three-and-A-Half Million U.S. Employees Have Been Mislaid: Or, an Explanation of Unemployment, 1934–1941. *Journal of Political Economy* 84 (February): 1–16.

Evans, Paul. (1982) The Effects of General Price Controls in the United States during World War II. *Journal of Political Economy* 90 (October): 944–66.

Friedman, Milton, and Anna Jacobson Schwartz. (1963). *A Monetary History of the United States, 1867–1960.* Princeton: Princeton University Press.

Friedman, Milton, and Anna Jacobson Schwartz. (1982) *Monetary Trends in the United States and the United Kingdom.* Chicago: University of Chicago Press.

Fussell, Paul. (1989) *Wartime: Understanding and Behavior in the Second World War.* New York: Oxford University Press.

Gordon, Robert J. (1969) $45 Billion of U.S. Private Investment Has Been Mislaid. *American Economic Review* 59 (June): 221–38.

Harris, Seymour E. (1945) *Price and Related Controls in the United States.* New York: McGraw-Hill.

Higgs, Robert. (1987) *Crisis and Leviathan: Critical Episodes in the Growth of American Government.* New York: Oxford University Press.

Higgs, Robert. (1993) Private Profit, Public Risk: Institutional Antecedents of the Modern Military Procurement System in the Rearmament Program of 1940–1941. In *The Sinews of War: Essays on the Economic History of World War II,* edited by Geofrey T. Mills and Hugh Rockoff. Ames, Ia.: Iowa State University Press, pp. 166–98.

Hughes, J. R. T. (1984) Stagnation without 'Flation': The 1930s Again. In *Money in Crisis: The Federal Reserve, the Economy, and Monetary Reform,* edited by Barry N. Siegel. Cambridge, Mass.: Ballinger, pp. 137–56.

Hughes, J. R. T. (1990) *American Economic History,* third edition. Glenview, Ill.: Scott, Foresman and Co.

Janeway, Eliot. (1951) *The Struggle for Survival: A Chronicle of Economic Mobilization in World War II.* New Haven: Yale University Press.

Jensen, Richard J. (1989) The Causes and Cures of Unemployment in the Great Depression. *Journal of Interdisciplinary History* 19 (Spring): 553–83.

Kendrick, John W. (1961) *Productivity Trends in the United States.* Princeton: Princeton University Press.

Krug, J. A. (1945) *Production: Wartime Achievements and the Reconversion Outlook.* Special report prepared for the U.S. War Production Board. Washington, D.C.: Government Printing Office.

Kuznets, Simon. (1945) *National Product in Wartime.* New York: National Bureau of Economic Research.

Kuznets, Simon. (1951) Government Product and National Income. In *Income and Wealth,* edited by Erick Lundberg. Cambridge: Bowes and Bowes, pp. 178–244.

Kuznets, Simon. (1952) Long-Term Changes in the National Income of the United States of America since 1870. In *Income & Wealth of the United States: Trends and Structure,* edited by Simon Kuznets. Cambridge: Bowes and Bowes, pp. 29–241.

Kuznets, Simon. (1961) *Capital in the American Economy: Its Formation and Financing.* Princeton: Princeton University Press.

Lebergott, Stanley. (1984) *The Americans: An Economic Record.* New York: W. W. Norton.

Manchester, William. (1980) *Goodbye Darkness: A Memoir of the Pacific War.* New York: Little, Brown.

Mansfield, Harvey C., and associates. (1947) *A Short History of OPA.* Washington, D.C.: Office of Price Administration.

Melman, Seymour. (1985) *The Permanent War Economy: American Capitalism in Decline,* revised edition. New York: Simon and Schuster.

Miller, John Perry. (1949) *Pricing of Military Procurements.* New Haven: Yale University Press.

Mills, Geofrey, and Hugh Rockoff. (1987) Compliance with Price Controls in the United States and the United Kingdom During World War II. *Journal of Economic History* 17 (March): 197–213.

Mises, Ludwig von. (1919, 1983) *Nation, State, and Economy: Contributions to the Politics and History of Our Time,* translated by Leland B. Yeager, first edition, 1919; translated edition, 1983. New York: New York University Press.

Mitchell, Wesley C. (1943) Wartime "Prosperity" and the Future. *National Bureau of Economic Research Occasional Paper 9.* New York: National Bureau of Economic Research.

National Bureau of Economic Research. (1972) *Economic Growth.* NBER General Series 96. New York: National Bureau of Economic Research.

Nelson, Donald M. (1946) *Arsenal of Democracy: The Story of American War Production.* New York: Harcourt, Brace and Co.

Niemi, Albert W., Jr. (1980) *U.S. Economic History: A Survey of the Major Issues,* second edition. Chicago: Rand McNally.

Nordhaus, William, and James Tobin. (1972) Is Growth Obsolete? In National Bureau of Economic Research, *Economic Growth,* NBER General Series 96. New York: National Bureau of Economic Research, pp. 1–80.

Novick, David, Melvin Anshen, and W. C. Truppner. (1949) *Wartime Production Controls.* New York: Columbia University Press.

Offer, Avner. (1987) War Economy. In *The New Palgrave: A Dictionary of Economics,* vol. 4, edited by John Eatwell, Murray Milgate, and Peter Newman. London: Macmillan, pp. 875–77.

Polenberg, Richard. (1972) *War and Society: The United States, 1941–45.* New York: J. B. Lippincott.

Puth, Robert C. (1988) *American Economic History,* second edition. Chicago: Harcourt Brace Jovanovich.

Rockoff, Hugh. (1978) Indirect Price Increases and Real Wages during World War II. *Explorations in Economic History* 15 (October): 407–20.

Rockoff, Hugh. (1984) *Drastic Measures: A History of Wage and Price Controls in the United States.* Cambridge: Cambridge University Press.

Schweitzer, Mary M. (1980) World War II and Female Labor Force Participation Rates. *Journal of Economic History* 40 (March): 89–95.

Smith, R. Elberton. (1959) *The Army and Economic Mobilization.* Washington, D.C.: U.S. Army.

Stein, Herbert. (1984) *Presidential Economics: The Making of Economic Policy from Roosevelt to Reagan and Beyond.* New York: Simon and Schuster.

U.S. Bureau of the Budget, War Records Section. (1946) *The United States at War: Development and Administration of the War Program by the Federal Government.* Washington, D.C.: Government Printing Office.

U.S. Bureau of the Census. (1975) *Historical Statistics of the United States, Colonial Times to 1970.* Washington, D.C.: Government Printing Office.

U.S. Civilian Production Administration [formerly War Production Board]. (1947) *Industrial Mobilization for War: History of the War Production Board and Predecessor Agencies, 1940–1945.* Washington, D.C.: Government Printing Office.

U.S. Council of Economic Advisers. (1990) *Annual Report, 1990.* Washington, D.C.: Government Printing Office.

U.S. Department of Commerce. (1954) *National Income, 1954 edition: A Supplement to the Survey of Current Business.* Washington, D.C.: Government Printing Office.

U.S. Department of Defense. (1987) *National Defense Budget Estimates for FY 1988/1989.* Office of the Assistant Secretary of Defense (Comptroller). Washington, D.C.: U.S. Department of Defense.

U.S. War Production Board. (1945) *American Industry in War and Transition, 1940–1950. Part II: The Effect of the War on the Industrial Economy.* Washington, D.C.: Government Printing Office.

Vatter, Harold G. (1985) *The U.S. Economy in World War II.* New York: Columbia University Press.

Vedder, Richard, and Lowell Gallaway. (1991) The Great Depression of 1946. *Review of Austrian Economics 2,* no. 2:3–31.

Walton, Gary M., and Hugh Rockoff. (1990) *History of the American Economy,* sixth edition. San Diego: Harcourt Brace Jovanovich.

Winkler, Allan M. (1986) *Home Front U.S.A.: America during World War II.* Arlington Heights, Ill.: Harlan Davidson.

Acknowledgments   For comments on previous drafts, I am grateful to Moses Abramovitz, Lee Alston, Alexander Field, Price Fishback, J. R. T. Hughes, Daniel Klein, Stanley Lebergott, Gary Libecap, Robert McGuire, Hugh Rockoff, Murray Rothbard, Randal Rucker, Andrew Rutten, Anna Schwartz, Julian Simon, Gordon Tullock, Harold Vatter, and Richard Vedder. I also thank the participants in seminars at the University of Arizona, the University of Washington, and Seattle University, and in presentations at the *Liberty* Magazine Editors' Conference (Richard Stroup, discussant) and the meetings of the Cliometric Society (John Wallis, discussant).

Wartime Socialization of Investment

*A Reassessment of U.S. Capital Formation
in the 1940s*

> There are circumstances which make the consumption of
> capital unavoidable. A costly war cannot be financed with-
> out such a damaging measure. . . . There may arise situations
> in which it may be unavoidable to burn down the house to
> keep from freezing, but those who do that should realize
> what it costs and what they will have to do without later on.
> *Ludwig von Mises,* Interventionism

DURING WORLD WAR II, the U.S. government dis-
placed private investors. According to National Income and Product
Accounts (NIPA) data for the period 1942–1945, net private investment
was minus $6.2 billion, and net government investment was plus $99.4
billion. Although economists have credited this government investment
with various contributions to wartime and postwar economic growth,
the bulk of it had little or no value beyond its immediate contribution
to winning the war. This episode dramatically exposes a fundamental,
but false, assumption that underlies official data on capital formation
(namely, that *all* expenditures for durable producer goods or munitions
form genuine capital).

In the oft-quoted final chapter of *The General Theory,* titled "Concluding Notes on the Social Philosophy Towards Which the General Theory
Might Lead," John Maynard Keynes declared: "The State will have to exercise a guiding influence on the propensity to consume partly through its
scheme of taxation, partly by fixing the rate of interest," and it will have

to undertake "a somewhat comprehensive socialisation of investment . . . though this need not exclude all manner of compromises and of devices by which public authority will co-operate with private initiative" (Keynes, 1936, p. 378). In composing this passage, Keynes surely had in mind a program by which the state would attempt to moderate the fluctuations of the peacetime macroeconomy, and in that sense, his vision went unrealized in Britain and the United States. Once in U.S. history, however, during World War II, Keynes's vision did achieve full-fledged realization. Although economists and historians have studied extensively the wartime tax measures and interest rate fixing, the government domination of investment that occurred in the United States from 1941 to 1945 has received much less attention.

Of course, it has not been overlooked entirely. Indeed, among contemporary analysts and early postwar writers, nearly all of whom subscribed to the "miracle of production" interpretation of the government's wartime economic management, the government's wartime takeover of capital formation received considerable, and generally favorable, recognition.

For example, R. Elberton Smith, author of the impressive official history *The Army and Economic Mobilization,* in describing the War Department's multifaceted involvement in capital accumulation, remarked that, "war plant expansion in the three years ending with 1943 was equal to half the investment in manufacturing facilities during the preceding two decades" (Smith, 1959, p. 440). In Smith's view, "the American economy in World War II exhibited the greatest capital expansion in its history—an expansion which went far toward guaranteeing the successful outcome of the war" (Smith, 1959, p. 475).

Speaking with pride of the more than $9 billion dollars that the Defense Plant Corporation (DPC), a Reconstruction Finance Corporation (RFC) subsidiary, had channeled into industrial capital formation during the war, RFC head Jesse Jones noted: "At the close of World War II, Defense Plant Corporation's investment alone embraced 96 per cent of the nation's synthetic rubber capacity, 90 per cent in magnesium metal, 71 per cent in the manufacture of aircraft and their engines, 58 per cent in aluminum metal, and nearly 50 percent of the facilities for fabricating aluminum" (Jones, 1951, p. 316). The War Department, the Navy Department, and other government agencies also financed massive industrial investments (Smith, 1959, pp. 447, 496–501; Connery, 1951, p. 345; and Smaller War Plants Corporation, 1946, p. 48).

In 1969, Robert J. Gordon shocked the economics profession by announcing that "$45 billion of U.S. Private Investment Has Been Mislaid." Of that "mislaid" amount—"an estimate of cumulative 1940–65 U.S. government expenditures on privately operated plant and equipment (in 1958 prices), minus the small portion already included in the official OBE [Office of Business Economics] capital stock data" (Gordon, 1969, p. 221)— some 62.5 percent had been spent from 1940 through 1945.[1] Gordon argued that "the existence of this vast amount of previously unmeasured capital explains in part how the private American economy produced so much during the war and early postwar years with such a small measured increase in the stock of capital relative to the level of the late 1920's" (Gordon, 1969, p. 232).

Recently, Gordon has refined his earlier estimates of the U.S. capital stock in the nonfarm, nonhousing private business sector, "changing from fixed to variable retirement, and . . . adding GOPO [government-owned, privately operated] and highway capital" (Gordon, 2000, p. 46). On the basis of his new estimates of the nonfarm, nonhousing private business capital stock, he concludes that, "instead of declining by 7.4 percent between 1930 and 1944, total capital input actually increases by 28 percent" a finding that he declares to be important and "highly relevant to the puzzle of how the United States succeeded in producing so much during World War II" (Gordon, 2000, pp. 46–7).

Like Gordon, Alexander J. Field has considered recently how taking properly into account the government's capital formation during World War II might help us to understand better the broad contours of U.S. productivity change in the twentieth century. Field observes: "There remains an unresolved dispute over the usefulness for civilian production of this capital after the war. Some have criticized the transfers to the private sector as sweetheart deals; the valuations reflected in the sales, however, have been defended on the grounds that substantial retrofitting was often required to make them suitable for civilian production" (Field, 2003, p. 1405).

The valuation of privatized government-financed plants and equipment is but one issue among many that bears on our understanding of the government's wartime capital formation and its consequences for the performance of the postwar economy. So far, however, students of this topic have overlooked a number of complications that cloud the meaning of the standard data used to study it.

My objective in this chapter is to display and discuss the official data that purport to measure wartime capital formation, to identify several problematic aspects of those data, and to indicate at least the direction, if not the precise magnitude, of some strongly warranted adjustments. The theme of my inquiry is that previous analysts have failed to take fully into account the incomparability of capital formation undertaken by private entrepreneurs and capital formation undertaken by government officials—an incomparability that looms especially large when the latter's projects are dedicated to highly specific military purposes. Here, as in so many other areas of economic analysis, we cannot penetrate to the essence of the matter unless we have a clear understanding of the economic principles that Ludwig von Mises and F. A. Hayek expounded in their contributions to the socialist calculation debate prior to World War II (Mises, 1935; Hayek, 1935). Unfortunately, the analytical insights that I present and the measurement corrections that I propose here may serve only to deepen some of the mysteries that previous analysts believed they had solved by taking into account the government's wartime capital formation.

Wartime Socialization of Investment

The basic data on which analysis usually rests appear in table 4-1. They come from the NIPA and are produced by the Bureau of Economic Analysis in the U.S. Department of Commerce.[2] The values are expressed in current dollars. In due course, I will say something about inflation-adjusted values—an especially tricky matter during the 1940s, because of the government's massive military mobilization, direct resource allocations, and price controls that substantially affected the greater part of the decade— but much of what we need to know does not require an attempt to arrive at "real" values.

As the data displayed in table 4-1 make clear, a massive shift occurred during the early 1940s in the sources of U.S. investment spending. In 1940, gross private domestic investment amounted to $13.6 billion ($5.6 billion net), whereas gross government investment came to just $4.4 billion ($2.9 billion net), including net national defense investment of an almost negligible $0.6 billion. In contrast, in 1943, at the peak of the government's investment surge, gross private domestic investment had dropped to $6.1 billion (–$4.0 billion net), whereas gross government investment had soared to $39.1 billion ($32.8 billion net), including net national defense investment of $32.9 billion. Plainly, this tremendous shift illustrates "the socialization of investment" with a vengeance.

For the four years from 1942 through 1945 as a whole, gross private investment fell to such low levels that it failed to compensate for the depreciation of the private capital stock. For that period, net private investment totaled minus $6.2 billion. In U.S. history, the only comparable evaporation of private capital occurred during the early years of the Great Depression.[3] For those same four war years, however, net government investment totaled $99.4 billion, of which net national defense investment amounted to slightly more than 100 percent (the government did not invest enough in its nondefense capital stock to compensate for its depreciation).

Then, even more quickly than the government had displaced private investors during the early 1940s, the latter displaced the government between 1945 and 1946, when net private domestic investment increased from approximately zero to $18.5 billion—an unprecedented amount—setting in motion an investment boom that continued thereafter for many years, restoring genuine prosperity to an economy that had wallowed for sixteen years in peacetime depression and wartime privation.[4] In stark contrast, between 1945 and 1946, gross government investment fell from $24.1 billion to just $3.5 billion (net from $13.9 billion to –$7.5 billion), and the national defense capital stock began a sustained decline that extended into the 1950s.

Table 4-1. Private and government fixed investment, 1940–1950 (billions of current dollars)

Year	Private domestic investment		Government investment				
					Net national defense		
	Gross	Net	Gross	Net Total	Net defense	Net defense structures	Net defense equipment
1940	13.6	5.6	4.4	2.9	0.6	0.5	0.1
1941	18.1	9.1	10.8	8.8	6.7	3.4	3.3
1942	10.4	0.3	28.5	25.0	24.3	10.0	14.3
1943	6.1	-4.0	39.1	32.8	32.9	5.3	27.6
1944	7.8	-2.6	36.6	27.7	28.3	1.9	26.4
1945	10.8	0.1	24.1	13.9	14.2	1.1	13.2
1946	31.1	18.5	3.5	-7.5	-7.4	-0.4	-7.0
1947	35.0	19.4	4.6	-6.1	-7.3	-0.7	-6.6
1948	48.1	29.8	7.0	-2.7	-5.1	-0.5	-4.5
1949	36.9	16.8	9.7	0.9	-3.1	-0.5	-2.6
1950	54.1	32.4	9.8	1.8	-2.9	-0.4	-2.5

Source: U.S. Department of Commerce, Bureau of Economic Analysis. *National Income and Product Accounts Tables.* Table 5.2. Gross and Net Investment by Major Type, available at http://www.bea.doc.gov/bea/dn/nipaweb/TableViewFixed.asp; accessed November 26, 2002.

Capital Is Capital?

As I have just shown, during the war the government spent huge amounts of money to purchase durable military and industrial assets, thereby adding substantially to the stock of government "capital." In the official accounts, no mystery attends the process of capital formation. If the government purchases a durable good, then ipso facto it adds to the gross capital stock, and therefore (given that the value of such purchases exceeds the value deducted as depreciation, according to standard accounting formulas) it increases the economy's future potential to produce valuable goods and services. In this so-called perpetual inventory method of accounting for capital formation, investment dollars flow like water into a capital stock bathtub from which, at the same time, depreciation causes a certain drainage (Wasson, Musgrave, and Harkins, 1970, p. 20). Just as all drops of water matter equally when one is filling or emptying a tub, so all dollars of investment spending count equally when one is constructing a time series of capital stock. Here, in its official accounting representation, capital becomes something like the "homogeneous mass" imagined by capital theorists such as Frank Knight—a dollar spent for "capital" is a dollar spent for "capital" (Hennings, 1987, p. 330).

Whatever virtues this view may have in relation to the economic theory of a market system—and hardly anything has been more hotly disputed by economists than capital theory (Hennings, 1987, pp. 327–33)—it has definite shortcomings in application to government capital formation. When private entrepreneurs make investments, they hazard their own property or the property that others have entrusted to them. Therefore, they must appraise carefully the prospect that the capital goods they purchase will give rise to an income stream sufficient to justify the present expense, the risks of loss, and the delays that they anticipate before they can appropriate future income. Ultimately, the success of any private investment turns on the ability to use capital goods in a way that, directly or indirectly, consumers validate by purchasing final goods in the market.

Government officials follow different stars in making their investment decisions: Politics, ideology, and even personal vanity ("empire building") have a much greater chance of carrying the day. As W. H. Hutt observed, "officials not only cannot have the necessary detailed awareness which market signals provide; but most important, they cannot be caused to lose property through error nor be rewarded by the acquisition of property through success" (Hutt, 1979, p. 76). For the government, no consumer-determined bottom line spells the difference between success and failure, because the government has the coercive power to extract taxes from citizens in order to finance the investments initially and to subsidize money-losing projects afterward, in defiance of consumer preferences.

Never does the contrast between the private investor and the government investor loom larger than it does during wartime, especially during a modern "total" war, such as World War II, when perceived military necessity counts heavily with those responsible for making government investments. The wartime investment program in the United States from 1940 through 1945 illustrates the contrast unmistakably. "This unprecedented expansion of industrial capacity was not directed by business executives; nor did dollar-a-year men exercise effective indirect control over it. Rather, it was semiautonomous bureaucrats in pursuit of national security goals and insulated within the increasingly powerful Pentagon who directed this effort."[5]

If it were possible, as some economists have maintained, for government officials to calculate all of the shadow prices needed to operate a centrally planned economy efficiently, and if the officials proceeded to make their decisions on the basis of those shadow prices, then matters would be different; but these conditions have never been established anywhere, and they certainly were not established in the United States during World War II, when the government's "investments" obeyed a different, starkly nonmarket logic. John Cochran has summarized the issues that are most pertinent here:

The concept of capital is not a category of all acting, but only a category of acting in a market economy. Capital is an essential element in entrepreneurial planning. It is an estimate of the market value at a definite date of a particular business plan. . . . A given business or entrepreneurial plan implies a time structure of production for the individual enterprise—a pattern of inputs (capital goods, labor and natural resources or land) applied at earlier dates followed by a pattern of outputs sold at later dates. . . . Without private ownership of the means of production, there can be no markets for resources, no money prices for resources, and thus no monetary calculation and no capital. (Cochran, 2003, pp. 3–4)

Therefore, whenever government officials undertake a massive investment program, we must expect them always to generate what Mises called "planned chaos" (Mises, 1949).

Thus, in March 1942, two military officers complained to the executive committee of the Army-Navy Munitions Board with regard to the vast industrial construction program that was then under way:

If we continue as at present, we shall have plants standing useless for lack of equipment or raw materials, or other things. Other plants will be turning scarce materials into items which cannot be used to oppose the enemy because of the lack of other things which should have been made instead. We shall have guns without gun sights, tanks without guns, planes without bomb sights, ships held up for lack of steel plates, planes which we cannot get to the field of battle because of lack of merchant bottoms.[6]

Of course, a government investment program *may* make some sense in relation to the achievement of strictly technological, military, or political objectives—arguably winning World War II was such a problem that the U.S. government solved, for the most part, by throwing gigantic amounts of money at it (Novick, Anshen, and Truppner, 1949, p. 9; Rockoff, 1996)— but in relation to economic rationality, it remains planned chaos, and its legacies must necessarily bear all of the marks of its essential character. Although the government planners made continuing adjustments to their planning apparatus throughout the war, and they improved it enough to permit the production of an enormous outpouring of munitions, the essential character of the planning system remained as devoid of economic logic near the end of the war as it had been at the beginning. Eliot Janeway referred, for example, to "the 1944 production crisis that saddled the war economy with surpluses while leaving it short of critical items," and he criticized "the fatal weakness in [Donald] Nelson's setup" for operating the War Production Board, the chief planning agency.[7]

In relation to the U.S. government's capital formation during World War II, the upshot is that many resources were completely wasted from the outset[8]; construction costs were pushed "substantially above normal levels"[9]; and many wartime investments proved to have little or no value after the war, despite the contrary impression that we might gain from an official time series of capital stock. For example, the Maritime Commission, which spent some $600 million (current dollars) to construct new shipyards, "decided to finance the emergency yards as if they were arsenals" because "it was believed that they would have little or no postwar value," and in fact, at the end of the war, "shipyards were a drug on the market," and "only a few found purchasers willing to pay even 12 per cent of what the yards cost" (Lane, 1951, pp. 108–9, 117). In addition, the Navy spent some $1.4 billion for shipyards, with similarly little to show for it at the end of the war (Lane, 1951, p. 397).

Simon Kuznets argued that when the government purchases durable military assets, "their survival beyond the initial year releases capital resources for other purposes, and while their services cannot be considered final product, the capital stock embodied in them, like other types of capital that serve a protective purpose, should be included" in estimates of overall capital formation (Kuznets, 1961, p. 470). It is difficult to see, however, how the mere physical survival of obsolete and permanently mothballed munitions, such as those thousands of otiose propeller-driven warplanes parked forever in the western deserts,[10] "released" anything or contributed in any way to a valuable purpose. To suppose otherwise would seem to entail making a fetish of physical durability at the expense of keeping genuine economic value at the center of our economic analysis.

The Composition of Wartime Government Investment

Although economists and historians have focused their analysis of the government's wartime investment on its purchases of industrial plants and equipment, the preponderance of the investment took other forms. As table 4-2 shows, outlays to construct strictly military facilities—so-called command installations, as opposed to industrial facilities—gobbled up $13.9 billion from 1941 through 1945, in contrast to $8.6 billion spent on industrial structures. By the end of the war, the War Department alone had invested in 2,996 command facilities (Smith, 1959, p. 448).

These spanned a wide range of uses:

> Some idea of the scope of the Army's far-flung empire of command installations in World War II may be inferred from the following

Table 4-2. Gross government fixed investment, 1940–1950
(billions of current dollars)

	All	National defense	National defense structures		
			All	Industrial buildings	Military facilities
1940	4.4	0.8	0.6	0.2	0.5
1941	10.8	7.2	3.6	1.3	2.1
1942	28.5	26.0	10.3	3.4	6.5
1943	39.1	37.4	5.8	1.9	3.3
1944	36.6	35.4	2.5	1.2	1.1
1945	24.1	22.7	1.7	0.8	0.9
1946	3.5	1.5	0.3	0.1	0.2
1947	4.6	0.9	0.2	0.1	0.3
1948	7.0	2.0	0.4	0.2	0.2
1949	9.7	2.9	0.4	0.2	0.2
1950	9.8	2.4	0.5	0.2	0.2

Source: U.S. Department of Commerce, Bureau of Economic Analysis. *National Income and Product Accounts Tables.* Table 5.14. Gross Government Fixed Investment by Type, available at http://www.bea.doc.gov/bea/dn/nipaweb/TableViewFixed.asp, accessed November 26, 2002.

partial list of establishments within the zone of interior alone: Army posts, camps, stations, forts, training and maneuvering areas, artillery and other ranges for the Ground Forces; airfields, air bases and stations, bombing and gunnery ranges for the Army Air Forces; storage facilities—from remote ammunition depots to metropolitan warehouses—for all branches of the Army; repair and maintenance stations for all types of equipment; hospitals, convalescent and recreation centers; military police camps, Japanese relocation centers, prisoner of war camps; a network of harbor defenses and other installations throughout the entire country for defense against enemy attack; holding and reconsignment centers, ports of embarkation, staging areas, and related facilities to mount the tremendous overseas expeditions of troops and supplies; local induction centers, radio stations, laundries, market centers, special schools and offices (including the $78 million Pentagon building); and, not to be overlooked, research laboratories, proving grounds, testing centers, and supersecret installations symbolized most completely by the atomic bomb. (Smith, 1959, p. 444)

Elsewhere, Smith also lists another category: 770 national cemeteries, occupying some 2,000 acres of land (Smith, 1959, p. 448). A similar itemization might have been compiled for the navy, whose bases, depots, repair yards, and other facilities spanned the globe.

Scanning the foregoing summary, one is struck by how many of the command facilities were highly specialized for aiding the operations of the wartime armed forces. Such facilities had little, if any, value for peacetime uses. Even those that the armed forces retained for strictly military purposes after the war proved grossly excessive, in view of the drastic reduction of military personnel strength after 1945. Small wonder that the Pentagon has spent more than half a century fighting (against local politicians and members of Congress, among others) to close bases still remaining from the massive base construction undertaken in the early 1940s to accommodate an armed force that eventually numbered more than 12 million men and women at its peak strength in 1945 (Twight, 1990; Edelstein,

2001, pp. 74–5). Even today, base closures continue to be made episodically, as political opportunities allow.

Industrial and military structures, together, account for less than one-fifth ($23.9 billion) of the total gross national defense investment ($128.7 billion) from 1941 through 1945 (see table 4-2). Clearly, the big gorilla of the government's wartime investment program consisted of the purchase of equipment (column 7 of table 4-1 shows this fact directly as a cumulative *net* investment of $84.8 billion in equipment during the same years). Again, as we have seen in relation to command facilities, the bulk of this investment (at least 90 percent) took the form of highly specialized military assets—combat airplanes, tanks, warships, guns, ammunition, and other such purely military durable goods—that had little, if any, value for use in peacetime activities.[11] In the workaday world, there's just not much call for phosgene-filled mortar shells, mustard gas-filled bombs, and white phosphorus-filled munitions,[12] not to mention the specialized equipment for producing atomic bombs.

Even the strictly military equipment, however, quickly became obsolete. Many readers will recall visiting or seeing photographs of the endless rows of aircraft parked in the western deserts or the scores of ships rusting peacefully at their moorage near the mouth of the Sacramento River in California. According to Kuznets's estimates, annual military capital consumption, which had been nearly negligible before the war, reached $6.35 billion in 1945 (compared with $19.1 billion of depreciation allowed for the economy's entire nonmilitary capital stock), and it continued to rise in the late 1940s, reaching $11.7 billion in 1950, as the wartime stock of munitions wore out, wasted away, or grew obsolete.[13]

Distortion of the Capital Structure

Notwithstanding the conventions of orthodox macroeconomics and the views of certain capital theorists, the actual capital stock is neither a homogeneous physical putty nor a financial mass of undifferentiated, fungible dollars. In a modern economy, with an extensive division of labor and highly articulated roundabout production, the capital stock consists of a vastly heterogeneous, intricately related collection of produced means of production. If the economy is to function effectively, the capital stock must assume a certain structure, so that the "planned chaos" I illustrated earlier does not cripple its operation. In general, whatever the usefulness of the government's wartime investment program for the immediate purpose of gaining military victory, the government investments gave rise to serious distortions of the capital structure, and therefore they had less value for postwar productive purposes than the sheer amounts spent on durable assets during the war might seem to imply.

Even though manufacturing accounted for less than 28 percent of the national income in 1940 (U.S. Bureau of the Census, 1975, p. 239), approximately nine-tenths of the government's wartime industrial investment flowed into that sector (Gordon, 1969, pp. 232–3), and within manufacturing, government investment went predominantly to a handful of industries: "aircraft, engines, and parts; explosives and shell loading; shipbuilding and repair; iron and steel and products; chemicals; nonferrous metals and products; ammunition, shells, bombs, etc.; guns; machinery and electrical equipment; petroleum and coal products; combat and motorized vehicles; and machine tools" (McLaughlin, 1943, pp. 100–9). As a contemporary analyst remarked, "In general, the proportion of public financing has been at a maximum for those industries whose expansions have been most disproportionate to probable postwar needs; . . . specialized war plants . . . possess questionable peacetime value; . . . [and] some of the special-purpose machinery will be worthless for peacetime operations" (McLaughlin, 1943, pp. 109, 114, 116). Some $12.2 billion of the government's total spending for industrial facilities ($17.2 billion), or approximately 71 percent, went into the metals and metal products industries.[14] According to a 1946 study by an analyst for the Board of Governors of the Federal Reserve System, "Prevailing opinion seems to be that about two-thirds of the Government owned war plants will not be adaptable to postwar production."[15]

Before the war, for example, the productive capacity of the aircraft industry had been almost negligible, but after swallowing more than $3 billion of the government's industrial investment outlays, the industry emerged from the war as a giant confronting only a tiny, ill-developed civilian market and a vastly shrunken government market for its products. Shipbuilding and repair experienced a similarly spectacular growth, and then a similarly anemic postwar demand for its products (U.S. Bureau of the Budget, 1946, p. 116; Smaller War Plants Corporation, 1946, pp. 43, 45–6; Lane, 1951, pp. 3–10 and passim; Hooks, 1991, pp. 158–60).

Besides producing unsustainable distortions in the sectoral and industrial composition of the capital stock, the government's wartime investment program created distortions in the locational distribution of the stock (McLaughlin, 1943, pp. 110–13). To some extent, these distortions reflected wartime security concerns, as when ordnance facilities were located more than 200 miles from the coast. Some locational distortions emerged "naturally," as reactions to other, unrelated government wartime actions that had brought about localized scarcities of labor, electrical power, or other resources. Some distortions arose from routine political pressures, especially by Roosevelt administration officials and by members of Congress, which continued to be exerted actively during the war (Jones, 1951; Eiler, 1997, p. 181; Lane, 1951, pp. 47, 96–7, 151–60, 190–201). As Glenn McLaughlin remarked in 1943, "Many war plants throughout the country will be physically appropriate for the manufacture of civilian products but geographically inappropriate" (McLaughlin, 1943, p. 117). Because the new industrial capacity that the government financed for war purposes did not conform to the locational pattern that would best meet the demands of the postwar market economy, standard accounting methods of computing its postwar value overstate its actual value.

"Real" Values and Insufficient Depreciation

At places in the foregoing discussion, I have added the current-dollar values of certain variables for various war years, notwithstanding the fact that the purchasing power of the dollar was falling throughout the war. For the purposes I was trying to serve, not much harm was done to my argument by those summations, but for other purposes, such as the determination of the net result of the government's wartime investment program, the use of current-dollar values will not suffice, and we must attend to the task of deflation. Unfortunately, wartime price indexes, in general, are unreliable, if indeed they have any validity at all (Higgs, 1992, pp. 49–52).

Matters are even worse in relation to the deflation of durable munitions, which, as we have seen, accounted for the great bulk of the government's wartime investment, according to the NIPA data. All economic statisticians seem to have recognized the essential futility of trying to construct a reliable price index for munitions output during World War II. Having made such an attempt in his 1945 monograph *National Product in Wartime,* Kuznets later decided to abandon the effort in his 1961 treatise *Capital in the American Economy,* remarking: "with the inclusion of additional war and nonwar years, it became exceedingly difficult to adjust the cost of military construction and munitions to levels comparable with normal, peacetime output. Instead, it seemed best to accept the price adjustment used in the Department of Commerce national income accounts" (Kuznets, 1961, p. 471). Unfortunately, the Commerce Department accountants themselves had already admitted that they could not do the job. In 1954, they had confessed that their "method of deflating munitions expenditures" has "severe limitations," in large part because "the price information relating to munitions is deficient, largely owing to the fact that there are insurmountable obstacles to the compilation of adequate time series on prices (or quantities) in this area which is characterized by extreme product change" (U.S. Department of Commerce, Office of Business Economics, 1954, p. 157). Therefore, the great bulk of the government's official capital formation during the war—its expenditures for durable munitions—cannot be deflated reliably. Because "insurmountable obstacles" cannot be surmounted, we need go no further down this path, except to emphasize the permanent dark cloud that hovers over all data that purport to represent in any way the real value of munitions outputs or stocks over time, especially for periods that include World War II.

Matters may not be so desperate with respect to the deflation of the government's wartime expenditures for industrial plants and equipment, in particular for the GOPO stock created during the war and, in part, sold to private owners during the immediate postwar years. Table 4-3 presents the most significant "real" data (expressed here in constant 1958 dollars), which are those pertaining to the private nonfarm business economy. In the Commerce Department report from which these data are drawn, four different estimates are given, based on two different deflators and two different depreciation formulas, but the four series all show essentially the same profile, and one variant will serve our purposes here well enough.

As table 4-3 shows, "real" privately owned capital fell from 1941 to 1944, rose slightly in 1945, and then grew rapidly in each of the next five years. "Real" GOPO capital mushroomed from near zero in 1940 to a

Table 4-3. Net fixed business capital (billions of 1958 dollars)

Year	Privately owned	Government owned, contractor operated	Total
1940	192.0	0.8	192.8
1941	195.9	5.9	201.8
1942	190.1	21.0	211.1
1943	182.4	36.7	219.1
1944	178.9	44.8	223.7
1945	181.8	50.2	232.0
1946	194.5	35.6	230.1
1947	211.6	27.3	238.9
1948	228.2	23.2	251.4
1949	239.5	19.4	258.9
1950	251.9	17.9	269.8

Note: Variant calculated by using straight-line depreciation and "constant cost 1." In these data, used assets acquired by business from government are valued at sales prices, not at the government's original cost of production.

Source: Wasson, Robert C, John C.. Musgrave, and Claudia Harkins. 1970. "Alternative Estimates of Fixed Business Capital in the United States, 1925–1968." *Survey of Current Business* 50 (April): 23, 36.

peak of $50.2 billion (in 1958 dollars) in 1945, and then began to decline rapidly, losing more than 60 percent of its value by 1949. The total privately operated stock of capital, shown in column 3 of the table, grew steadily from 1940 to 1945, fell slightly in 1946—a decline attributable entirely to the estimated decline of nearly 30 percent in the real value of GOPO capital, a substantial part of that decline representing the transfer of assets to private owners—and then grew steadily for the remainder of the decade. From 1940 to 1945, the estimated total stock increased by 20 percent and then, from 1945 to 1950, by 16 percent.

It is almost certain that the Commerce Department figures overstate the increase in the privately operated capital stock during the first half of the 1940s, because the standard formulas for computing depreciation fail to take into account certain extraordinary conditions during the war, especially "the accelerated depreciation resulting from intensive plant use and scarcity of replacement parts" (McLaughlin, 1943, p. 113). According to a War Production Board report:

> [P]lant utilization in the munitions industries increased sharply after Pearl Harbor. . . . [T]he average utilization of facilities in the metal products industries late in 1944 was about two-thirds above the prewar level, after having reached nearly twice the prewar level in the spring of 1943; the increase in the remaining industries, though smaller, was still substantial. . . . *[T]he increased utilization of existing facilities contributed nearly as much to the increase of total industrial output during the war as did the construction of new facilities;* though the contribution made by more intensive utilization was much more important in the earlier part of the period, particularly in 1940 and 1941, than it was in 1943 and 1944.[16]

Double-shift and even triple-shift operation of plants became much more common during the war (U.S. War Production Board, 1945, pp. 31–2). For example, shipyard facilities, which had been worked at most one shift per day before the war, supported three shifts per day during the war (Lane, 1951, p. 232).

Recently, Lee Ohanian, citing a 1963 study by Murray F. Foss, also has noted that "capital utilization increased substantially during the war" (Ohanian, 1997, p. 33). Foss had reported, among other things, that in a comparison of conditions in 1934–39 and those in 1940–44, hours of usage per year increased by 53 percent for railroad freight cars, by 54 percent for freight locomotives, and by 34 percent for passenger locomotives (Foss, 1963, p. 15). Hours of usage per year per spindle in the cotton textile industry increased by about two-thirds during the war years (Foss, 1963, p. 9).

At the same time that the capital stock was being used far more intensively, the lack of replacement parts and repair materials kept producers from doing the normal upkeep on their property. In the housing sector, rent controls induced landlords to forgo ordinary repairs. For apartment houses and small structures, index numbers of repair and maintenance expenditures fell some 20 percent during the war (Rockoff, 1984, p. 156). The motor-carrier industry during the three peak war years obtained "only 195,000 new trucks and buses," which amounted to "less than 10 percent of the number it would normally require for replacements and expansions," while increasing its loads each year and thereby hastening wear and tear on its fleet of vehicles (Director of War Mobilization and Reconversion, 1945, p. 39). At the beginning of 1945, the Director of War Mobilization and Reconversion confirmed that "wear and tear on [industrial] plants has been far above normal, while repairs and replacements have been below normal" (Director of War Mobilization and Reconversion, 1945, p. 50).

We can gain a rough idea of the effect of this accelerated wartime depreciation by making some conservative adjustments to the Commerce Department's capital consumption allowances. From the gross and net investment figures shown in table 4-1, we can infer that the official allowances for depreciation of the private capital stock during the five wartime production years were as follows, in current dollars: $9.0 billion in 1941, $10.1 billion in 1942, $10.1 billion in 1943, $10.4 billion in 1944, and $10.7 billion in 1945. If we adjust these estimates by adding just 10 percent in 1941, and 20 percent in each year from 1942 through 1945, the total *additional* depreciation for the entire wartime period comes to $9.1 billion, a far from trivial sum—consider, for example, that it offsets approximately

53 percent of the amount ($17.2 billion) that the government spent on new industrial facilities (structures, equipment, and reconversions) from July 1940 through June 1945.[17] In addition, we may presume that the official depreciation formulas also failed to capture fully the actual wartime depreciation of government-financed industrial facilities, which were also operated at extraordinary intensity, probably more so than the private capital stock as a whole. Given that more than half of the government's industrial investment had been completed by the end of 1942 (Smaller War Plants Corporation, 1946, p. 37), an allowance for extra depreciation of the GOPO industrial capital might easily add another $1 billion to the total adjustment for wartime understatement of actual depreciation, bringing that total to more than $10 billion in current dollars, or approximately $20 billion in 1958 dollars.[18]

If we deduct just *half of* this amount—$10 billion in 1958 dollars—from the total net fixed (privately operated) business capital estimate shown in table 4-3 for 1945 (which represents only part of the nation's total privately operated capital stock), the total falls to $222.0 billion. One implication, then, is that the total net fixed (privately operated) business capital stock increased between 1940 and 1945, not by the 20 percent implied by the official figures, but by just 15 percent. Moreover, given the new figure for 1945 (and a corresponding adjustment of the data for later years), another implication is that the total increased between 1945 and 1950, not by the 16 percent implied by the official figures, but by 17 percent. In my judgment, a complete and precise adjustment—which would require an enormous research effort to produce, if it is possible to produce at all, given the sorts of data that would be required—almost certainly would be greater than my crude, exploratory adjustment here.

By taking into account the undoubted measurement errors in the wartime depreciation allowed in the Commerce Department figures shown in table 4-3, which are caused by the inappropriate application of uniform, standard depreciation schedules, we may conclude that the actual drop in the privately owned net stock of capital was even greater than shown for the war years and that the increase in that stock during the second half of the 1940s was greater than shown. For the privately operated capital stock

(GOPO capital being incorporated with privately owned capital), as for the economy's real output (Higgs, 1992; Higgs, 1997; Higgs, 1999), the official data have misled us by making the wartime expansion appear bigger than it really was and the postwar expansion smaller than it really was.

Conclusion

Contemporaries greatly exaggerated the heroic achievements of the wartime socialization of investment. Their exaggeration reflected, in part, an unwarranted concentration of attention on the manufacturing sector. Although that sector undoubtedly played a central role in the production of munitions, it represented less than one-third of the entire prewar economy, and the other two-thirds got very short shrift indeed from the government's wartime investment program. Even *within* manufacturing, the nonmunitions industries suffered wartime privations of capital formation. Most important, of course, we must recognize that the great bulk (some 83 percent) of the apparent capital formation, as officially recorded (see tables 4-1 and 4-2), consisted not of industrial structures or equipment, but of military structures (some 14 percent) and durable munitions (some 69 percent)— weapons platforms, guns, ammunition, and auxiliary equipment and supplies. To have counted such military output as capital formation was always, at best, an extremely dubious practice, and the justifications for doing so that Kuznets and others have advanced are not convincing. If we take into account only those parts of the wartime capital formation that had value beyond their sheer immediate usefulness in winning the war, and if we give appropriate weight to the significant measurement errors that I have described, then we may conclude with reasonable confidence that, in fact, real capital formation during the first half of the 1940s was not proportionally greater than that during the latter half of the decade; indeed, it was more likely a good deal less. The wartime socialization of investment served a definite purpose in allowing the U.S. military-industrial complex to triumph over the nation's enemies in World War II. Beyond that, its achievements had little, if anything, to recommend them.

Notes

1. My calculation from data in Gordon (1969, p. 233).
2. Available online at www.bea.doc.gov/bea/dn/nipaweb/TableViewFixed.asp.
3. For periodized data from 1891 to 1989, see Edelstein (2000, pp. 390–1).
4. For an extended analysis of this generally misunderstood macroeconomic experience, see Higgs (1997). On the reconversion miracle itself, see Higgs (1999).
5. See Hooks (1991, p. 140). On the most important of these bureaucrats, Under Secretary of War Robert P. Patterson, see Eiler (1997). I do not intend to suggest that civilian demands had no influence on the wartime planners. On the contrary, conflicts raged between civilian interests and military interests throughout the war period; those conflicts are what Hooks was referring to when he subtitled his book "World War II's Battle of the Potomac." Such conflicts arose with regard to price controls, taxation, materials allocations, rationing, and countless other matters. In addition to the works by Hooks and Eiler, see Polenberg (1972), Higgs (1987, pp. 196–236), Higgs (1993), Edelstein (2001), and the many primary sources cited in these works. My point here is that regardless of these expressed civilian demands, to which some government officials responded actively, the planners, absent unrestricted private property rights and the relative prices to which trading in such rights gives rise, had no means of making decisions in an economically rational manner. Whatever their desires about the division of outputs between civilians and the military, they had no way to know the true cost of anything. Using "old" prices from the prewar economy was better than using random numbers, but using old prices was scarcely suitable for the achievement of an economically rational outcome, because the old prices could not possibly represent the actual underlying rates of substitution in consumption and production under the radically transformed demand-and-supply conditions of the wartime economy.
6. Quoted in Smith (1959, p. 453).
7. Janeway (1951, p. 353). For details about the continuing foul-ups that plagued wartime economic planning and the production program, see also, among many other sources, U.S. Bureau of the Budget (1946), Catton (1948), Novick, Anshen, and Truppner (1949), Lane (1951), and Eiler (1997).
8. For striking examples, see Jones, with Angly (1951, pp. 342–44), Lane (1951, pp. 627–36), and McCartney (1988, pp. 56–70).
9. Smith (1959, p. 502), citing evidence from the Truman Committee hearings; see also Lane (1951, p. 796).
10. Photos in Cohen (1991, p. 405).
11. Of the government's total wartime investment (1940–45) in industrial facilities, $8.8 billion went for structures (data in my table 4-2, column 4). Government spending for industrial plants, equipment, and reconversions totaled $17.2 billion (as reported in Smaller War Plants Corporation [1946, p. 38], citing War Production Board data). Therefore, no more than $8.4 billion went for industrial equipment. This compares to $105 billion spent for all national defense equipment (calculated from my table 4-2, columns 2 and 3).

12. Items among those dealt with during the deactivation of the Huntsville Arsenal in the late 1940s; see http://www.redstone.army.mil/history/studies/ viii.html.
13. Kuznets (1961, p. 499). I do not intend to suggest that none of the surplus military equipment left over in 1945 had any usefulness for subsequent military purposes, because some of it clearly did have such usefulness. Leebaert (2002, p. 97) reports, for example, that during the Korean War, some "ships had to be drawn from the two thousand vessels mothballed between 1946 and 1951" to carry supplies to U.S. troops in Korea. Also, some of the ammunition produced during the war must have been used during the post-1945 decade in military training and in the Korean War. If Kuznets's assumption (1961, p. 498) of a nine-year life for munitions is accurate, however, the ammunition left over in 1945 must have been lost, for the most part, to consumption, age, or obsolescence by 1954. Later, during the 1980s, all four *Iowa* class battleships were recommissioned. Such subsequent usage, however, was definitely the exception to the rule. None of this, of course, has any bearing whatever on the government's wartime contribution to the *industrial* capital stock, which is the more pertinent matter at issue here.
14. Smaller War Plants Corporation (1946, p. 38), citing War Production Board data.
15. Dirks (1946, p. 14); for a more optimistic judgment, see Smaller War Plants Corporation (1946, pp. 39–40).
16. U.S. War Production Board (1945, p. 7), emphasis added.
17. Smaller War Plants Corporation (1946, pp. 37–38), citing War Production Board data.
18. Adjustment for price-level change made here by using the implicit deflator for private nonresidential fixed investment; see U.S. Council of Economic Advisers (1970, p. 180).

References

Catton, Bruce. (1948) *The War Lords of Washington.* New York: Harcourt, Brace and Co.

Cochran, John P. (2003) Sound Money and the Business Cycle. Address delivered to the Austrian Scholars Conference, Auburn, Ala., March 15, 2003. Available as Mises.org Daily Article for March 24, 2003, at http://mises.org/articles.asp.

Cohen, Stan. (1991) *V for Victory: America's Home Front during World War II.* Missoula, Mont.: Pictorial Histories Publishing Co.

Connery, Robert H. (1991) *The Navy and the Industrial Mobilization in World War II.* Princeton: Princeton University Press.

Director of War Mobilization and Reconversion. (1945) *Problems of Mobilization and Reconversion* (First Report to the President, the Senate and the House of Representatives, January 1, 1945). Washington, D.C.: Office of War Mobilization and Reconversion.

Dirks, Frederick C. (1946) Postwar Capital Formation and Its Financing in Manufacturing and Mining Industries. In *Private Capital Requirements* (Postwar Economic Studies, No. 5). Washington, D.C.: Board of Governors of the Federal Reserve System.

Edelstein, Michael. (2000) War and the American Economy in the Twentieth Century. In *The Cambridge Economic History of the United States,* edited by Stanley L. Engerman and Robert E. Gallman, vol. III. New York: Cambridge University Press, pp. 329–405.

Edelstein, Michael. (2001) The Size of the U.S. Armed Forces during World War II: Feasibility and War Planning. *Research in Economic History* 20: 47–96.

Eiler, Keith E. (1997) *Mobilizing America: Robert P. Patterson and the War Effort, 1940–1945.* Ithaca, N.Y.: Cornell University Press.

Field, Alexander J. (2003) The Most Technologically Progressive Decade of the Century. *American Economic Review* 93 (September): 1399–1413.

Foss, Murray F. (1963) The Utilization of Capital Equipment: Postwar Compared With Prewar. *Survey of Current Business* 43 (June): 8–16.

Gordon, Robert J. (1969) $45 Billion of U.S. Private Investment Has Been Mislaid. *American Economic Review* 59 (June): 221–38.

Gordon, Robert J. (2000) Interpreting the "One Big Wave" in U.S. Long-term Productivity Growth. In *Productivity, Technology, and Economic Growth,* edited by Bart van Ark, Simon Kuipers, and Gerard Kuper. Boston: Kluwer Publishers, pp. 19–65.

Hayek, F. A. (1935) The Present State of the Debate. In *Collectivist Economic Planning: Critical Studies of the Possibilities of Socialism,* edited by Friedrich A. Hayek. London: Routledge & Kegan Paul, pp. 210–43.

Hennings, K. H. (1987) Capital as a Factor of Production. In *The New Palgrave: A Dictionary of Economics,* edited by John Eatwell, Murray Milgate, and Peter Newman. New York: Stockton Press, pp. 327–33.

Higgs, Robert. (1987) *Crisis and Leviathan: Critical Episodes in the Growth of American Government.* New York: Oxford University Press.

Higgs, Robert. (1992) Wartime Prosperity? A Reassessment of the U.S. Economy in the 1940s. *Journal of Economic History* 52 (March): 41–60.

Higgs, Robert. (1993) Private Profit, Public Risk: Institutional Antecedents of the Modern Military Procurement System in the Rearmament Program of 1940–1941. In *The Sinews of War: Essays on the Economic History of World War II,* edited by Geofrey T. Mills and Hugh Rockoff. Ames: Iowa State University Press, pp. 166–98.

Higgs, Robert. (1997) Regime Uncertainty: Why the Great Depression Lasted So Long and Why Prosperity Resumed after the War. *The Independent Review* 1 (Spring): 561–90.

Higgs, Robert. (1999) From Central Planning to the Market: The American Transition, 1945–1947. *Journal of Economic History* 59 (September): 600–23.

Hooks, Gregory. (1991) *Forging the Military-Industrial Complex: World War II's Battle of the Potomac.* Urbana: University of Illinois Press.

Hutt, W. H. (1979) *The Keynesian Episode: A Reassessment*. Indianapolis, In.: Liberty Fund.

Janeway, Eliot. (1951) *The Struggle for Survival: A Chronicle of Economic Mobilization in World War II*. New Haven: Yale University Press.

Jones, Jesse H., with Edward Angly. (1951) *Fifty Billion Dollars: My Thirteen Years with the RFC (1932–1945)*. New York: Macmillan.

Keynes, John Maynard. (1936) *The General Theory of Employment, Interest and Money*. New York: Harcourt, Brace & World.

Kuznets, Simon. (1945) *National Product in Wartime*. New York: National Bureau of Economic Research.

Kuznets, Simon. (1961) *Capital in the American Economy: Its Formation and Financing*. Princeton: Princeton University Press.

Lane, Frederic C. (1951) *Ships for Victory: A History of Shipbuilding under the U.S. Maritime Commission in World War II*. Baltimore: Johns Hopkins Press.

Leebaert, Derek. (2002) *The Fifty-Year Wound: The True Price of America's Cold War Victory*. Boston: Little, Brown.

McCartney, Laton. (1988) *Friends in High Places: The Bechtel Story: The Most Secret Corporation and How It Engineered the World*. New York: Simon and Schuster.

McLaughlin, Glenn E. (1943) Wartime Expansion in Industrial Capacities. *American Economic Review* 33; supplement (March): 108–18.

Mises, Ludwig von. (1935) Economic Calculation in the Socialist Commonwealth, translated by S. Adler from an original German publication of 1920. In *Collectivist Economic Planning: Critical Studies of the Possibilities of Socialism,* edited by Friedrich A. Hayek. London: Routledge & Kegan Paul, pp. 87–130.

Mises, Ludwig von. (1940) *Interventionism: An Economic Analysis*. Irvington-on-Hudson, N.Y.: Foundation for Economic Education, 1998; original edition.

Mises, Ludwig von. (1947) *Planned Chaos*. Irvington-on-Hudson, N.Y.: Foundation for Economic Education.

Novick, David, Melvin Anshen, and W. C. Truppner. (1949) *Wartime Production Controls*. New York: Columbia University Press.

Ohanian, Lee E. (1997) The Macroeconomic Effects of War Finance in the United States: World War II and the Korean War. *American Economic Review* 87 (March): 23–40.

Polenberg, Richard. (1972) *War and Society: The United States, 1941–1945*. New York: J. B. Lippincott.

Rockoff, Hugh. (1984) *Drastic Measures: A History of Wage and Price Controls in the United States*. New York: Cambridge University Press.

Rockoff, Hugh. (1996) The Paradox of Planning in World War II. Cambridge, Mass.: NBER Historical Working Paper No. 83, May.

Smaller War Plants Corporation. (1946) *Economic Concentration and World War II.* Washington, D.C.: U.S. Government Printing Office. Smith, R. Elberton. (1959) *The Army and Economic Mobilization.* Washington, D.C.: U.S. Government Printing Office.

Twight, Charlotte. (1990) Department of Defense Attempts to Close Military Bases: The Political Economy of Congressional Resistance. In *Arms, Politics, and the Economy: Historical and Contemporary Perspectives,* edited by Robert Higgs. New York: Holmes & Meier, pp. 236–80.

U.S. Bureau of the Budget. (1946) *The United States at War: Development and Administration of the War Program by the Federal Government.* Washington, D.C.: U.S. Government Printing Office.

U.S. Bureau of the Census. (1975) *Historical Statistics of the United States, Colonial Times to 1970.* Washington, D.C.: U.S. Government Printing Office.

U.S. Council of Economic Advisers. (1970) *Annual Report of the Council of Economic Advisers.* Washington, D.C.: U.S. Government Printing Office.

U.S. Department of Commerce, Bureau of Economic Analysis. *National Income and Product Accounts Tables.* Available at http://www.bea.doc.gov/bea/dn/nipa web/ TableViewFixed. asp.

U.S. Department of Commerce, Office of Business Economics. (1954) *National Income, 1954 Edition.* Washington, D.C.: U.S. Government Printing Office.

U.S. War Production Board. (1945) *American Industry in War and Transition, 1940–1950. Part II. The Effect of the War on the Industrial Economy.* Document No. 27; July 20. Washington, D.C.: U.S. War Production Board.

Wasson, Robert C., John C. Musgrave, and Claudia Harkins. (1970) Alternative Estimates of Fixed Business Capital in the United States, 1925–1968. *Survey of Current Business* 50 (April): 18–36.

Acknowledgments   For pointing me toward or helping me lay hands on some of the data analyzed in this article, I am grateful to Robert J. Gordon, Barbara M. Fraumeni, Lee J. Alston, and Andres Gallo. For substantive critical comments on a previous draft, I am indebted to Michael Edelstein, Alexander Field, and Hugh Rockoff.

5

From Central Planning to the Market

The American Transition, 1945–47

> At the end of 1946, less than a year and a half after VJ-day, more than 10 million demobilized veterans and other millions of wartime workers have found employment in the swiftest and most gigantic change-over that any nation has ever made from war to peace.
>
> *Harry S. Truman,* Economic Report, *8 January 1947*

THE COMPLEX, AND OFTEN FITFUL, transition from central planning to the market in China and the Warsaw Pact countries has been a hot topic since 1989. Notably, the United States made a similar transition after World War II. Indeed, the reconversion from a wartime command economy to a market-oriented postwar economy, a transition accomplished with astonishing speed and little apparent difficulty, constitutes one of the most remarkable events in U.S. economic history. Nevertheless, economists and economic historians have devoted little attention to that episode, and their explanations of it are, on close inspection, extremely problematic. With few exceptions, scholars have not yet recognized the problems inherent in dealing with that great event.[1] In this chapter, I consider some major issues of measurement and explanation related to the reconversion of the U.S. economy between 1945 and 1947, a transition that laid the groundwork for the prosperity of the following half century.

The Orthodox Story

To illustrate briefly the long-established view of the reconversion, I quote from the economic history textbook by Gary M. Walton and Hugh Rockoff:

> It was widely expected that the Great Depression would return once the war was over. After all, it seemed as if enormous levels of government spending during the war were the only thing that had gotten the country out of the depression. Many, perhaps most, economists agreed with this analysis. . . . The expected depression did not materialize. During the war, people had accumulated large stores of financial assets, especially money and government bonds. . . . Once the war was over, these savings were released and created a surge in demand that contributed to a postwar rise in prices and to the reintegration of workers from the armed forces and from defense industries into the peacetime labor force. Government policy also played a role in smoothing the transition. The so-called "G.I. Bill of Rights" . . . delayed the reentry of many former servicemen into the labor force and provided them with improved skills.[2]

As this statement illustrates, the orthodox account maintains, first, that the economy did not revert to depression after the war boom and, second, that the expected postwar bust failed to materialize, primarily because consumers employed the financial assets accumulated as "forced savings" during the war to give vent to their "pent-up demand" for goods, primarily durables, whose supply had been restricted or prohibited during the war. Government policy played a lesser role in "smoothing the transition," mainly by temporarily removing men from the labor force.[3]

Spurious Prosperity, Spurious Depression

Notwithstanding the orthodox story, the economy seemingly did plunge into depression in 1946—at least, that is the conclusion one must reach if one takes seriously the official gross domestic product (GDP) data on which economists and historians normally base their accounts of macroeconomic fluctuations. As figure 5-1 shows, the economy began to contract in 1945, when real GDP fell by 4 percent from its wartime peak in 1944. Then, in 1946, the bottom fell out: Real GDP dropped by 20.6 percent, by far the largest annual fall ever in U.S. economic history, exceeding even that of the worst year (1932) of the Great Contraction.[4] Real GDP continued to fall slightly, by 1.5 percent, in 1947, before finally beginning to recover in 1948.

Before one dismisses the apparent postwar economic collapse as a misleading statistical peculiarity, one ought to recognize that the same system of economic accounts that gives rise to that oddity also generates the evidence of the "wartime prosperity" (figure 5-1), evidence that economists and historians alike have long credited. According to the official national product accounts, real GDP grew at astonishingly high rates—about 20 percent annually—in 1941, 1942, and 1943, and at the still remarkable rate of 8.4 percent in 1944. If we dismiss as spurious the GDP data that indicate a postwar depression, are we warranted as well in dismissing the GDP data that indicate a wartime boom?[5]

A glance at figure 5-2 suggests that something may be askew in the data series indicative of wartime prosperity and a postwar slump. Figure 5-2 shows the annual percentage growth rates of the private portion of real GDP, that is, GDP minus government purchases of newly produced final goods and services. Comparison of those growth rates with the growth rates of total GDP in figure 5-1 shows that the differences were slight for the years 1930–40. In 1941, however, a large gap opened. The gap became enormous in 1942 and 1943, when private output fell sharply—by 10.6 percent and 3.7 percent, respectively—even though total output increased by 20 percent each year. After converging in 1944, the growth rates of total and private GDP diverged in the opposite direction in 1945 and 1946. In the latter year, while total GDP fell by 20.6 percent, private GDP leaped upward by an astonishing 29.5 percent, a growth rate never approached before or since. From 1948 to 1950, the two growth rates again tracked closely, as they had before the war. Figure 5-3 allows one to see at once how, and how

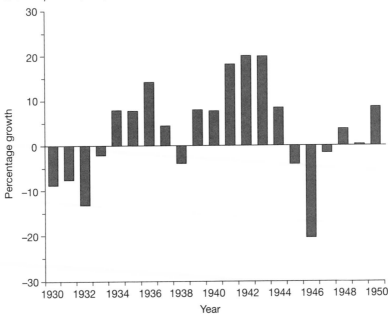

Figure 5-1. Percentage growth of real (1987$)
gross domestic product, 1930–50.

Note: Data all figures in this chapter are the author's calculations
from basic data in U.S. Council of Economic Advisors (1995, p. 406).

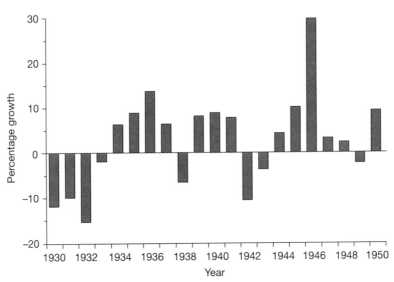

Figure 5-2. Percentage of growth of real (1987$)
private gross domestic product, 1930–50.

greatly, the private economy and the total economy (that is, that including government purchases) deviated in their officially calculated growth performance from 1941 to 1947.

Despite the widespread and long-standing acceptance of official GDP data indicative of wartime prosperity from 1941 to 1945, those data have no sound scientific basis.[6] Although the estimates have defects of various sorts, the fundamental problem is that meaningful national product accounting requires market prices, and the command economy of the war years rendered all prices suspect and many of them, especially the prices paid by the government for goods and services, manifestly arbitrary.[7] To suppose that this problem can be solved by employing the market prices generated at another time or in another place is to lose sight of what a national product estimate is supposed to tell us—namely, the aggregate valuation placed on final outputs, with each output being valued at its existing margin of

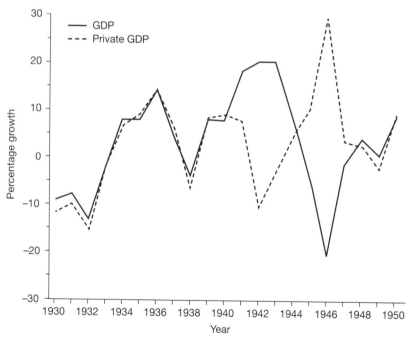

Figure 5-3. Percentage growth of real gross domestic product and real private gross domestic product, 1930–50.

production by the people composing an economy that approximates a competitive equilibrium and operates with the resources, tastes, technologies, and institutions specific to its own time and place. Other difficulties, such as the index number problem and the gross inaccuracy of wartime price indexes, only compound the fundamental problem.[8]

Simply by sniffing the data for the years 1941–46, one ought to have smelled a rat. Consider that between 1940 and 1944, real GDP increased at an average annual rate of 13 percent—a growth spurt wholly out of line with any experienced before or since. Moreover, that extraordinary growth took place notwithstanding the movement of some 16 million men (equivalent to 28.6 percent of the total labor force of 1940) into the armed forces at some time during the war and the replacement of those prime workers mainly by teenagers, women with little or no previous experience in the labor market, and elderly men (U.S. Bureau of the Census, 1975, p. 1140; Ballard, 1983, pp. 129–30). Is it plausible that an economy subject to such severe and abruptly imposed human-resource constraints could generate a growth spurt far greater than any other in its entire history? Further, is it plausible that when the great majority of the servicemen returned to the civilian labor force—some 9 million of them in the year following V-J Day—while millions of their relatively unproductive wartime replacements left the labor force, the economy's real output would fall by 22 percent from 1945 to 1947?[9] The utter implausibility of such developments suggests that scholars have placed far too much weight on the metaphor of a wartime production "miracle."

One way to gauge the trend of an economy's capacity to produce is to connect the outputs achieved in peak years of the business cycle by a constant-rate-of-growth line. For example, by linking the outputs for the benchmark years 1929 and 1948, one can construct a capacity-trend line. Performing this exercise on the real GDP data shown in figure 5-4, one finds, not surprisingly, that the economy during the 1930s performed well below its capacity-trend line. But one also finds—*mirabile dictu*—that from 1942 to 1945, the economy performed far above its capacity to produce.[10] Although one might speculate that various ad hoc events of the war years temporarily raised the economy's capacity to produce, a

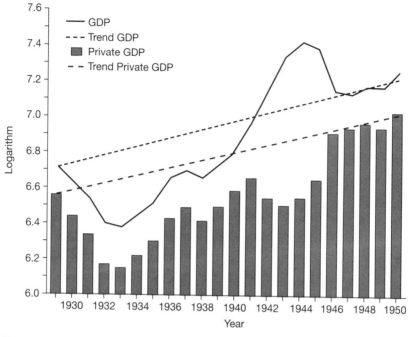

Figure 5-4. Log real gross domestic product, log real private gross domestic product, and 1929-48 trends.

far more compelling conclusion is simply that the apparent super-trend wartime boom in output was an artifact of an unjustifiable accounting system. No doubt Americans produced an abundance of munitions during the war: If one accepts the national-product estimates at face value, it transpires that nearly 40 percent of GNP consisted of war-related ouputs from 1942 to 1945.[11] But such national-product estimates should not be accepted at face value.

In brief, the war boom, as typically comprehended, did not occur; nor did the corresponding "crash of 1946" that is so evident in the standard GDP data. It is hardly surprising that contemporary Americans experienced 1946 as a gloriously prosperous year that had nothing in common with 1932. Economists and historians, notwithstanding their reliance on faulty national-product data to describe the "wartime prosperity" have properly disregarded such data when considering the postwar transition and correctly concluded that the much-feared postwar depression did not materialize. In light of the foregoing critique, let us now consider why the postwar transition took place so swiftly and smoothly.

Recovery of the Private Economy

Returning to figure 5-4, note that a trend line connecting the values of (the logarithm of) private GDP for 1929 and 1948 shows that the private economy languished far below its capacity trend throughout the 1930s and the first half of the 1940s. Then, because of the spectacular 29.5 percent leap that occurred in 1946, the private economy reached the trend line and continued along it for the rest of the decade, except during the brief, mild recession of 1949. Clearly, the bulk of the postwar transition took place when the private economy made its magnificent recovery—a recovery that had been sixteen years in coming—during 1946.

Why the Postwar Consumption Boom?

Recall that the orthodox story of the postwar transition places heavy weight on the drawing down of accumulated liquid assets to finance consumers' satisfaction of their so-called pent-up demands. In the words of Walton and Rockoff, quoted earlier in a longer passage, "During the war, people had accumulated large stores of financial assets, especially money and government bonds. . . . Once the war was over, *these savings were released and created a surge in demand*" (emphasis added). No doubt many people did urgently desire to purchase, among other things, new cars, household appliances, and houses, which had been unavailable or in tightly limited supply during the war.[12] But the idea that postwar consumers paid for such goods by drawing down their liquid-asset holdings runs up against several difficulties.

The most serious flaw in that part of the orthodox story is that, in fact, individuals did not reduce their holdings of liquid assets after the war. Let us define liquid assets as currency held by the public, demand and time deposits in commercial banks, deposits in mutual savings banks, and deposits in the postal savings system. In November 1945, liquid assets, so defined, reached an all-time high of $151.1 billion. By December 1946, they had risen to $161.6 billion, and by December 1947, they had increased to $168.5 billion (Friedman and Schwartz, 1963, pp. 717–18). Every component of liquid assets, so defined, also increased during that two-year period. Of course, so long as the total amount of money was increasing, the public, as a whole, could not "draw down" its holdings: What one member of the public gave up, another acquired.

If people did not, indeed, could not, reduce their holdings of liquid assets, perhaps they tried to do so, thereby driving up the velocity of monetary circulation. Not so. Neither the velocity of money defined as M1 nor the velocity of money defined as M2 rose in those years. For the four years 1945–48, the velocity of M1 took the values 1.75, 1.52, 1.62, and 1.73, respectively; the velocity of M2 took the values 1.37, 1.16, 1.23, and 1.31, respectively (Friedman and Schwartz, 1963, p. 774). Thus, people were actually holding the average dollar longer during the three postwar years than they had during the war years.[13]

Perhaps consumers were liquidating their bond holdings? No. At the end of 1945, individuals held $64.0 billion of the public debt; at the end of 1946, $64.1 billion; and at the end of 1947, $65.7 billion. It is true that the amount of federal debt outstanding declined between 1945 and 1948, but the decline occurred almost entirely because of reductions in the holdings of commercial banks and of corporations other than banks and insurance companies.[14]

How, then, did consumers finance their surge of spending during the postwar recovery of the private economy? The answer is, in nominal terms, by a combination of increased personal income and a reduced rate of savings; in real terms, simply by reducing the rate of personal savings. Between 1945 and 1946, when personal consumption spending increased by $23.7 billion, annual personal savings dropped by $14.4 billion, and personal taxes fell by $2.2 billion; increased (nominal) personal income financed the balance of the increased consumption. Between 1946 and 1947, when personal consumption spending increased by $17.3 billion, annual personal savings dropped by $5.2 billion, and personal taxes rose by $2.7 billion; increased (nominal) income financed the balance of the increased consumption. Between 1947 and 1948, when personal consumption spending increased by $12.9 billion, increased (nominal) personal income accounted for more than the entire increase, because personal taxes fell by just $0.2 billion and annual personal savings actually increased by $6.1 billion. Clearly, during the critical first two years after the war, the ability of consumers to spend more nominal dollars ($41.0 billion) for consumer goods depended overwhelmingly on just two sources: increased personal income (+$20.5 billion) and reduced annual saving ($19.7 billion).[15]

The potential for a reduction of the personal saving rate (personal savings relative to disposable personal income) was huge after V-J Day. During the war, the personal saving rate had risen to extraordinary levels: 23.6 percent in 1942, 25.0 percent in 1943, 25.5 percent in 1944, and 19.7 percent in 1945. Those rates contrasted with prewar rates, which had hovered around 5 percent during the more prosperous years (e.g., 5.0 percent in 1929, 5.3 percent in 1937, 5.1 percent in 1940). After the war, the personal saving rate fell to 9.5 percent in 1946 and 4.3 percent in 1947, before rebounding to the 5 to 7 percent range characteristic of the next two decades (U.S. Council of Economic Advisers, 1970, p. 194). After having saved at far higher rates than they would have chosen in the absence of the wartime restrictions, households quickly reduced their rate of saving when the war ended. Note, however, that *they did not dissave.* Even at the low point in 1947, the saving rate was 4.3 percent, not much below the prewar norm for relatively prosperous years.

Why the Postwar Investment Boom?

The postwar resurgence of the private economy rested on an investment boom as well as a consumer spending surge. In current dollars, gross private domestic investment leaped from $10.6 billion in 1945 to $30.6 billion in 1946, $34.0 billion in 1947, and $46.0 billion in 1948. Relative to GNP, that surge pushed the private investment rate from 5.0 percent in 1945 (it had been even lower during the previous two years) to 14.7 percent in 1946 and

1947 and 17.9 percent in 1948 (U.S. Council of Economic Advisers, 1970, p. 177). As a standard for comparison, the investment rate had been nearly 16 percent during the latter half of the 1920s, before hitting the skids during the depression (Swanson and Williamson, 1972, p. 55).

Firms could finance their increased investment spending, in part, because, unlike individuals, they did unload some of the government securities that they had acquired during the war. Between 1945 and 1946, holdings of public debt by corporations (exclusive of banks and insurance companies) fell by $6.9 billion; they fell by another $1.2 billion in 1947, before rising by $0.7 billion in 1948 (U.S. Council of Economic Advisers, 1970, p. 255).

Moreover, thanks to a reduced tax liability—the Revenue Act of 1945 lowered the top corporate income-tax rate and repealed the excess-profits tax—corporations enjoyed rising after-tax profits from 1946 through 1948.[16] During the years 1941–44, after-tax corporate profits had held steady in the range of $10 billion to $11 billion annually. After-tax profits dropped to $9.0 billion in 1945, as the government canceled procurement contracts and many firms incurred extraordinary expenses to reconvert their production facilities. Then, after-tax profits rose to $15.5 billion in 1946, $20.2 billion in 1947, and $22.7 billion in 1948. Those postwar profits compared nicely with the $8.6 billion recorded in 1929, even after adjustment for inflation (which had diminished the value of the 1948 dollar by 37 percent relative to the 1929 dollar).[17] With greater after-tax profits to draw on, businesses increased their retained earnings.[18] Gross business savings increased from $15.1 billion in 1945 and $14.5 billion in 1946 to $20.2 billion in 1947 and $28.0 billion in 1948 (U.S. Council of Economic Advisers, 1970, p. 198). The additional retained earnings provided an important source of financing for the higher business investment after the war.

Corporations also returned to the capital markets in a big way. Stock and bond offerings, which only once had exceeded $3.2 billion in the years 1935–44 (the exception being $4.6 billion in 1936), jumped to $6.0 billion in 1945, $6.9 billion in 1946, $6.6 billion in 1947, and $7.1 billion in 1948.[19] Public confidence in future corporate earnings also manifested itself in higher stock prices. The Standard & Poor's index of 500 stocks, having fallen steadily from 1939 to 1942 before regaining the lost ground in 1943 and 1944, shot up by 21.6 percent in 1945, and then by 12.6 percent in 1947, before falling back to the 1946 level for the remainder of the decade (U.S. Council of Economic Advisers, 1970, p. 267). A price index of all common stocks, having reached a trough in 1942 before beginning a slow ascent, rose (fourth quarter to fourth quarter) by 31.1 percent in 1945. That index rose another 10 percent in the first half of 1946, before peaking and then retreating later in the year to a plateau, where it remained, still nearly twice its wartime low, for the balance of the 1940s (Balke and Gordon, 1986, p. 805). Purchasers of corporate bonds expressed their vote of confidence by keeping bond prices so high that the effective (nominal) yield remained in the narrow range of 3.0 to 3.5 percent between 1945 and 1949 (Balke and Gordon, 1986, p. 783).

In sum, the corporate investment boom of the postwar transition years received its financing from a combination of the proceeds of sales of previously acquired government bonds, increased current retained earnings (attributable, in part, to reduced corporate tax liabilities), and the proceeds of corporate securities offerings. Higher postwar stock market values and low effective yields on corporate bonds validated the optimism that underlay the investment boom. According to President Truman's economic report of January 1948, "the extraordinary rate of business income in general allowed investment to proceed at record levels. Even greater expansion was prevented mainly by lack of material rather than by lack of intention to invest or lack of financial resources" (Truman, 1948, p. 25).

Real Private Sector Recovery Officially Underestimated

The data depicted in figures 5-1 to 5-4 and all of the "real" data to which I have previously referred in this chapter embody adjustments for changes in the price level that are based on the implicit deflators computed by the Commerce Department. Like the more familiar price indexes, the Consumer Price Index and the Producer Price Index, those deflators rest ultimately on price data collected by government agents. All scholars who have seriously considered the matter agree that during the war the more or less comprehensive price controls that were being enforced gave rise to substantial understatement of the actual inflation, especially for the private portion of the national product (Higgs, 1992, pp. 51–52). In the words of Milton Friedman and Anna J. Schwartz:

> [P]rices, in any economically meaningful sense, rose by decidedly more than the "price index" during the period of price control. The jump in the price index on the elimination of price control in 1946 did not involve any corresponding jump in "prices"; rather, it reflected largely the unveiling of price increases that had occurred earlier. Allowance for the defects in the price index as a measure of price change would undoubtedly yield a decidedly higher rate of price rise during the war and a decidedly lower rate after the war. (Friedman and Schwartz, 1963, p. 558)

One upshot of correcting for the biases of the official price indexes during and immediately after the war is that the estimated real growth of private product during the war is thereby diminished and the estimated real growth of private product after the war is thereby increased—the miracle of 1946 was even greater than the official data (depicted in figures 5-2, 5-3, and 5-4) indicate. According to the official implicit deflator for private product, the price level increased by 21.8 percent between 1945 and 1947 (U.S. Council of Economic Advisers, 1970, p. 1881). Friedman and Schwartz's estimated deflator for net national product (NNP), which probably overstates the inflation for private product alone, increased by just 9 percent during the two-year period (Friedman and Schwartz, 1963, p. 125). Richard K. Vedder and Lowell E. Gallaway's estimated deflator for GNP, which probably overstates the inflation for private product alone, increased by just 10.6 percent during that two-year period (Vedder and Gallaway, 1991, p. 155). If one assumes that the private-sector price level actually rose by 10 percent between 1945 and 1947, which may well overstate the true increase, then real private product increased during those two years by a mind-boggling 44.5 percent, rather than the 33.8 percent implied by the data underlying figures 5-2, 5-3, and 5-4 (taken from the Council of Economic Advisers' 1995 report). No wonder nobody was complaining about a slump, even though the official GDP data depicted a Great Contraction in 1946. In reality—that is, when output is evaluated at prices validated by free consumer choice—1946 was the most fabulously expansive year in U.S. economic history.

Labor Market Shifts

Although the arbitrariness of prices and the suppression of voluntary resource allocation in a command economy preclude meaningful straightforward comparisons of wartime and peacetime national products, we can gain some understanding of the postwar transition by examining the changing size, composition, and employment of the labor force in the 1940s. No doubt, many scholars and laypersons alike have viewed the wartime economic conditions as prosperous because of the "full employment" that prevailed. But that aspect of the so-called wartime prosperity also tends to mislead us, because for the most part it reflected nothing more than the buildup of a huge armed force, mainly by conscription.[20] After V-J Day, however, the armed forces demobilized rapidly, shrinking from 12.12 million uniformed personnel in mid-1945 to 1.58 million in mid-1947. Simultaneously, civilian employment by the armed forces fell from 2.63 million persons to 0.86 million, and military-related employment in industry dropped from 11.0 million persons to 0.79 million. Therefore, total military-related employment fell, in just two years, from 25.75 million (39.2 percent of the total labor force) to 3.23 million (5.3 percent of the total labor force) [U. S. Department of Defense, 1990, pp. 124, 126, 128].

Between 1945 and 1947, the civilian labor force increased from 53.9 million persons to 60.2 million. Nonetheless, civilian unemployment increased only from 1.0 million persons (1.9 percent of the civilian labor force) to 2.4 million (3.9 percent) [U.S. Bureau of the Census, 1975, p. 126). During the same period, civilian nonmilitary-related employment increased from 39.1 million persons to 55.4 million, an increase of 16.3 million (41.7 percent increase) in just two years (U.S. Department of Defense, 1990, p. 126). After the war, the ratio of nonmilitary-related employment to civilian labor force reached a level indicative of private-sector prosperity for the first time since 1929 (U.S. Bureau of the Census, 1975, p. 126). Whereas the American economy had eliminated unemployment during the war by reallocating labor resources to the production of military goods and services, it retained a low level of unemployment during the postwar transition because service-men and munitions workers moved into nonmilitary-related employment and because many people left the labor force. (The total labor force, which comprises the armed forces and the civilian labor force, fell by about 5.7 million.) It was no miracle to herd 12 million men into the armed forces and to attract millions of men and women to work in munitions plants during the war. The real miracle was to reallocate a third of the total labor force to serving private consumers and investors in just two years. That event, whose reality is unambiguous, is unique in U.S. economic history.

Vedder and Gallaway, who are among the few to have grappled se-riously with the problems of measurement and explanation that are at issue here, maintain that the smooth labor-market adjustment during the postwar transition occurred because the aggregate productivity-adjusted real wage fell (Vedder and Gallaway, 1991, pp. 168–70). To demonstrate the robustness of that explanation, they calculate their wage index un-der a variety of assumptions about wages, price-level changes, and labor productivity. Unfortunately, every variant, including the indirect variant (labor's share of income or product), requires that one treat wartime na-tional product and postwar national product as directly comparable. As I have already argued, national product estimates for a command economy are essentially arbitrary. Therefore, the change of Vedder and Gallaway's calculated wage index between 1945 and 1946 cannot bear the interpreta-tive weight placed on it. Moreover, Vedder and Gallaway's analysis rests on a model that assumes "labor supply is highly inelastic . . . [and] moves over time slowly and predictably with demographic and other trends"— assumptions that contrast starkly with the sharp changes in labor supply conditions that occurred from 1945 to 1947 (Vedder and Gallaway, 1991, p. 16). The model simply does not apply to the experience of the period 1941–47, as Vedder and Gallaway themselves come close to admitting at several points.[21]

All we can say with confidence is that, given the economic conditions that existed during the transition and the expectations held at that time by consumers, investors, and enterprise managers, firms appraised the value of labor services highly enough that, in the aggregate, they were willing to employ nearly all workers seeking employment at the prevailing wages. Whether the real wage as perceived at that time by actors in the labor market was higher or lower than what they perceived it to have been during the war had no relevance. Decisions to offer or accept employment are forward-looking, not retrospective.[22] The wartime economy, with its Byzantine, constantly changing structure of prohibitions, priorities, scheduling, physical allocations, conservation and limitation orders, quotas, set-asides, subsidies, price controls, commodity rationing, credit rationing, interest rate pegging, conscripted and draft-exempted labor, and massive direct government investment in industrial facilities, was—or soon would be—a bygone. After the war, private decision makers looked to a future in which they would again have room to maneuver.

Postwar Expectations

Although scholars sometimes refer to the expectation of a postwar depression as if they take it to have been widely entertained at the end of the war, in fact, that expectation prevailed most notably among the Keynesian theorists and econometricians who were newly ensconced in agencies such as the War Production Board, the Bureau of the Budget, and the Federal Reserve Board (Sapir, 1949, pp. 289, 340; Jones, 1972, pp. 129–30). Other economists, including W. S. Woytinsky and Rufus S. Tucker, turned out to have had a more prescient view of the postwar economy. Michael Sapir, himself a government forecaster, remarked later that "economists of an older vintage tended to do better because they relied more on history" (Sapir, 1949, p. 317). [History did not provide a perfect guide, however. People who, like the average business economist in Joseph Livingston's survey, continued for years to expect a postwar deflation, probably did so because of what they knew had happened after previous wars, especially after World War I.]

For determining the actual course of events, the expectations of economists, right or wrong, mattered far less than the expectations of consumers and investors, especially the latter. Unless private investment recovered, no postwar prosperity could last long—after all, it was the failure of private investment to recover fully that had kept the economy from getting out of the Great Depression in the 1930s. Fortunately, as Sapir noted, "business men's expectations about the economic climate were much more optimistic than those of the Washington economists whose views commanded most attention; and actual developments may constantly have exceeded even those expectations, thus leading to further upward revisions of investment plans" (Sapir, 1949, p. 297; Ballard, 1983, pp. 19–22).

In 1944 and 1945, the *Fortune* poll of business executives registered widely prevailing confidence about postwar economic conditions. In May 1944, a national sample of executives was asked: "In general, does it seem to you that after the war the prospects of your company will be better, or worse, or about the same as they were before?" Of the respondents, 51.2 percent said that prospects would be better, 8.5 percent said that they would be worse, and 36.8 percent said that they would be about the same (Cantril, 1951, p. 1121). In February 1945, a national sample of executives was asked: "How, in your judgment, will employment in your company after the war compare with wartime and with prewar employment?" Relative to their wartime employment, 33.9 percent expected greater employment and 26.7 percent expected less (39.4 percent did not answer the question); relative to prewar employment, 48.2 percent expected greater employment and 5.6 percent expected less (46.2 percent did not answer the question) [Cantril, 1951, p. 902].

Unlike the brash young Keynesian economists, businessmen in 1945 and 1946:

> could not believe that a serious "slump" was around the corner just because the government had stepped out of the market so fast—

after all, they had a large and growing volume of unfilled orders for peacetime products. . . . Expectations of price increases, tax reductions, and large volume sales apparently far outweighed in business minds the impact of reduced government spending. (Sapir, 1949, pp. 320–1)

After two years of the postwar boom, businessmen remained confident. According to President Truman's economic report for 1948, "business sentiment now appears to entertain the expectation of strong markets for as far ahead as it can see" (Truman, 1948, p. 43).

Sapir also noted that soon after V-J Day "a climate of expectations looking to much freer markets was implanted in business" (Sapir, 1949, p. 314). He seemingly failed to appreciate, however, that those expectations arose, not only from postwar developments suggesting that the government would move quickly to abandon or loosen war-related controls, but also from a closely related factor, the altered character of the federal administration. During the war, businessmen and administrators who were friendly to business had largely taken over the management of the command economy, displacing especially the ardent New Dealers who had surrounded President Franklin D. Roosevelt from 1935 until the military buildup of 1940–41 (Higgs, 1987, pp. 203–4, 211–15; Higgs, 1993, pp. 186–94; Hooks, 1991, pp. 80–224; Riddell, 1990; Jeffries, 1990; Jeffries, 1996; Brinkley, 1995, pp. 175–200). After the war, with FDR dead and the federal administration in less hostile hands, businessmen perceived a much diminished threat to their property rights.[23] Investors were then much more willing to hazard their private property than they had been before the war, as both survey data and financial market data confirm.[24]

In 1946, the electorate gave the Republicans, who had campaigned for lower taxes and reduced government spending, a majority in both houses of Congress, thereby ensuring that even if the Truman administration were to move toward strengthening the New Deal, it would not get far. In pushing for lower taxes after the war, the Republicans hoped to starve to death at least some parts of the bloated federal bureaucracy that had grown up between 1933 and 1945. As Senator Robert A. Taft said in 1947, "the best reason to reduce taxes is to reduce our ideas of the number of dollars the government can properly spend in a year, and thereby reduce inflated ideas of the proper scope of bureaucratic authority."[25] That message came as music to the ears of potential investors, reassuring them that the federal government no longer posed the potentially disastrous threat to their property rights that they had perceived it to pose when it was controlled by the zealous, business-hating leaders and advisers of the Second New Deal.[26] Passage of the Taft-Hartley Act in 1947 curtailed the ability of unions to interfere in the operation of business and allowed businessmen and investors to breathe even easier.

Toward a More Defensible Understanding of the Postwar Transition

Having analyzed the reconversion and the failure of the government forecasters to come even close to predicting its actual macroeconomic contours, in the late 1940s, Sapir wrote, "Looking backward it seems incredible that we could have missed the signs so badly" (Sapir, 1949, p. 321). Even more incredible is that economists and economic historians, with few exceptions, have continued for fifty years to misunderstand what happened during the war and reconversion, relying on theoretically groundless government-product data and error-ridden private-product data for the command economy and continuing to represent the "wartime prosperity" as having validated the basic Keynesian model, but failing to notice that the events of the reconversion totally discredited such a model. Even Vedder and Gallaway, who have explicitly recognized the entrenched errors and tried to avoid them, have failed to break completely free of them.

A basic reason for the continuing deficiencies of economic scholarship on the war and reconversion is that analysts have continued to think in terms such as "the 1944–47 business cycle experience" (Vedder and Gallaway, 1991, p. 158). As that expression reveals, scholars treat the events of the war and reconversion years as if they composed a segment, directly comparable with other segments, in a longer-running economic process. More specifically, economists and economic historians treat the macroeconomic events of the war and reconversion segment as if those events resulted from causal forces common to and reverberating through the longer-running economic process, thereby imparting to it certain dynamic properties (e.g., a characteristic "cyclical" movement). They fail to comprehend that the drastic institutional discontinuities of the wartime command economy rendered it sui generis and, hence, not directly comparable with either the prewar or the postwar economy. If it is to be understood, it must be understood on its own terms.

Retrospectively describing the wartime economic expansion, War Production Board economists in 1945 seemed to appreciate the nature of the beast, observing that:

> This expansion is unique, not only because of its magnitude and the relatively high level from which it started, but also because of its institutional basis. To a much greater extent than during the peacetime cyclical upswings—or even the expansion during World War I—this expansion has depended upon Government's readiness to provide most of the fixed and much of the working capital needed in war production; upon the existence of what amounts to a guaranteed market for anything that could be produced; and in general, upon Government's initiative, support, guidance and control. (U.S. War Production Board, 1945, p. 4)

In short, as all contemporary sources attest, the American economy became essentially a command economy during 1941 and 1942; it operated as such during 1943, 1944, and 1945; and it made the transition back to a mainly market-oriented configuration between, roughly, mid-1945 and mid-1947.[27] Of course, in various respects, the government never surrendered the powers that it had assumed during the war.[28] The point here, however, is that by the latter half of 1947, the economy had reverted to operating as a market system about as far as it ever would, and at that time, it was far less subject to government control than it had been during the war. Between 1940 and 1947, the U.S. economy passed through an institutional cycle (market-command-market) and a corresponding output cycle (butter-guns-butter). Because of that extreme cycling of its institutional structure and its output composition, the economy's performance during those years simply cannot be compared in any unambiguous manner with that of either the pre-1941 economy or the post-1946 economy. Nor can we justifiably impose any macroeconomic model on a long period that includes the years 1941–46 as a subperiod: Any model appropriate for analyzing the subperiod is inappropriate for analyzing the other years, and vice versa. Command economies and market economies do not—to employ a positivist figure of speech—obey the same laws. In the face of this fundamental analytical difficulty, we must recognize that some questions simply cannot be answered; at least, they cannot be answered if posed in the usual way (e.g., Was real GDP greater in 1944 or 1948?).

Still, we can make reasonable conjectures and bring pertinent evidence to bear as we strive to understand how the reconversion proceeded so quickly and successfully as gauged by, say, the low unemployment rate that prevailed throughout the transition. Some causes I have already suggested, including the impetus to private investment that arose from postwar reductions of taxes on corporate earnings. The government deserves additional credit for the speed with which it released men from the armed forces, canceled and settled extant munitions contracts, sold many government production facilities to private parties, transformed its budget deficit into a surplus, removed wartime controls, and assisted military personnel in making the transition to civilian life immediately after their mustering out.[29]

Under provisions of the G.I. Bill, which historians have often credited with helping to keep transitional unemployment low by paying veterans to attend college, the government did support some 800,000 veterans who enrolled as students in September 1946 (U.S. Office of War Mobilization and Reconversion, 1946, p. 62). Even if all of those enrolling veterans had instead been unemployed, however, they would have raised the unemployment rate by only 1.4 percentage points. Moreover, the law did more than simply remove veterans from the labor market. Historians have generally failed to appreciate that the G.I. Bill's provisions for veterans' unemployment benefits—$20 per week for as many as 52 weeks—amounted to an unemployment subsidy for veterans who were in the labor force and, therefore, caused measured unemployment to be greater than it otherwise would have been. In August 1945, about 900,000 veterans were counted as unemployed, constituting about 44 percent of the total number of persons who were unemployed (U.S. Office of War Mobilization and Reconversion, 1946, pp. 59–60).

Too often, however, even the government's helpful transition measures have been seen either as ad hoc measures or as the fruits of foresighted government planning during the war. It is important to recognize that those measures were precisely the sort one ought to have expected to be taken by the men who controlled the administration, the Congress, and the war-specific economic agencies during the transition. As I have emphasized earlier and documented elsewhere, the upper reaches of the wartime command economy came under the control of men who were sympathetic to business, even before the United States became a declared belligerent (Higgs, 1993; Higgs, 1997). By the manner in which they exercised their power, those men—thousands of whom were themselves businessmen on leave from their firms—transformed the climate in which investors and businessmen formed their expectations about postwar political and economic conditions. Therefore, even though the wartime administrators imposed extraordinarily pervasive and forceful controls on the economy, investors and businessmen confidently regarded those controls as temporary.

The speed with which the controls were removed—most of them in 1945 and most of the rest in 1946—validated that confidence and encouraged investors and businessmen to act, for the first time since the early 1930s, as if their property rights in their capital and the income it generated would remain reasonably secure. Without that outlook, which elsewhere I have called "regime certainty," the other measures that tended to make the transition a success would have availed relatively little. Restoring the regime certainty of investors and business people was a necessary condition for the transition to a prosperous postwar economy; nothing could substitute for it, and without it, the economy probably would have fallen back into depression before long, if not immediately.[30]

One interesting, empirically verifiable implication of the foregoing interpretation can be tested against the results of surveys of wage expectation. In November 1943, the American Institute of Public Opinion (AIPO) asked a national random sample of employed persons: "Do you think the wages now being paid in industries producing war materials will continue to be as high when these same industries produce peacetime goods?" Of the respondents, 9 percent said yes and 85 percent said no (6 percent had no opinion) [Cantril, 1951, p. 1013]. In May 1944, AIPO asked a national random sample of employers and employees who worked in war plants and planned to continue working after the war: "Do you think you will get the same rate of pay as you are now getting, or will you probably have to take less?" Of the respondents, 45 percent said that the rate of pay would stay the same, 39 percent said that it would be less, and 6 percent said that it would be more (10 percent had no opinion) [Cantril, 1951 p. 900]. In June 1945, AIPO asked a national random sample: "After the war, are you expecting the general level of wages to be higher, lower, or about the same as it is now?" Of the respondents, 5 percent said that it would be higher, 63 percent said that it would be lower, and 27 percent said that it would be about the same (5 percent had no opinion) [Cantril, 1951, p. 1014]. Clearly, the central tendency of wage expectations was that wages would be lower after the war.[31]

That expectation probably inclined workers to accept more readily the lower wage rates offered to them after the war. Had they tended to expect the same or even higher wages, they would have been more likely to hold out for higher wage offers than they received after the war and, therefore, they would have been more likely to be unemployed. It is not difficult to imagine that, had the federal government been under the sway of politicians more closely allied with organized labor, as it had been between 1935 and 1941, workers would have anticipated and therefore held out for higher wages.

The CIO wanted an immediate 20 or 30 percent wage increase at the end of the war to make up for the elimination of overtime pay, and many old New Dealers, such as Commerce Secretary Henry Wallace and Robert Nathan of the Office of War Mobilization and Reconversion, considered such an increase essential to maintain living standards and avoid the long-feared postwar downturn. (Lichtenstein, 1989, p. 135)

Clearly, in the labor market, as in the investment domain, the character of the postwar regime helped to establish conditions consistent with a smooth transition to a high-employment civilian economy.

Indeed, the labor-market developments exemplify just one of the many areas in which the perceived temporariness of the wartime controls contributed to postwar behavior consistent with a smooth transition. In many other ways as well, the transition would have been far more painful had the government been dominated by the same "long-haired boys" who had occupied its upper reaches during the Second New Deal. Those men shared "the conviction that government must exercise an increased level of authority over the structure and behavior of private capitalist institutions"; even in the late 1930s, at the high tide of their policies, they believed that "the New Deal had not gone far enough."[32] Such devotees of government planning and control would have fought to retain many of the wartime controls, as, indeed, those who remained in the government actually did in 1945 and 1946.[33] As Michael J. Lacey has written, however, "Truman and his Fair Dealers were generally reconciled to the existing structure of the economy. Feats of wartime production had restored the public image of business leadership, and a general willingness to concede economic leadership to the corporate sector reemerged" (Lacey, 1989, p. 5).

To sum up, the success of the transition hinged on the expeditious abandonment of the government's command-and-control apparatus and the return to resource allocation via the price system. It required sufficient confidence in the future security of private property rights that investors would once again place high volumes of resources at risk in long-term projects. Such a transition could go forward successfully only under a regime that was far more dedicated to the market system than the dominant faction of the latter half of the 1930s had been. Ironically, the war had brought into power a coalition that was much more congenial to the market, and many of the most zealous New Deal planners had been pushed onto the periphery or completely out of the government. Though the postwar regime was, by no means, devoted to laissez-faire and the economy remained subject to a host of government restrictions, participants in the postwar market economy had enough confidence in the security of their property rights and enough room to maneuver that they could succeed in reinvigorating the private economy for the first time since the 1920s.

Notes

1. Exceptions include Skousen (1988), Vedder and Gallaway (1991), Vedder and Gallaway (1997, pp. 150–75), and Smiley (1994, pp. 197–206).
2. Walton and Rockoff (1994, pp. 580–81). I have no intention to single out Walton and Rockoff for special censure; most textbooks of U.S. economic history contain similar passages. I myself once wrote: "The immediate postwar period was prosperous not because of shrewd fiscal management by the federal government but because consumers, starved by years of depression and wartime restrictions on the production of civilian durable goods and bloated with bank accounts and bonds accumulated during the war, produced an expansive market and encouraged a private investment boom" (Higgs, 1987, p. 227). On the contemporary forecasts, see Sapir (1949).
3. For a well-documented account of the origins and perpetuation of the orthodox story, see Vedder and Gallaway (1997, pp. 161–64).
4. Basic data from U.S. Council of Economic Advisers (1995, p. 406).
5. Since World War II, the relative price of munitions has tended upward. Therefore, each time the GDP deflator has been updated and the real GDP figures recomputed for the 1940s, the magnitudes of both the war boom and the postwar bust have become greater, as Vedder and Gallaway have illustrated (1991; 1997, pp. 150–75). That statistical phenomenon is interesting and, for certain purposes, important, but the main points I seek to make in this chapter are distinct, and they remain, regardless of the deflator employed. My critique rests more on a comparative-institutions foundation than on a merely statistical basis.
6. My argument for this conclusion, which builds on earlier critiques, especially that of Simon Kuznets, appears most fully in Higgs (1992, pp. 44–9).
7. As Ellen O'Brien has written, "the treatment of the government sector put in place in 1947 (which has remained standard practice in the US since that date) was initiated by estimators in order to assess the impact of the tremendous increase in war expenditures on the economy. While World War II may have focused attention on the role and finance of government spending, theoretical debates from the pre-war period continued through 1947 and were never fully resolved." See O'Brien (1994, p. 242).

8. The conclusion that the low unemployment rates during the war evidenced wartime prosperity is similarly flawed. The buildup of the armed forces, overwhelmingly by conscription, accounts fully (and then some) for the decline of unemployment. See Higgs (1992, pp. 42–4).

9. "On VJ-day 2 million veterans were employed. Today more than 10 million of them have jobs." About 900,000 were unemployed, and "about 1 million veterans—aside from those in school—have not yet started to look for work" (U.S. Office of War Mobilization and Reconversion, Director of War Mobilization and Reconversion, 1946, Eighth Report, 1 October, p. 60). On departures from the labor force, see Ballard (1983, p. 131).

10. Although the deflator is different and therefore the "real" values are affected somewhat, the trend real (1972$) GNP data computed by Nathan S. Balke and Robert J. Gordoiv derive from this technique and tell the same story. For their data, see Balke and Gordon (1986, pp. 782–3).

11. Calculated from current-dollar data in U.S. Council of Economic Advisers (1970, p. 177). For a detailed list of physical quantities of munitions produced during the war, see Krug (1945, pp. 29–32).

12. For graphic representations of how consumer spending for durables, non-durables, and services deviated from their prewar consumption functions during the war years, see Sapir (1945, pp. 304–5). Note, too, that during the first year of reconversion, "the phenomenal and quite unexpected rise in *nondurable* expenditures . . . [was] most striking" (p. 308, emphasis added).

13. Friedman and Schwartz speculate about "a continued fear of a major contraction and a continued belief that prices were destined to fall." Hence, "the public acted from 1946 to 1948 as if it expected deflation. . . . [T]his fear or expectation . . . induced [the public] to hold larger real money balances than it otherwise would have been willing to" (Friedman and Schwartz, 1963, pp. 583–4). For evidence of expectations of deflation in the late 1940s, see the Livingston survey data in Gordon (1980, p. 112).

14. U.S. Council of Economic Advisers (1970, p. 255). Thus, consumer behavior accorded with the findings of the National Survey of Liquid Assets conducted for the Federal Reserve Board by the Bureau of Agricultural Economics early in 1946. According to Sapir (1949, pp. 312–13), that study tended "to support the idea that on the whole families did not intend and did not want to spend their liquid assets in 1946 on such things as automobiles, refrigerators, and consumer goods generally. Apparently people preferred if possible to buy out of income, or perhaps borrow on short-term (by means of installment credit)."

15. The source for all data analyzed in this paragraph is U.S. Council of Economic Advisers (1970, pp. 194–5).

16. Repeal of the excess-profits tax was no small matter. From 1941 through 1945, net payments of that tax cumulated to $40 billion. See U.S. Bureau of the Census (1975, p. 1109).

17. U.S. Bureau of the Census, *Historical Statistics* (1975), p. 260 (corporate profits and taxes) and p. 181 (implicit price deflator for private national product).

18. "Business corporations, while paying out a record amount in dividends, retained the remarkably high proportion of five-eighths of their profits after taxes in 1947" (Harry S Truman [14 January 1948], *The Economic Report of the President*, p. 24).

19. U.S. Council of Economic Advisers (1970, p. 266). In addition, short-term funds could be borrowed at very low rates: 0.75 percent in 1945, 0.81 percent in 1946, and 1.03 percent in 1947 for 4- to 6-month prime commercial paper. Data source is Balke and Gordon (1986, p. 783). Even if the true rate of inflation was much lower than reported, those nominal rates of interest implied substantially negative real rates of interest.

20. See Higgs (1992, pp. 42–4). See also Vedder and Gallaway (1991, p. 168). ("The wartime unemployment rates of under 2 percent were low, at least in part, because the normal rules of noncoercive labor-market participation did not apply.")

21. Vedder and Gallaway (1991): "these results . . . are highly suspect because the underlying data are almost certainly replete with significant distortions" (p. 152); "enormous distortions [were] associated with the substitution for market-valued economic activity of command-economy activity not formally measured at true market prices" (pp. 156–7); and "we have only limited faith in the estimates of falling adjusted real wages" (p. 170).

22. As Ludwig von Mises wrote, "the anticipation of future prices of the products . . . determines the state of prices of the complementary factors of production. . . . The fact that yesterday people valued and appraised commodities in a different way is irrelevant" (Mises, 1966, pp. 336–7).

23. See Lacey (1989, pp. 5–6, 76, 136–7).

24. For an extensive presentation of evidence for this claim, see Higgs (1997, pp. 561–90).

25. Taft, as quoted in Isbell (1995, p. 177).

26. Of the Second New Deal (that is, 1935–40) bureaucrats, James Burnham wrote in his book *The Managerial Revolution* (1941), "they are, sometimes openly, scornful of capitalists and capitalist ideas. . . . They believe that they can run things, and they like to run things" (quoted in Hayek, 1997, p. 251).

27. Many contemporary sources are cited in Higgs (1992, p. 54, fn. 40).

28. For enduring legacies, see Higgs (1987, pp. 225–34).

29. On all of these reconversion policies, see Ballard (1983).

30. See Higgs (1993, 1997). Rockoff has written about "a new macroeconomic regime" that, he argues, undergirded postwar prosperity, but his discussion applies not so much to the immediate postwar years as to the much longer post war era. Indeed, prior to the Federal Reserve-Treasury Accord of 1951, the monetary regime continued to feature the same Fed subordination to the Treasury that had begun at the outset of the war. See Rockoff (1998, pp. 115–18). In any event, the "regime certainty" at issue here, essentially a political and property-rights phenomenon, differs from the "new macroeconomic regime" hypothesized by Rockoff.

31. Workers might have expected lower postwar wages simply by anticipating the effect of a drastic reduction of war-related work, which paid relatively high wages. According to Claudia Goldin (citing a 1946 study of women workers by the Department of Labor), "the earnings premium for war-related over consumer-related manufacturing was between 25 percent and 45 percent in 1944/45, depending on the war production area" (Goldin, 1991, p. 743, fn. 1).

32. See Brinkley (1995, p. 56). The "long-haired boys" were also known as "the liberal crowd" and, by association with their patron saint, Felix Frankfurter, "the Harvard crowd." George Peek called them the "boys with their hair ablaze" (Brinkley, 1995, p. 51).

33. For example, Chester Bowles, among other prominent New Dealers, fought to retain price controls. See Goodwin (1989, pp. 90–9) and Lichtenstein (1989). See also Jones (1972, p. 130). As Brinkley has written, the hardcore New Dealers embraced government planning "with almost religious veneration" (1995, p. 47).

References

Balke, Nathan S., and Robert J. Gordon. (1986) Appendix B: Historical Data. In *The American Business Cycle: Continuity and Change,* edited by Robert J. Gordon. Chicago: University of Chicago Press, pp. 781–810.

Ballard, Jack Stokes. (1983) *The Shock of Peace: Military and Economic Demobilization after World War II.* Washington, D.C.: University Press of America.

Brinkley, Alan. (1995) *The End of Reform: New Deal Liberalism in Recession and War.* New York: Knopf.

Cantril, Hadley. (1951) *Public Opinion 1935–1946.* Princeton, N.J.: Princeton University Press. Friedman, Milton, and Anna Jacobson Schwartz. (1963) *A Monetary History of the United States, 1867–1960.* Princeton, N.J.: Princeton University Press.

Friedman, Milton, and Anna Jacobson Schwartz. (1982) *Monetary Trends in the United States and the United Kingdom.* Chicago: University of Chicago Press.

Goldin, Claudia. (1991) The Role of World War II in the Rise of Women's Employment. *American Economic Review* 81 (4): 741–56.

Goodwin, Craufurd D. (1989) Attitudes toward Industry in the Truman Administration: The Macroeconomic Origins of Microeconomic Policy. In *The Truman Presidency,* edited by Michael J. Lacey. New York: Woodrow Wilson International Center for Scholars and Cambridge University Press, pp. 89–127.

Gordon, Robert J. (1980) Postwar Macroeconomics: The Evolution of Events and Ideas. In *The American Economy in Transition,* edited by Martin Feldstein. Chicago: University of Chicago Press, pp. 101–62.

Hayek, F. A. (1997) *The Collected Works of F. A. Hayek,* vol. 10. *Socialism and War: Essays, Documents, Reviews,* edited by Bruce Caldwell. Chicago: University of Chicago Press.

Higgs, Robert. (1987) *Crisis and Leviathan: Critical Episodes in the Growth of American Government.* New York: Oxford University Press.

Higgs, Robert. (1992) Wartime Prosperity? A Reassessment of the U.S. Economy in the 1940s. *Journal of Economic History* 52 (1): 41–60.

Higgs, Robert. (1993) Private Profit, Public Risk: Institutional Antecedents of the Modern Military Procurement System in the Rearmament Program of 1940–1941. In *The Sinews of War: Essays on the Economic History of World War II,* edited by Geofrey T. Mills and Hugh Rockoff. Ames: Iowa State University Press, pp. 166–98.

Higgs, Robert. (1997) Regime Uncertainty: Why the Great Depression Lasted So Long and Why Prosperity Resumed after the War. *The Independent Review* 1 (Spring): 561–90.

Hooks, Gregory. (1991) *Forging the Military-Industrial Complex: World War II's Battle of the Potomac.* Urbana: University of Illinois Press.

Isbell, Steven B. (1995) The 1948 Tax Cut: Prelude to Reaganomics. *Essays in Economic and Business History* 13:169–80.

Jeffries, John W. (1990) The "New" New Deal: FDR and American Liberalism, 1937–1945. *Political Science Quarterly* 105 (3): 397–418.

Jeffries, John W. (1996) A "Third New Deal"? Liberal Policy and the American State, 1937–1945. *Journal of Policy History* 8 (4): 387–409.

Jones, Byrd L. (1972) The Role of Keynesians in Wartime Policy and Postwar Planning, 1940–1946. *American Economic Review* 62 (2): 125–33.

Krug, J. A. (1945) *Production: Wartime Achievements and the Reconversion Outlook.* War Production Board Document No. 334, 9 October.

Lacey, Michael J. (1989) Introduction and Summary: The Truman Era in Retrospect. In *The Truman Presidency,* edited by Michael J. Lacey. New York: Woodrow Wilson International Center for Scholars and Cambridge University Press, pp. 1–18.

Lichtenstein, Nelson. (1989) Labor in the Truman Era: Origins of the "Private Welfare State." In *The Truman Presidency,* edited by Michael J. Lacey. New York: Woodrow Wilson International Center for Scholars and Cambridge University Press, pp. 128–55.

Mises, Ludwig von. (1966) *Human Action: A Treatise on Economics,* third revised edition. Chicago: Henry Regnery.

O'Brien, Ellen. (1994) How the "G" Got into the GNP. In *Perspectives on the History of Economic Thought,* vol. 10. *Method, Competition, Conflict and Measurement in the Twentieth Century,* edited by Karen I. Vaughn. Aldershot, England: Edward Elgar, pp. 241–55.

Riddell, Kelly. (1990) The State, Capitalism, and World War II: The U.S. Case. *Armed Forces & Society* 17 (1): 53–79.

Rockoff, Hugh. (1998) The United States: From Ploughshares to Swords. In *The Economics of World War II: Six Great Powers in International Comparison,* edited by Mark Harrison. Cambridge: Cambridge University Press, pp. 81–131.

Sapir, Michael. (1949) Review of Economic Forecasts for the Transition Period. In National Bureau of Economic Research, Conference on Research in Income and Wealth, *Studies in Income and Wealth,* vol. 11. New York: National Bureau of Economic Research, pp. 273–351.

Skousen, Mark. (1988) Saving the Depression: A New Look at World War II. *Review of Austrian Economics* 2: 211–26.

Smiley, Gene. (1994) *The American Economy in the Twentieth Century.* Cincinnati: South-Western Publishing.

Swanson, J. A., and S. H. Williamson. (1972) Estimates of National Product and Income for the United States Economy, 1919–1941. *Explorations in Economic History* 10 (1): 53–73.

Truman, Harry S. (Various dates) *The Economic Report of the President,* Washington, D.C.: Government Printing Office.

The Truman Presidency, edited by Michael J. Lacey. 1989. New York: Woodrow Wilson International Center for Scholars and Cambridge University Press.

U.S. Bureau of the Census. (1975) *Historical Statistics of the United States, Colonial Times to 1970.* Washington, D.C.: Government Printing Office.

U.S. Council of Economic Advisers. (Various years) *Annual Report.* Washington, D.C.: Government Printing Office.

U.S. Department of Defense, Office of the Comptroller. (1990) *National Defense Budget Estimates for FY 1991.* March.

U.S. Office of War Mobilization and Reconversion, Director of War Mobilization and Reconversion. (Various dates) *Report to the President, the Senate, and the House of Representatives.* Washington, D.C.: Government Printing Office.

U.S. War Production Board, General Economics and Planning Staff. Program and Statistics Bureau. (1945) *American Industry in War and Transition, 1940–1950. Part II. The Effect of the War on the Industrial Economy.* Document 27, July 20.

Vedder, Richard K., and Lowell E. Gallaway. (1991) The Great Depression of 1946. *Review of Austrian Economics* 5 (2): 3–31.

Vedder, Richard K., and Lowell E. Gallaway. (1997.) *Out of Work: Unemployment and Government in Twentieth-Century America,* updated edition. New York: New York University Press for The Independent Institute.

Walton, Gary M., and Hugh Rockoff. (1994) *History of the American Economy,* seventh edition. Fort Worth, Tex.: Dryden Press.

Acknowledgments   For comments on previous drafts, I am grateful to Lee J. Alston, Donald J. Boudreaux, Burton Folsom, Daniel B. Klein, Gary D. Libecap, Hugh Rockoff, Mark Thornton, two anonymous referees, seminar participants at Seattle University, and the audience at the 1998 annual meeting of the Economic and Business History Society. Thanks, too, to Susan Isaac.

6

The Cold War Economy
*Opportunity Costs, Ideology,
and the Politics of Crisis*

> Our government has kept us in a perpetual state of fear—
> kept us in a continuous stampede of patriotic fervor—
> with the cry of grave national emergency. Always there
> has been some terrible evil at home or some monstrous
> foreign power that was going to gobble us up if we did not
> blindly rally behind it by furnishing the exorbitant funds
> demanded. Yet, in retrospect, these disasters seem never to
> have happened, seem never to have been quite real.
>
> *General Douglas MacArthur,* A Soldier Speaks

FOR FOUR DECADES, the government of the United
States waged the Cold War. Doing so brought about massive changes in
the allocation of resources, with effects on many dimensions of the nation's
economic performance. Despite all that has been written by economists,
historians, political scientists, and others about the Cold War economy,
economic historians have given little attention to it as such. Most textbooks
devote scant, if any, space to discussing it.[1] Now that it can be viewed as a
distinct phase of U.S. economic history, an analytical survey is in order.

In the first part of this chapter, I present such a survey in the form of
a statistical anatomy accompanied by a brief narrative of related political
and military events. I deal with the magnitudes of defense spending, both
absolutely and relative to national product, as well as the trends and cycles
of those magnitudes. Next, I examine opportunity costs, identifying how
changes in the military share of national product were related to changes

in the private share or the government nonmilitary share, both from year to year and over the course of distinct periods of military buildup and cutback. Finally, I consider how the Cold War economy's performance looks when we reconsider the measurement of national product along lines that I, among others, consider more defensible than the orthodox ones.

In the second part of the chapter, I turn more explicitly to issues of political economy. The Cold War economy derived from resource allocation by government. But in the context of American political institutions, the government's actions cannot be fully understood apart from the public's preferences and the politics that connected the rulers and the ruled. Post-World War II American military affairs—preparation for as well as actual involvement in war—gave rise to characteristic political processes. In analyzing those processes, I focus on information and ideology. Who knew what, and who believed what, about national defense requirements and capabilities? How was the existing information used in the political processes that determined the broad societal allocation of resources? How stable were public preferences, and what made them change as they did? How were conflicts between the national security elite and the public resolved?

A Statistical Anatomy of the Cold War Economy

Terms of Reference

To inquire into how the costs of Cold War military activities were distributed between the private sector and the government nonmilitary sector, I extend the familiar guns versus butter metaphor slightly, dividing the gross national product (GNP) into three exhaustive classes: government military purchases (G-M); all government—federal, state, and local—nonmilitary purchases (G-NM); and all private purchases, whether for consumption or investment (or net exports) [P].[2] This categorization permits us to view the societal opportunity costs of military purchases very broadly. The military purchases include only newly produced final goods and services, as designated under the "national defense" heading in the National Income and Product Accounts. Hence, at the beginning of the analysis, I am examining the division of the entire national flow of output, as conventionally measured.

To provide empirical terms of reference for the analysis, I consider periods of military mobilization to be defined by a rapid, uninterrupted, multiyear increase in real military outlays, and periods of demobilization to be defined by a substantial, uninterrupted, multiyear decrease in real military outlays. In the United States, during the Cold War, three mobilizations occurred, during 1950–53, 1965–68, and 1978–87, each followed by a demobilization.

An increase in the share of G-M in GNP can occur at the expense of the share of P, the share of G-NM, or both. For expositional convenience, let us employ the usual terms, calling G-M "guns," and P, "butter." G-NM will be called "roads." A distinction may be drawn between "butter-sacrificing" mobilizations, when the P share declines, and "roads-sacrificing" mobilizations, when the G-NM share declines. Demobilizations may be viewed in parallel terms as "butter-enhancing" or "roads-enhancing."

Military Spending: Magnitudes and Shares

World War II cast an enormous shadow over the years that followed in the United States. In addition to the immense economic consequences, the war's institutional and Constitutional legacies loomed very large.[3] The ideological effects were also tremendous. Benjamin Page and Robert Shapiro, in their massive survey of public opinion data, describe World War II as "the most pervasive single influence on public opinion" in the entire period since the mid-1930s. Among other things, it "transformed American public opinion concerning virtually all aspects of foreign affairs" (Page and Shapiro, 1992, p. 332). In the dominant view that emerged from the war, "isolationism" and "appeasement" were completely discredited. Within the federal government, the president gained power and discretion, especially in foreign affairs—people would later speak of an "imperial presidency." In these respects, important groundwork was laid for a greatly expanded

American role in world affairs. In the latter half of 1945 and throughout 1946, however, the rapid demobilization of the awesome wartime military machine raised doubts as to whether the United States would possess the means to achieve its newly embraced global goals.

Culminating the demobilization, real military spending hit its postwar low in calendar year 1947 at $10 billion in current dollars, equivalent to about $45 billion in 1982 dollars, or 4.3 percent of GNP. (Henceforth, unless otherwise indicated, all dollar amounts are expressed in 1982 purchasing power.)[4] But in 1947, relations with the Soviet Union were deteriorating, especially in the eyes of the president and officials at the Department of State and the newly created Department of Defense (Huntington, 1961, pp. 33–39). Already, Winston Churchill had warned that an iron curtain was descending between Soviet-controlled Europe and the West. For the people on Main Street, however, other concerns had priority. "Though the polls showed growing awareness of Soviet aggressiveness, most Americans were still not ready to undertake the dangerous, expensive job of opposing Russia. . . . The Republicans had gained control of Congress in November [1946] by promising a return to normalcy, not an assumption of Britain's empire."[5] To convince the public, and thereby Congress, of the need for additional defense spending to implement the proclaimed Truman Doctrine of containing communist expansion around the world, the administration needed a more visible crisis. The confrontations over Greece and Turkey, which had flared up in 1947, could not carry the full burden of justification required.

Events came to the administration's rescue when the communists took over the Czechoslovakian government early in 1948. Also, Lieutenant General Lucius Clay, military governor of the U.S. Zone in Germany, helped to create a war scare by sending a telegram, which was subsequently publicized, warning that war between the United States and the Soviet Union might occur "with dramatic suddenness." In March, President Truman called for a supplemental defense appropriation of more than $3 billion (current dollars), which Congress quickly approved (Huntington, 1957, p. 425; Kolodziej, 1966, pp. 74–81; Mosley, 1985, p. 7). Hoping for a rally-'round-the-flag response from the citizenry as he sought reelection, Truman gave a major speech that stressed the danger of war with the Soviets. He denounced their "ruthless action" and their "clear design" to dominate Europe.[6]

With these events, the Cold War had definitely begun. Congress approved defense appropriations for fiscal year 1949 that were about 20 percent higher than those for fiscal year 1948 (U.S. Bureau of the Census, 1975, p. 1114). The Berlin crisis that began in mid-1948, the communist conquest of China, the Soviet nuclear test, and the formation of NATO in 1949, and the outbreak of the Korean War in mid-1950 ensured that the superpower rivalry and confrontation that came to be known as the Cold War—a state of chronic national emergency and sustained military readiness that was without precedent in American history—would remain the dominant reality of U.S. foreign and defense affairs for the next four decades, ending only with the breakup of the East Bloc and then of the Soviet Union itself in 1990 and 1991, respectively.

Notwithstanding the sharp jump in real military purchases in calendar year 1949, the first rapid multiyear mobilization of the Cold War era did not begin until after the outbreak of the Korean War (figure 6-1). Previously, administration officials had encountered stiff resistance from Congress to their pleas for a substantial buildup along the lines laid out in NSC-68, a landmark document of April 1950. The authors of this internal government report took a Manichaean view of America's rivalry with the Soviet Union, espoused a permanent role for the United States as world policeman, and envisioned U.S. military expenditures amounting to perhaps 20 percent of GNP.[7] Congressional acceptance of the recommended measures seemed highly unlikely in the absence of a crisis. In 1950, "the fear that [the North Korean] invasion was just the first step in a broad offensive by the Soviets proved highly useful when it came to persuading Congress to increase the defense budget." As Secretary of State Dean Acheson said afterward, "Korea saved us."[8] The buildup reached its peak in 1953, when the stalemated belligerents in Korea agreed to a truce.

The ensuing demobilization lasted just two years, leaving annual defense outlays during the next decade nearly three times higher than they had been in the late 1940s (see figure 6-1). During the period 1947–50, real annual military spending never exceeded $60 billion; after 1952, it never

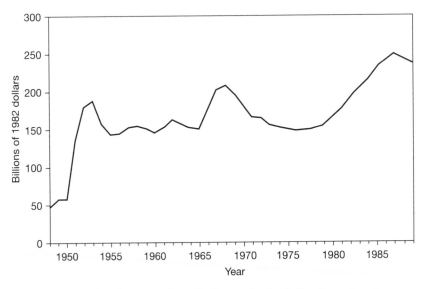

Figure 6-1. Real military outlays (billions of 1982 dollars), 1948–1989.

fell below $143 billion, and usually was substantially higher (the average for 1956–65 was $168 billion). Samuel Huntington, a leading student of U.S. defense policy, speculated that, "without the war, the increase probably would have been about the size of that of 1948–1949," that is, 20 percent, instead of nearly 200 percent (Huntington, 1961, p. 201).

During the period 1955–65, U.S. military policy underwent substantial recasting. First, the Eisenhower administration's New Look put major emphasis on massive nuclear retaliation by the Strategic Air Command's long-range bombers and intercontinental ballistic missiles; then, the Kennedy administration's plan tilted toward flexible nuclear response, counterinsurgency, and forces tailored to limited wars. But these shifts had only minor impacts on overall defense spending, which fluctuated within a range of $143 billion to $163 billion. After JFK took office, a much-vaunted buildup raised spending by 11 percent between 1960 and 1962, but the decline during the next three years brought the real spending of 1965 below the amount spent in 1957. Because the Kennedy buildup was so brief, so small, and so transient, I do not regard it as belonging in the same category with the three mobilizations identified earlier.

After 1965, the Vietnam War buildup carried real defense purchases to a mobilization peak in 1968, up by more than one-third. The ensuing demobilization is harder to date with certainty. I put its completion at 1971, when the military share of GNP had fallen below the premobilization share of 1965 (figure 6-2). After holding its own in 1972, however, the amount of real military spending continued downward until it hit bottom in 1976. (The G-M share of GNP hit bottom in 1978.) Despite this resumption of the decline that first began after 1968, it would be unwarranted to describe the decline that occurred between 1972 and 1976 as part of the Vietnam War demobilization as such.[9] Although this latter phase of decline certainly reflected, in part, disillusionments and convictions engendered by the Vietnam experience, it applied more to the military establishment in general, especially the procurement accounts, than to forces in or supporting military action in Southeast Asia (Korb, 1979, pp. 53–4, 62–4; Gansler, 1980, pp. 21–2, 26). In January 1973, with only 30,000 U.S. military personnel remaining in Vietnam, the Nixon administration

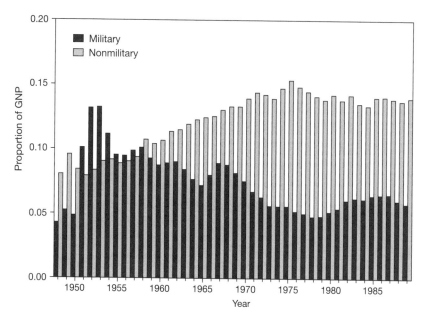

Figure 6-2. Government military shares (dark bars) and nonmilitary shares (light bars) of GNP, 1948–1989.

terminated the draft, and the Paris Peace Agreement provided for the withdrawal of all remaining U.S. forces from Vietnam (Stubbing, 1986, pp. 297, 310; Ambrose, 1985, pp. 234–5, 242–54). The bulk of the military retrenchment in 1972–76 reflected public and congressional revulsion against militarism and the Cold War, as evidenced by such events as the passage of the War Powers Resolution in 1973 and the National Emergencies Act in 1976, rather than savings associated with the reduction and eventual cessation of U.S. engagement in the Vietnam War.

Finally, after 1978, the Carter-Reagan buildup is obvious in the spending data (see figure 6-1). Between 1978 and 1980, real military outlays increased by $15.7 billion, or 10.4 percent; between 1980 and 1987, they increased by $84.4 billion, or 50.7 percent. For the entire nine-year buildup, annual outlays went up by $100.1 billion, or 66.4 percent. (Recall that these figures are expressed in 1982 dollars.) Not being associated with a major shooting war, this vast military spending surge had no precedent in American history.

Before proceeding, one should note two important points. First, I have computed the data on real military spending by deflating nominal-dollar defense purchases by the GNP deflator. (All data are for calendar, not fiscal, years.) Although this procedure does not permit one to claim that the resulting real spending series accurately portrays the growth of real defense "quantity"—whatever that might mean—it does permit one to approximate the opportunity cost of military spending in terms of real nonmilitary output forgone.[10] Second, the military spending being analyzed here is for purchasing newly produced goods and services, including foreign military assistance. This component of the national income and product accounts is not the same as the budgetary outlays of the Department of Defense, which include substantial sums for transfer payments, such as military retirement pay and purchases of land. Also, some defense purchases originate in other federal departments, for example, the Energy Department (previously the Atomic Energy Commission), which purchases goods and services to produce nuclear reactors and warheads for the armed forces.[11]

For the entire Cold War period, 1948–89, real military purchases cumulated to a total of $7,051 billion—equivalent to nearly $13 trillion in

2005 dollars—averaging $168 billion per year. There was, obviously, substantial fluctuation: The standard deviation was $44.6 billion. The trend was slightly upward. A trend equation fitted to the data reveals a tendency for defense purchases to increase by $2.6 billion per year, on average.

From 1948 to 1989, real GNP increased at an average rate of 3.1 percent per year. (This rate and others given in this paragraph were computed from a linear regression of the logarithm of the variable on time.) Average growth rates of the component shares of the real GNP were as follows: real private spending, 3.0 per year; real government nonmilitary spending, 4.5 percent per year; and real military spending, 1.9 percent per year. Thus, while private spending, by far the largest component of GNP, almost maintained its share of the total, the share of G-NM tended to increase, while the share of G-M tended to diminish.

By focusing on the long-term trends of the shares, however, one overlooks the abrupt changes that occurred early in the period: The share of G-M jumped from 5.0 in 1950 to 13.1 percent in 1952 and to 13.2 percent in 1953, after which a gradual downward trend is clear (see figure 6-2); the private share, in contrast, fell from 86.5 percent in 1950 to 77.7 percent in 1953, recovered to 81.5 in 1955 (a private share never again reached), and then leveled off for the long term at about 80 percent. In short, one finds that the composition of real output, as conventionally measured, underwent a permanent once-and-for-all shift in the early 1950s, when the private share lost about six percentage points at the expense of, first, an abrupt increase in the government military share, and then a gradual, long-term increase in the government (federal, state, and local) nonmilitary share, which trended upward until the mid-1970s, and then leveled off at about 14 percent (see figure 6-2).

Table 6-1 shows that, in some respects, one's description of GNP shares during the Cold War depends heavily on whether or not one includes the years 1948–50 in the long period. With those three years excluded, the private share shows no long-term tendency to decline, and its standard deviation is much smaller; the military share falls significantly faster, with the annual figures deviating much less from the trend line. In describing the long-term changes in the G-NM share, in contrast, it matters little

Table 6-1. Gross national product share
characteristics for two long periods

	1948–1989	1951–1989
Private share		
Mean	0.803	0.798
Standard deviation	0.020	0.010
Trend change per decade	−0.006	0.001
R^2 of trend equation	0.121	0.007
Government military share		
Mean	0.075	0.077
Standard deviation	0.022	0.022
Trend change per decade	−0.010	−0.016
R^2 of trend equation	0.332	0.733
Government nonmilitary share		
Mean	0.122	0.125
Standard deviation	0.022	0.021
Trend change per decade	0.016	0.016
R^2 of trend equation	0.780	0.736

whether one includes or excludes the years 1948–50. As a stylized description of the Cold War shares, one comes close to the truth as follows: P share = 80 percent; G-M share = 7.6 percent; G-NM share = 12.4 percent.

If one begins in 1948, the long-term tendency was for the G-NM share to gain at the expense of both the private share and the military share, with the military share absorbing almost two-thirds of the shift. (Because the three shares exhaust the entire GNP, their trend rates of change must add to zero, which—except for rounding error—they do in table 6-1.) Excluding the years 1948–50 from the long term, one finds that the long-term tendency was for the G-NM share to gain exclusively at the expense of the military share, while the private share remained approximately constant over the long period from 1951 to 1989. Thus, if the United States during the Cold War was simultaneously a warfare state and a welfare state, it is clear that the welfare part expanded much more robustly than the warfare part after the initial military surge of the early 1950s.[12]

Given the overarching trends, one may proceed to ask whether increases in the G-M share during military mobilizations occurred at the expense of the G-NM share or the P share. The answer is clear. There was no systematic tendency at all for the G-NM share to fall when the G-M share rose during mobilizations. In fact, during military buildups, the G-NM share of GNP was more likely to rise than to fall. The G-NM share was higher in 1953 than it had been in 1950, and higher in 1968 than it had been in 1965. During the Carter-Reagan buildup, the G-NM share fluctuated in a narrow band, sometimes rising and sometimes falling, but the share at the end (13.88 percent in 1987) was nearly the same as it had been before the buildup began (14.06 percent in 1978). A regression of the annual changes in the G-NM share on the annual changes in the G-M share has a slope coefficient that does not differ significantly from zero (t = 0.355) and an R2 of just 0.003, which shows that the annual changes in the two variables bore no contemporaneous linear relationship to one another.

The behavior of the private share was quite different. Changes in the G-M and P shares were almost exactly offsetting. A trade-off equation fitted to the annual changes during 1948–89 has a tight fit (R2 = 0.814) and shows that the implicit cost of a one-percentage-point increase in the military share was a reduction of one percentage point in the private share: The regression slope coefficient is minus 1.004, with a standard error of 0.077; hence, one cannot reject the hypothesis that the slope equals one at any customary level of Type I error. (Deletion of the years 1948–50 from the data set has no effect on this conclusion.) Figure 6-3 plainly shows the two offsetting changes to be deviations from a horizontal line, representing a zero sum of the two changes. In short, during the Cold War, the private sector alone bore the full cost of annual increases in the military share of total output, as conventionally defined.

In the metaphors explained earlier, one may describe the buildup of 1950–53 as completely butter-sacrificing and the demobilization of 1953–

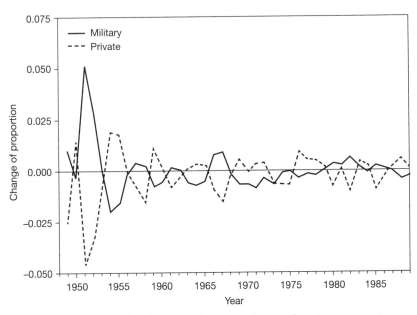

Figure 6-3. Change of military and private shares of GNP, 1949–1989.

55 as completely butter-enhancing. But because the magnitude of the military upswing greatly exceeded that of the subsequent retrenchment, over the full cycle of 1950–55 the net change in the private share was minus 5.1 percentage points. The buildup of 1965–68 was also completely butter-sacrificing. The ensuing demobilization was 50 percent butter-enhancing if it is considered complete in 1971, and 59 percent butter-enhancing if it is considered complete in 1976. Over the complete cycle of 1965–71, the net change in the private share was minus 1.4 percentage points; over the period 1965–76, it was minus 0.4 percentage points. The Carter-Reagan buildup of 1978–87 was 89 percent butter-sacrificing: the private share fell by 1.5 percentage points, while the military share rose by 1.7 percentage points. During the Reagan portion of the buildup alone, from 1980 to 1987, the mobilization was 76 percent butter-sacrificing, because the private share fell by 1 percent, while the military share rose by 1.3 percent. The post-1987 demobilization continued as the Cold War came to an end.

Cold War Economy: Unconventionally Viewed

To this point, my analysis has proceeded by making use of the conventional categories of the national income and product accounts. I now take a different tack. In the conventional accounting framework, the government's spending for national defense enters fully into GNP. The soundness of this accounting practice can be, and often has been, questioned. The challenges apply, in some cases, to the accounting treatment of all government spending (Spindler, 1982), and in other cases, to defense spending, in particular (Dumas, 1990). Some critics would deduct all government spending from GNP, and others, only a portion; likewise for defense spending alone. Whether or not one accepts the arguments of the critics, it is worthwhile to consider the grounds of the arguments and to assess how our view of the economy's performance would be changed by adopting alternative accounting conventions. Among the several bases for rejecting the usual accounting conventions, the following may be noted.

First, because the prices paid for defense goods and services generally are not—and, in some cases, cannot be—determined within a competitive market framework, all such prices are suspect. What do they mean? Is there any reason to suppose that they approximate consumers' marginal rates of substitution or producers' marginal costs? If not, why should the actual prices paid be regarded as appropriate weights for the purpose of aggregating physically incommensurable goods and services? The prices paid for conscripted soldiers' services are only the most incontestable example of a wide class of prices that deviate from competitive equilibrium levels. For many items procured, the government and the supplier compose a bilateral monopoly, and the prices reflect only the relative bargaining power of the transactors—not to speak of the supplier's political pull.

Second, even if the pricing problem can be disregarded, defense purchases measure input, not output. Obviously, what people value is national security, not the mere devotion of resources to the ostensible production of national security. Because no one knows the production function for national security, and because under certain conditions (e.g., arms races), more military spending may be associated with less, rather than more, security, one may not suppose even that the relation between spending and security is necessarily monotonic; far less may one assume what the specific form of the function might be (Weidenbaum, 1992, pp. 124–5; Weida and Gertcher, 1987, pp. 46–50, 54, 164–5, 202–03). Moreover, how one might aggregate individuals' valuations of security to arrive at a societal value for national security is problematic in theory, as well as practice.

Third, defense output, even if it were measurable, ought to be regarded as an intermediate rather than a final good, and on this basis, excluded from GNP. As James Tobin and William Nordhaus put it, extending an argument embraced earlier by Simon Kuznets, defense is a "necessary regrettable," not a source of final utility to anyone. If there were no external threat, all defense spending could be eliminated and no one would be the worse. To the extent that defense spending serves to preserve the social and economic framework within which nondefense production can go forward, its value is already incorporated into the market prices of civilian goods.[13]

Finally, following lines of argument that are familiar in public choice theory (bureaucratic behavior à la Niskanen and rent-seeking à la Tullock), one may argue that political and bureaucratic allocation of resources tends toward the dissipation of net value for all services provided by the government. Hence, at the margin, the observed defense spending amounts to transfer payments rather than payments for net additions to the real national product (Spindler, 1982). Students of the politics of maintaining obsolete military bases and other defense boondoggles have demonstrated that at least a substantial portion of defense spending makes no genuine net contribution to national security (Higgs, 1988; Higgs, 1989; Twight, 1990).

The preceding arguments, although not widely accepted within the mainstream economics profession, are scarcely the wild-eyed notions of crackpots. At least three Noble laureates in economic science (Kuznets,

Tobin, and Buchanan) are on record as proponents of some or all of the preceding arguments, and many other respectable economists also have subscribed to them. Especially weighty is the position of Simon Kuznets in opposition to the now-standard way of treating defense spending in the national product accounts, because Kuznets was the acknowledged leader in the original development of the accounts. Except for World War II, which he treated as a unique event, Kuznets always insisted on using a "peacetime concept" of GNP.[14]

For assessing the long-run trend of real GNP during the Cold War, it matters little whether one examines conventional real GNP or real GNP*, the latter being real GNP minus all defense spending. The two series exhibit a similar upward tendency. Between 1948 and 1989, real GNP grew at an average rate of 3.10 percent per year, and real GNP*, at an average rate of 3.21 percent per year. (Again, growth rates are obtained from linear regressions of log output on time.) On the basis of this difference, one has little to choose, because the growth rate of orthodox total output and that of civilian output alone differed by just 0.11 percentage points per year.

Notwithstanding the similarities of their long-run trends, the two series moved quite differently in particular years and, on one occasion, over the course of a conventionally demarcated business cycle. Comparing the annual percentage growth rates of real GNP and real GNP*, one finds that they differed by one percentage point or more in six years, and in several other years, they differed by enough to make a substantial difference in, say, the predictive performance of a macro model fitted to them. A linear regression of the growth rate of real GNP* on the growth rate of real GNP accounts for less than 80 percent of the variance $(R^2 = 0.796)$ and has a standard error of estimate of 1.2 percentage points. So, how one defines GNP can make an important difference in one's understanding of the patterns of real output fluctuations in the postwar era. Empirical macroeconomists appear to be oblivious to this issue.

As figure 6-4 shows, the differences tended to diminish with the passage of time. The early 1950s witnessed the greatest deviations between the growth rate of orthodox real GNP and that of civilian real GNP. The

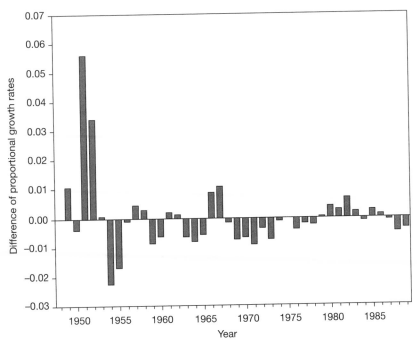

Figure 6-4. Difference between growth rates of real GNP
and real GNP*, 1949–1989.

differences were considerably smaller from the mid-1950s to the mid-1970s, and then even smaller between 1974 and 1989. To some extent, the diminution reflected the diminishing share of military spending in GNP (see figure 6-2).

For the early 1950s, the choice of an output concept makes a major difference in the description of the business cycle (figure 6-5). The conventional concept gives rise to a description that shows an expansion from 1950 through 1953, a mild recession in 1954, and a strong recovery in 1955. Real GNP*, in contrast, shows a much slower pace of expansion in 1951 and virtually no growth in 1952. The year 1953 looks the same for both measures, but 1954 does not. Moving from real GNP to real GNP* transforms 1954 from a mild recession to a weak expansion—a minus 1.3 percent change becomes a plus 1.0 percent change. Both series show

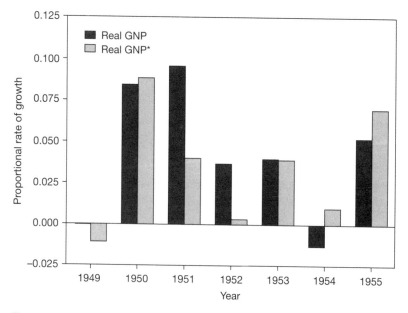

Figure 6-5. Growth rates of real GNP (dark bars)
and real GNP* (light bars).

strong recovery in 1955, with civilian growth outpacing that of GNP, including the military component.

One may not wish to accept GNP* as a replacement for conventional GNP,[15] but the point remains. Whether or not one wishes to exclude defense spending from the measure of total output, one must recognize that some years look good or bad merely because of variations in defense spending—a type of spending with a very tenuous relation to the well-being of consumers, investors, and the beneficiaries of governmentally purchased civilian goods and services. The year 1951 was far better for guns than it was for butter or roads. The year 1952 saw only minuscule growth of road output and actual decline of butter output; the year 1954, a bad one for guns, brought slight improvements in the rates of output of both roads and butter. What we call these differences matters little, so long as we are clear, but appreciating the existence of the differences is important for understanding and evaluating the actual performance of the economy during the Cold War.

The Political Economy of the Cold War

The foregoing evidence and analysis raise a variety of questions about the political economy of the Cold War, only a few of which can be considered here. I shall focus on issues related to ideology, information, and the conflict between governing elites and the public.

Consider first the profile of resource allocation to the military during the Cold War. One might ask: (1) What accounts for the unprecedentedly enormous base spending level, that is, the level when the nation was not involved in a shooting war? (2) What accounts for the deviations from that base, that is, for the buildups? Until the late 1970s, the answers seem fairly transparent. The high base level of spending resulted from the Cold War ideology of global anti-communism and the foreign policy doctrines and military commitments that flowed from that ideology. The spending deviations were associated with the extraordinary costs of engagement in two major shooting wars in Asia.[16] The Carter-Reagan buildup is a different matter. Set in motion by a unique combination of external events, astute partisan political action, and information management, and kept in motion by executive determination and bureaucratic tenacity, it bore little resemblance to the two preceding buildups.[17]

During the "normal" years of the post-Korean War period, 1955–65, and the post-Vietnam War period, 1972–78, when neither substantial mobilization nor demobilization was occurring, real defense spending fluctuated within a range of $144 billion to $166 billion. This contrasted with the $48 billion to $60 billion range of the years 1948–50. One may conclude that the establishment of the full-fledged Cold War regime caused real defense spending almost to triple. Shooting wars entailed marginal expenditures of another $20 billion to $60 billion per year. Even without the periodic buildups, the "normal" expense of a military establishment requiring $150 billion per year for forty years would have cumulated to $6 trillion (1982 dollars). This staggering sum is equivalent to the entire GNP of the United States in the two-year period 1977–1978.

From 1948 to the late 1960s, the dominant Cold War ideology and a bipartisan consensus on defense and foreign policy, focused on global containment of communism and deterrence of a Soviet attack on Western Europe or the United States, gave support to the unprecedented allocation of resources to the "peacetime" military establishment (Huntington, 1961; Liggio, 1972; Neu, 1987, pp. 91–2, 100–1; Rockman, 1987, pp. 18, 28–9). Having weakened somewhat under the strains of the Vietnam War controversy and its political aftermath, both the ideology and the consensus persisted, subject to a good deal of fraternal squabbling, notably within Congress.[18] President Reagan's rhetorical hostility toward the Soviet Union's "evil empire" and the generally hawkish stance of his administration, especially during Reagan's first term, gave renewed luster to the tarnished Cold War ideology. Despite the public's waning enthusiasm for foreign military adventures after the near-hysteria of 1980, events such as the U.S. invasion of Grenada and the Soviet downing of Korean Airlines flight 007 in 1983 were "carefully managed and interpreted by the [Reagan] administration" and "proved crucial, at least long enough to save the weapons buildup" (Page and Shapiro, 1992, p. 273).

The ideological milieu was important, indeed essential, in maintaining high levels of resource allocation to defense, but it was not sufficient. Ordinary citizens, almost none of whom had any direct contact with conditions or evidence bearing on national security, easily came to suspect that the nation's security did not really require such vast expenditures and that military interests, especially the uniformed services and the big weapons contractors, were using bogus threats as a pretext for siphoning off the taxpayers' money. Countless political cartoons, featuring bloated generals bedecked with rows of medals, promoted precisely such an attitude. Citizens did not need to be natural cynics. The problem of creeping skepticism was inherent in the remoteness of the subject from their immediate experience. In addition, as Huntington remarked, "The longer a given level of military force is apparently adequate for deterrence, the greater is the temptation to assume that a slightly lower level might be equally adequate" (Huntington, 1961, p. 205).

Frequent newspaper and television reports of waste, fraud, mismanagement, and bribery fostered the public's tendency, absent a crisis, to doubt what the defense authorities said. Popular books explained how the military-industrial-congressional complex formed an "iron triangle," exploiting the taxpayers, distorting defense policies, and blocking progress toward multilateral arms reductions.[19] As Gordon Adams explained, because no one knew the production function for national security, it was "difficult to correlate military expenditure levels to distinct improvements in national security. Citizens [could] only spend and hope." But "the indeterminate nature of the need to spend," along with the underlying Cold War ideology, created a potential for political leaders periodically to arouse the public's slumbering apprehensions.[20]

The tendency of chronic background threat to lose its efficacy in supporting high levels of military spending could be offset by episodic crises. In a perceived crisis, public opinion became volatile. Many people suspended their reason, critical faculties, and long-term judgment, reacting emotionally and with heightened deference to political leaders.[21] As Senator Arthur Vandenberg observed when Truman was first attempting to persuade the public to support a policy of containment in 1947, gaining such support required that national leaders "scare hell out of the American people" (Ambrose, 1985, p. 87). Sometimes the outside world presented an inviting opportunity to take advantage of a crisis, as when the North Koreans crossed the 38th parallel in 1950 or when the Soviets invaded Afghanistan at the end of 1979. Usually, however, the world did not supply such clear-cut cases, and the national security managers had to take matters into their own hands.

During the Cold War, the authorities alerted the public to a series of ominous "gaps."[22] Just after World War II, U.S. leaders exaggerated Soviet force levels and offensive capabilities. Of the fearsome 175 Soviet divisions, a third were undermanned and another third were ill-equipped militia (Kolodziej, 1966, p. 77; Isaacson and Thomas, 1986, p. 503). Then came a bomber gap in the mid-1950s and a missile gap between 1958 and 1961, followed within a few years by an antimissile gap and a first-strike missile gap. All were revealed in due course to have been false alarms. Meanwhile, the American people received an almost wholly fictitious account of incidents in the Gulf of Tonkin in 1964, which stampeded Congress into giving its blessing to what soon became a major war.[23] Subsequent gaps were alleged with regard to bombers (again), thermonuclear megatonnage, antisubmarine capabilities, and missile throw weights. An influential group of Republican hawks, calling themselves the Committee on the Present Danger, declared the 1970s to have been a "decade of neglect" that opened a dangerous "window of vulnerability." According to Secretary of Defense Caspar Weinberger, speaking in 1987, an "enormous gap" had "emerged since 1970 between the level of Soviet defense activities and our own," though, fortunately, the Reagan administration had "managed to close much of this gap."[24] Still, as the Cold War passed through its waning years, government spokesmen were warning that the country faced a Star Wars gap that could be closed only by spending vast amounts of money.[25]

Although not every gap scare led directly to a corresponding U.S. response, the drumbeat succession of such episodes helped to sustain an atmosphere of tension, distrust, and insecurity that fostered the maintenance of an enormous ongoing arms program. Claims about gaps placed the burden of argument on relatively ill-informed opponents of military spending. Among the general public, mood substituted for information—a situation that well suited the purposes of the defense establishment.

Throughout the Cold War, the national security elite, including the president; the National Security Council (NSC); the Joint Chiefs of Staff and a few other military leaders; a few congressional leaders; high officials of the State Department, the Defense Department, and the Central Intelligence Agency (CIA), plus the heads of other intelligence organizations; various aides, arms contractors, scientists, and consultants—altogether a small group of persons among whom only the president and vice-president held elective office—possessed a close hold on critical defense-related information. This situation sprang from origins in the National Security Act of 1947, which created the NSC and the CIA and "set in motion a cult of secrecy, a far more pervasive system of classifying information than had ever existed previously, and a growing executive determination to withhold sensitive information from the public and from Congress."²⁶ An NSC member once declared, "Policy decisions of the National Security Council are not a fit subject for public discussion" (Huntington, 1961, p. 183).

The need for a certain amount of secrecy was obvious to everybody, but many people suspected that, as Sidney Lens observed, "mostly, secrecy [was] used against the people of the United States."²⁷ Strategic decision-making was not the only area that was kept secret. A substantial portion of the spending for weapons development, intelligence gathering, and covert operations was financed from a "black budget" that, by the late 1980s, amounted to more than $30 billion per year. This budget was entirely shielded from congressional and public debate. As Harvey Sapolsky noted, "what no one knows, no one can criticize."²⁸

In view of their exclusive possession of critical information and their perceived need to "sell" their preferred policies to the public, the national security elite did not shrink from dissembling. As J. Russell Wiggins put it, "Our government repeatedly resorts to lies in crises, where lies seem to serve its interests best."²⁹ This easily documented observation, which may shock some citizens even in our own, less gullible times, does not surprise political scientists. Lance Bennett has observed that "Information about public issues is an inherently political commodity. It is concealed, revealed, leaked, released, classified, declassified, jargonized, simplified, and packaged symbolically according to the political interests of those ubiquitous 'informed sources' who have a stake in the outcome of the issue in question."³⁰ Manipulation of information is central to what modern governing elites do. Senator Daniel Patrick Moynihan, himself no stranger to the inner sanctums of government power, observed that "knowledge is power, and the ability to define what others take to be knowledge is the greatest power."³¹

The national security elite's close hold on critical information would not have been particularly noteworthy if the interests of the elite and the interests of the public had corresponded closely. But nothing in the workings of U.S. political institutions ensured that a close correspondence would always exist, and abundant historical evidence shows that it frequently did not. Plainly, leaders of the defense elite had interests of their own—

personal, political, institutional, material, and ideological—interests that they could serve through strategic retention, dissemination, or misrepresentation of the information to which they alone had access.[32]

They did not hesitate to exploit the advantages of their privileged access to information. The Iran-Contra affair and the Pentagon briberies and influence-peddling brought to light during the late 1980s were only two episodes in a long series of actions shielded by self-serving mendacity. "The entire sequence of decisions concerning the production and use of atomic weaponry," for example, took place "without any genuine public debate, and the facts needed to engage in that debate intelligently [were] officially hidden, distorted, and even lied about."[33] Beginning in World War II, the government operated a complex of facilities for manufacturing nuclear materials and weapons. These operations caused a variety of radioactive and other toxic contaminations of the surrounding air, water, and soil; yet, the managers of the facilities repeatedly misrepresented and lied about the hazards to citizens living nearby. In at least one case of huge significance—the so-called "green run" at Hanford, Washington, in 1949—the operators deliberately released a large quantity of nuclear materials, including some 7,780 curies of iodine 131, onto the unwitting residents of the surrounding area, as part of an experiment.[34]

Nothing in what I have just said means that the national security elite could do anything they wished. If they could have, retrenchments of the military establishment would not have occurred after the buildups. Certainly, the steep decline of 1968–76, especially its later phase, which defense interests stoutly opposed, would not have been so steep. The fact that the allocation of resources to defense did sometimes fall, and fall substantially, refutes radical arguments that allege the exercise of hegemony by the national security establishment.[35] Although one must appreciate the tremendous political resources possessed by the defense elite, it is possible—and not unusual—to overestimate its strength. It lost some political battles, too. That is why, during the late 1980s, notwithstanding the preceding buildup, the defense share of GNP never exceeded 7 percent (see figure 6-2). Defense interests had the political savvy to appreciate that proposals or actions that were widely perceived as excessively grasping and strategically unjustified would be imprudent and counterproductive. More important, however, were the domestic factors that constrained the defense managers in spite of their unique control of information and their consequent ability to mold, rather than respond to, public opinion.[36]

The biggest problem for defense authorities who were intent on exploiting ideology, controlling information, and molding public opinion arose from that proverbially inevitable duo: death and taxes. Those were the most evident forms taken by the costs of extensive commitments of resources to military purposes. Of the two, death was the more important. John Mueller fitted statistical models to public opinion data gathered during the Korean War and the Vietnam War, and he found that, in both cases, "every time American casualties increased by a factor of 10, support for the war dropped by about 15 percentage points" (Mueller, 1973, pp. 60–1). Robert Smith reported public opinion data showing that "complaints about taxes were high during the two limited wars and increased as the wars progressed."[37]

As Smith's data illustrate, opportunity costs constantly constrained military activities throughout the Cold War. In the crisis of 1948, and immediately afterward, Truman resisted recommendations for a huge increase in military spending facilitated by either increasing taxes or imposing economic controls because "he was convinced that these courses were not economically or politically feasible" (Kolodziej, 1966, pp. 91, 119–20). In the wake of the Soviets' Sputnik success, Eisenhower opposed the Gaither Committee's recommendation for a big buildup because he had "a nagging fear that the American people would balk at paying the bill."[38] Given this abiding popular resistance, it was only to be expected that, as Hugh Mosley noted, the Johnson administration "was reluctant to resort to increased taxes to finance the [Vietnam] war for fear of losing public support for its policy of military escalation."[39] Nixon was said to have "realized that for economic reasons (the war was simply costing too much) and for the sake of domestic peace and tranquility he had to cut back on the American commitment to Vietnam"; the retrenchment was "forced on [him] by public opinion" (Ambrose, 1985, pp. 242–3). Jacques Gansler observed that, during the 1970s, "the will of the people, who were fed up with the war in Vietnam, was to devote all available resources toward improving the peacetime life of the nation."[40] Yet, at the same time, rising real marginal tax rates inspired tax revolts, limiting the capacity of government to supply more nonmilitary goods. Something had to give. Of the political factions struggling, in effect, over the three grand categories of GNP, the pro-military faction proved the weakest, at least until 1979.

When the national security elite lacked persuasive rationales to present to the public, they could only draw on the pool of patriotism. But that was not a bottomless reservoir, and without replenishment from sources that the public could understand and support, it tended to run dry (Rosecrance, 1986, pp. 38, 131, 158; Higgs, 1987, pp. 64–5; Ambrose, 1985, pp. 249–50). When it did, public opinion could not be effectively controlled by the authorities. As the opinion balance became strongly negative, it worked its way through political processes, reaching both Congress and the administration, to affect the allocation of resources to the military.[41]

Figure 6-6, which is based on 193 comparable, nationally representative surveys in which people were asked whether they would prefer that defense spending be increased, decreased, or kept the same, shows a summary variable, opinion balance, which is defined as the percentage of respondents stating that they want an increase minus the percentage stating that they want a decrease. Despite the gaps in the record, the figure shows clearly the positive (but sometimes just barely positive) support for increased spending in the 1950s and 1960s (through 1967); the strong preference for reduced spending, at least from 1968 until the late 1970s; the strong support for increased spending from 1979 through 1981; and the substantial balance in favor of reduced spending thereafter.[42]

Political histories also provide evidence that the wartime administrations reacted, with variable lags, to swings of public opinion. The Korean War made President Truman increasingly unpopular as it dragged on (Mueller, 1973, p. 199; Rees, 1970, pp. 386–87). Eisenhower gained election to the presidency in 1952 largely on the strength of his promise to end the war, a promise he hastened to keep (Huntington, 1957, p. 391; Cotton, 1986,

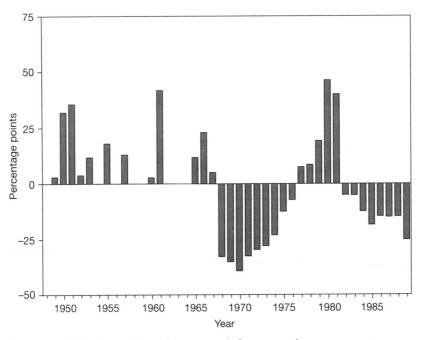

Figure 6-6. Public opinion balance on defense spending, 1949–1989.

p. 630). Johnson declined to seek reelection in 1968 because of mounting opposition to his war policy (Berman, 1989, pp. 176–203; Cotton, 1986, pp. 630–1; Russett and Graham, 1989, p. 252; Matusow, 1984, pp. 376–94). The Nixon administration devoted itself to winding down American participation in the fighting, ending the draft, and eventually withdrawing all U.S. forces from Vietnam, for which it was rewarded with a landslide re-election in 1972 (Cotton, 1986, pp. 631–2). At the very peak of the Reagan buildup, Secretary of Defense Caspar Weinberger complained that "new weapons can be developed by our adversaries . . . much more rapidly because [in the USSR] there are no funding restraints imposed by public opinion" (Weinberger, 1987, p. 16). Ultimately, not even the national security elite could control public opinion, which responded to the heightened opportunity costs of defense programs and actual warfare just as a rational consumer would move toward the northwest along a demand curve.[43]

Conclusion

The Cold War era witnessed a new relation of military activity to the political economy of the United States. Before World War II, the allocation of resources to military purposes remained at token levels, typically no more than 1 percent of GNP, except during actual warfare, which occurred infrequently. Wartime and peacetime were distinct, and during peacetime—that is, nearly all the time—the societal opportunity cost of "guns" was nearly nil. The old regime ended in 1940. The massive mobilization of the early 1940s drove the military share of GNP to more than 41 percent at its peak in 1943–44.[44] Despite an enormous demobilization after the war ended, in 1947, at the postwar trough, the military sector still accounted for 4.3 percent of GNP, three times the 1939 share. Following the Korean War, military purchases reached an unprecedented level for "peacetime" and, while fluctuating, remained at or above this elevated level ever afterward. During the period 1948–89, military purchases cumulated to more than $7 trillion (1982 dollars), averaging about $168 billion annually, or 7.5 percent of GNP. The trend tilted slightly upward for absolute real spending and slightly downward for spending as a share of GNP. Increases in the military share of GNP during the Korean War and the Vietnam War came entirely at the expense of the private share. The government nonmilitary share increased during the first two post-World War II military buildups, and remained approximately constant during the third. Examining GNP*, defined as GNP minus all defense spending, one finds that this measure of national product often moved differently from conventional GNP. The largest discrepancies occurred during the early 1950s. These discrepancies suggest the desirability of reassessing the business cycle in its relation to economic well-being during those years. After the mid-1950s, the difference between the growth rates of GNP and GNP* tended to diminish, becoming nearly negligible during the 1980s.

The high base level of defense spending during the Cold War resulted from the dominant ideology of global anti-communism, which called forth various foreign policy doctrines (e.g., the Truman Doctrine, massive retaliation, the Reagan Doctrine) and military commitments (e.g., NATO, bilateral defense treaties, U.S. military "advisers" in Latin America). The ideology alone, however, was an insufficient prop, and episodic crises played an essential part in maintaining public support for vast military expenditures. The national security elite warned of one "gap" after another, most of which turned out to be exaggerated or nonexistent. Given the secrecy in which much defense-related information was held, it was inevitable that the national security elite would use its unique access to information to promote its own interests, which were sometimes in conflict with public preferences. There were limits, however, and in political struggles, military interests sometimes lost. The authorities could not always effectively mislead the citizenry, especially when many deaths and increasing taxes (including unanticipated inflation) were involved. But the constraints on policymakers, being subject to informational and ideological displacement and responsive to perceived crisis, were themselves elastic and manipulable.

Notes

1. On my own bookshelf I have ten textbooks on American economic history that were published between 1972 and 1990. Of these, none has a chapter or even a section on the Cold War economy as such, though one has two pages devoted to "Planning and Stability: The Role of Military Spending" and another has a two-paragraph section on "The Role of Military Spending" in relation to the postwar growth of government. Only one has an entry for "Cold War" in the index, but the reference is to a merely incidental mention. Most make only passing comments on the Korean War and the Vietnam War and no remarks at all on military activities or expenditures during the "peacetime" years since World War II.

2. I am not concerned in this chapter with how the opportunity costs of changes in the military part of GNP were divided between consumption and investment. For an analysis of this question, see Edelstein (1990). Edelstein's conclusion that private consumption, rather than private investment, absorbed the full cost of additional defense spending in the period from 1946 to 1979 is consistent with the conclusion of Murray Weidenbaum (1992, p. 115) and sources cited there. Because of the heavy debt financing that accompanied the Reagan buildup in the 1980s, I suspect that some crowding out of investment occurred then, even if not earlier.

3. See Higgs (1992) and Higgs (1987, pp. 220–36) and sources cited there.

4. The source of all basic data for GNP, its components, and the implicit GNP deflator, unless otherwise indicated, is U.S. Council of Economic Advisers (1991, pp. 286–90).

Notice that here and hereafter in this essay national defense spending is defined rather narrowly, as in the national income and product accounts. Other analysts have included some or all of the government's spending for space exploration, research, education, and veterans' services, as well as the costs of the Department of State and foreign aid. For some purposes, it is appropriate to add some or all of these items. Because of the uncertainty with respect to how much of them ought to be considered "national defense" expenditures and because the narrower definition used here allows one to make a better grounded, more conservative case, these more problematical items are left out of the present analysis. For the same reason, I make no adjustment for the fact that a substantial part of military manpower was conscripted between 1948 and 1972. Obviously, conscription gives rise to an accounting understatement of the opportunity costs of military activities, but making a reliable estimate of the amount of the understatement would require research far beyond the scope of the present essay.

5. See Isaacson and Thomas (1986, pp. 393–4). See also Kolodziej (1966, pp. 35–6, 67–8) and Ambrose (1985, pp. 71, 79–82, 93–4).

6. See Donovan (1977, pp. 357–61), Ambrose (1985, pp. 95–7), Kolodziej (1966, p. 72), and Page and Shapiro (1992, pp. 200–1, 206–9). Page and Shapiro (p. 209) conclude that "during the early Cold War [in the late 1940s], U.S. public opinion can be said, to a significant extent, to have been manipulated"—that is, deliberately misled by the authorities. This is not to say, of course, that the events propelling the United States into the Cold War were completely concocted—far from it—but then, as often thereafter, the foreign policy decision makers, perceiving a need to respond to threats, found it useful to exaggerate the threats when dealing with the public and Congress.

7. See Huntington (1957, p. 384), Huntington (1961, pp. 47–53), Mosley (1985), and Ambrose (1985, pp. 113–15). According to Morton Halperin, the authors of NSC-68 "made a deliberate decision to exaggerate possible dangers" (Halperin, as quoted by Schneider, 1988, p. 67). At the same time, they steered clear of revealing how great the costs would be. Secretary of State Dean Acheson instructed Paul Nitze, the principal author of NSC-68, not to mention costs in the report (Weiner, 1990, p. 30).

8. Isaacson and Thomas (1986, p. 504 [Acheson quote p. 513]). See also Huntington (1957, pp. 364, 382–4, 445–6), Huntington (1961, pp. 53–64), Mosley (1985, pp. 11, 13, 173), Ambrose (1985, pp. 113–31), Kolodziej (1966, pp. 124–56), and Page and Shapiro (1992, pp. 209–14).

9. Here I part company with, among others, Richard A. Stubbing (1986, pp. 14, 97). But Stubbing's own account seems inconsistent; compare pp. 299, 327–30. See also Mosley (1985, pp. 174–7).

10. Mosley (1985, p. 29). Economic statisticians have identified serious shortcomings in the construction of deflators for defense purchases. Statisticians at the Commerce Department's Bureau of Economic Analysis, who created such an index at the request of the Defense Department, have themselves stated that the index is inappropriate for calculating reliable weapons-specific price changes. Existing indexes do not deal satisfactorily with quality changes in equipment, among other things. See Weida and Gertcher (1987, p. 63) and Smith (1989, pp. 350–1). Ziemer and Galbraith (1983, pp. 147–99) offer a more complacent view (the authors are employed by the Bureau of Economic Analysis), but see the comment by Manser that follows their essay.

11. For a discussion of the various sources and measures of military spending, see Mosley (1985, pp. 17–44).

12. Of course, the more characteristic type of spending of the welfare state, government transfer payments, increased even more enormously. But because these payments are not for immediate purchase of currently produced goods and services—that is, they are not components of GNP—they lie outside the scope of the present analysis. My analysis here and in the following three paragraphs disagrees fundamentally with the interpretation of similar data by Du Boff (1989, pp. 6–7).

13. In personal communications, Stanley Lebergott and Hugh Rockoff reminded me that many privately purchased goods also ought to be viewed as intermediate. Indeed, the approaches to consumer theory pioneered by Kevin Lancaster and Gary Becker proceed from precisely this understanding. One can grant this objection and still insist that national security differs so greatly from the typical private good in this respect as to present a qualitatively different case.

14. Ultimately, Kuznets seems to have concluded that GNP even for a period that includes World War II should be measured by a "peacetime concept." For a discussion of Kuznets's arguments, see Higgs (1992).

15. As Hugh Rockoff has told me, it depends on the question. For example, one might want to use standard GNP rather than GNP* in estimating the demand for money.

16. See Ostrom (1978, p. 955), Domke, Eichenberg, and Kelleher (1983, pp. 30- 31), and Ostrom and Marra (1986, pp. 824–39). Schneider (1988) assesses several other factors as well.

17. Informative analyses of the Carter-Reagan buildup include Korb (1979, pp. 151–64), Stubbing (1986, pp. 12–30), Mosley (1985, pp. 145–60), Ostrom and Marra (1986, pp. 819–42), Kaufmann (1986), Lurtwak (1984), and Page and Shapiro (1992, pp. 264–71, 335, 368). The external events included (what was perceived to be) a rapid Soviet arms buildup, the Iranian hostage-taking at the U.S. embassy, and the Soviet invasion of Afghanistan. The rest of the momentum derived from the Reagan team and its political supporters, before as well as after Reagan took office.

18. All sides agree. For testimony from a variety of ideological perspectives, see Isaacson and Thomas (1986, pp. 369, 725, and passim), Ambrose (1985, pp. 221–2 and passim), Rosenberg (1973), Sanders (1973, pp. 176–7, 186–7, 201–2), U.S. Senate, Staff of the Committee on Armed Services (1985, p. 573), Lens (1987, pp. 43–4), Cypher (1982, pp. 10–15), Navarro (1984, pp. 259–62, 273–5), and Weinberger (1987, pp. 15, 41–50).

19. Prominent examples include Mills (1956), Fitzgerald (1972), Adams (1982), and Lens (1987).

20. See Adams (1977, p. 467). See also Mancur Olson, as quoted in Mosley (1985, p. 19), and Weida and Gertcher (1987, pp. 50, 54, 78). From an analysis of public opinion data for the six years from 1973 to 1978, a period lacking any great foreign-policy crisis, Kriesberg and Klein (1980, pp. 106–7) concluded that "a latent readiness to support defense spending . . . can be evoked and sustained by established authority figures" and that, although instrumental thinking is sometimes important, "ideology also contributes significantly to explaining variations in attitudes about defense spending."

21. See Huntington (1961, pp. 202,214–15), Bennett (1980, pp. 113–17, 216–19), Higgs (1987, pp. 17–18, 62–7, and passim), and Rockman (1987, pp. 21–7, 32, 36–7). Page and Shapiro

(1992, p. 222) note that "abrupt opinion changes occur most often in times of war or international turmoil, not in times of peace."

22. Huntington described U.S. military forecasts between 1946 and 1960 as "a series of prophecies of disaster which never materialized" (1961, pp. 428–9).

23. See Ambrose (1985, pp. 212–13); Lens (1987, pp. 73–4, 123); and Kwitney (1984, pp. 357–359). Page and Shapiro (1992, p. 227) call the Tonkin Gulf affair "a classic case of opinion manipulation." They note that (p. 228) "the administration had made contingency plans for striking at North Vietnam and had prepared a draft congressional resolution for introduction at the appropriate moment."

24. See Weinberger (1987, p. 17). Page and Shapiro (1992, p. 269) observe that the Reagan administration "misrepresented the arms balance long enough to take credit for 'restoring' U.S. strength."

25. On the gaps, compare Navarro (1984, p. 240), Stubbing (1986, pp. xiii, 14–25), Lens, (1987, pp. 170–1), Huntington (1961, pp. 428–9 and passim), Ambrose (1985, p. 168), and Weiner (1990, pp. 19–45).

26. See Carpenter (1986, p. 6). See also Huntington (1961, pp. 184–8), Mills (1956, pp. 293–4, 355), Lens (1987, p. 38), Sanders (1973, pp. 206–7), Adams (1977, pp. 467–74, 486; 1982, pp. 95–6), Stubbing (1986, pp. 56, 110), and Neu (1987, pp. 89–90, 98–100).

27. See Lens (1987, p. 44). For an insightful analysis of national security policymaking that proceeds from an explicit recognition of the distinction between the nation and the government that rules the nation, see Hummel and Lavoie (1990).

28. See Sapolsky (1987, p. 122). On the black budget, see Weiner (1990).

29. Wiggins, as quoted by Lens (1987, p. 119; see also pp. 122, 130, 168, 172). For a well-documented survey of the landmark foreign- and defense-policy events involving what they call the "manipulation" (deliberate misleading) of public opinion by government leaders during a period of fifty-five years since the beginning of scientific polling, see Page and Shapiro (1992, pp. 172–284, 367–72).

30. See Bennett (1980, p. 311). See also "Lies: The Government and the Press," in Kwitney (1984, pp. 355–78).

31. Moynihan, as quoted by Stubbing (1986, p. 5). See also Mills (1956, pp. 220, 222).

32. Friendly critics have pointed out to me that defense policy is not especially outstanding in these regards: any kind of political interest group, whether inside or outside the government, tries to control or slant information in the service of its policy ends. The distinction I insist on, however, arises from the unique capacity of defense policymakers to determine what information others can acquire about specific facts and to distort the public's understanding of the context within which the policy will be implemented. In domestic policy, the closeness of the policy context to a variety of observers, some of whom are partisan opponents of the officials in power, makes information distortion and management much less rewarding for the authorities.

33. Mills (1956, p. 355). See also Huntington (1957, pp. 382–4; 1961, pp. 113–14, 303, 305) and Weiner (1990, pp. 19–28).

34. See Marshall (1986, pp. 613–15), Steele (1988, pp. 17–23), and Stenehjem (1990, pp. 6–22). On a closely related subject, see Shulman (1992).

35. For arguments that strongly suggest, if they do not explicitly allege, that such hegemony was exercised, see Lens (1987), Adams (1977), and Cypher (1982).
36. On the resistance of public opinion to official manipulation, see Page and Shapiro (1992, pp. 274–81). These researchers observe that (p. 279) "when information is available that can support critical analyses, especially when elites differ, opinion manipulation is very difficult"
37. See Smith (1971, p. 250). See also Kolodziej (1966, pp. 156–7) and Page and Shapiro (1992, pp. 213, 237–42, 333–4).
38. Eisenhower, as quoted by Huntington (1961, p. 113). See also Neu (1987, p. 89).
39. Mosley (1985, p. 153). See also Matusow (1984, pp. 153–79).
40. Gansler (1980, p. 22). See also Neu (1987, pp. 100).
41. See Ostrom (1978, p. 954); Ostrom and Marra (1986, pp. 830–9); and Russett (1990, 98–100). More definitive documentation and analysis of the asserted relation between public opinion and defense spending appears in the essay by Higgs and Kilduff (1993).
42. Figure 6-6 is based on opinion survey data underlying the work of Higgs and Kilduff (1993). The figure indicates that public opinion tended to turn against support for further military buildup as each buildup proceeded, but it also shows that the three highest peaks of pro-military opinion all occurred in conjunction with a crisis: the North Korean and Chinese invasions in Korea in 1950, the Berlin crisis of 1961, and the aftermath of the Iranian hostage-taking and the Soviet invasion of Afghanistan in November and December 1979.
43. For an analytical survey of the extensive literature on the relation of public opinion to defense policy, see Russett and Graham (1989). The authors conclude that "governments lose popularity directly in proportion to the length and cost (in blood and money) of the war" (pp. 243, 245). Public opinion unquestionably affects policy, but the relation is complex. "Leaders in a real sense interact with public opinion, both responding to it and manipulating it." See also Russett (1990, pp. 87–118). From a statistical and historical study, Cotton (1986, p. 632), concludes: "Over the past century war has had a significant, detrimental, and independent [electoral] effect on elected leaders of the 'war party.' The degree of the effect seems to have depended on the level of commitment of the nation's resources to the war effort." Finally, see Page and Shapiro's extensive historical analysis of public opinion in relation to foreign and defense policy (1992, pp. 172–284 and passim).
44. For reasons discussed by Higgs (1992), the 41 percent figure can be taken only as suggestive. No genuinely meaningful national product accounting is possible in the institutional context of a command economy, which is what the United States had from 1942 through 1945.

References

Adams, Gordon M. (1977) Disarming the Military Subgovernment. *Harvard Journal on Legislation* 14: 459–503.

Adams, Gordon M. (1982) *The Politics of Defense Contracting: The Iron Triangle.* New Brunswick, N.J.: Transaction. Ambrose, Stephen E. (1985) *Rise to Globalism: American Foreign Policy Since 1938,* fourth edition. New York: Penguin.

Bennett, W. Lance. (1980) *Public Opinion in American Politics.* New York: Harcourt Brace Jovanovich.

Berman, Larry. (1989) *Lyndon Johnson's War: The Road to Stalemate in Vietnam.* New York: W. W. Norton.

Carpenter, Ted Galen. (1986) Global Interventionism and a New Imperial Presidency. *Cato Institute Policy Analysis No. 71* (May 16).

Cotton, Timothy Y. C. (1986) War and American Democracy: Electoral Costs of the Last Five Wars. *Journal of Conflict Resolution* 30: 616–35.

Cypher, James M. (1982) Ideological Hegemony and Modern Militarism: The Origins and Limits of Military Keynesianism. *Economic Forum* 13: 1–20.

Domke, William K., Richard C. Eichenberg, and Catherine M. Kelleher. (1983) The Illusion of Choice: Defense and Welfare in Advanced Industrial Democracies, 1948–1978. *American Political Science Review* 77: 19–35.

Donovan, Robert J. (1977) *Conflict and Crisis: The Presidency of Harry S Truman, 1945–1948.* New York: W. W. Norton.

Du Boff, Richard B. (1989) What Military Spending Really Costs. *Challenge* (September/October): 4–10.

Dumas, Lloyd J. (1990) Economic Power, Military Power, and National Security. *Journal of Economic Issues* 24: 653–61.

Edelstein, Michael. (1990) What Price Cold War? Military Spending and Private Investment in the US, 1946–1979. *Cambridge Journal of Economics* 14: 421–37.

Fitzgerald, A. Ernest. (1972) *The High Priests of Waste.* New York: W. W. Norton.

Gansler, Jacques S. (1980) *The Defense Industry.* Cambridge, Mass.: M.I.T. Press.

Higgs, Robert. (1987) *Crisis and Leviathan: Critical Episodes in the Growth of American Government.* New York: Oxford University Press.

Higgs, Robert. (1988) Hard Coals Make Bad Law: Congressional Parochialism versus National Defense. *Cato Journal* 8: 79–106.

Higgs, Robert. (1989) Beware the Pork-Hawk. *Reason* 21: 28–34.

Higgs, Robert. (1992) Wartime Prosperity? A Reassessment of the U.S. Economy in the 1940s. *Journal of Economic History* 52: 41–60.

Higgs, Robert, and Anthony Kilduff. (1993) Public Opinion: A Powerful Predictor of U.S. Defense Spending. *Defence Economics* 4: 227–38.

Hummel, Jeffrey Rogers, and Don Lavoie. (1990) National Defense and the Public-Goods Problem. In *Arms, Politics, and the Economy: Historical and Contemporary Perspectives,* edited by Robert Higgs. New York: Homes & Meier for The Independent Institute, pp. 37–60.

Huntington, Samuel P. (1957) *The Soldier and the State: The Theory and Politics of Civil-Military Relations.* Cambridge, Mass.: Harvard University Press.

Huntington, Samuel P. (1961) *The Common Defense: Strategic Programs in National Politics.* New York: Columbia University Press.

Isaacson, Walter, and Evan Thomas. (1986) *The Wise Men: Six Friends and the World They Made—Acheson, Bohlen, Harriman, Kennan, Lovett, McCloy.* New York: Simon and Schuster.

Kaufmann, William W. (1986) *A Reasonable Defense.* Washington: Brookings.

Kolodziej, Edward A. (1966) *The Uncommon Defense and Congress, 1945–1963.* Columbus, Ohio: Ohio State University Press.

Korb, Lawrence J. (1979) *The Fall and Rise of the Pentagon: American Defense Policies in the 1970s.* Westport, Conn.: Greenwood.15Kriesberg,

Louis, and Ross Klein. (1980) Changes in Public Support for U.S. Military Spending. *Journal of Conflict Resolution* 24: 79–111.

Kwitney, Jonathan. (1984) *Endless Enemies: The Making of an Unfriendly World.* New York: Congdon and Weed.

Lens, Sidney. (1987) *Permanent War: The Militarization of America.* New York: Schocken.

Liggio, Leonard P. (1972) American Foreign Policy and National-Security Management. In *A New History of Leviathan: Essays on the Rise of the American Corporate State,* edited by Ronald Radosh and Murray N. Rothbard. New York: E. P. Dutton, pp. 224–59.

Luttwak, Edward N. (1984) *The Pentagon and the Art of War.* New York: Simon and Schuster.

MacArthur, Douglas. (1965) *A Soldier Speaks: Public Papers and Speeches of General of the Army Douglas MacArthur,* edited by Vorin E. Whan, Jr. New York: Praeger.

Manser, Marilyn. (1983) Comment. In *The U.S. National Income and Product Accounts: Selected Topics,* edited by Murray F. Foss. Chicago: University of Chicago Press, pp. 199–203.

Marshall, Eliot. (1986) The Buried Cost of the Savannah River Plant. *Science* 233: 613–15.

Matusow, Allen J. (1984) *The Unraveling of America: A History of Liberalism in the 1960s.* New York: Harper and Row.

Mills, C. Wright. (1956) *The Power Elite.* New York: Oxford University Press.

Mosley, Hugh G. (1985) *The Arms Race: Economic and Social Consequences.* Lexington, Mass.: D. C. Heath.

Mueller, John E. (1973) *War, Presidents, and Public Opinion.* New York: John Wiley.

Navarro, Peter. (1984) *The Policy Game: How Special Interests and Ideologues Are Stealing America.* New York: John Wiley.

Neu, Charles E. (1987) The Rise of the National Security Bureaucracy. In *The New American State: Bureaucracies and Politics since World War II,* edited by Louis Galambos. Baltimore: Johns Hopkins University Press, pp. 85–108.

Ostrom, Charles W. (1978) A Reactive Linkage Model of the U.S. Defense Expenditure Policymaking Process. *American Political Science Review* 72: 941–57.

Ostrom, Charles W., and Robin F. Marra. (1986) U.S. Defense Spending and the Soviet Estimate. *American Political Science Review* 80: 824–39.

Page, Benjamin L, and Robert Y. Shapiro. (1992) *The Rational Public: Fifty Years of Trends in Americans' Policy Preferences.* Chicago: University of Chicago Press.

Rees, David. (1970) *Korea: The Limited War.* Baltimore: Penguin.

Rockman, Bert A. (1987) Mobilizing Political Support for U.S. National Security. *Armed Forces & Society* 14: 17–41.

Rosecrance, Richard. (1986) *The Rise of the Trading State: Commerce and Conquest in the Modern World.* New York: Basic Books.

Rosenberg, Douglas H. (1973) Arms and the American Way: The Ideological Dimension of Military Growth. In *Military Force and American Society,* edited by Bruce M. Russett and Alfred Stepan. New York: Harper and Row, pp. 170–92.

Russett, Bruce M. (1990) *Controlling the Sword: The Democratic Governance of National Security.* Cambridge, Mass.: Harvard University Press.

Russett, Bruce M., and Thomas W. Graham. (1989) Public Opinion and National Security Policy: Relationships and Impacts. In *Handbook of War Studies,* edited by Manus I. Midlarsky. Boston: Unwin-Hyman, pp. 239–57.

Sanders, Ralph. (1973) *The Politics of Defense Analysis.* New York: Dunellen.

Sapolsky, Harvey M. (1987) Equipping the Armed Forces. *Armed Forces & Society* 14: 113–28.

Schneider, Ernest. (1988) Causal Factors in Variations in US Postwar Defense Spending. *Defense Analysis* 4: 53–79.

Shulman, Seth. (1992) *The Threat at Home: Confronting the Toxic Legacy of the U.S. Military.* Boston: Beacon Press.

Smith, Richard B. (1971) Disaffection, Delegitimation, and Consequences. In *Public Opinion and the Military Establishment,* edited by Charles C. Moskos, Jr. Beverly Hills, Calif.: Sage, pp. 221–51.

Smith, R. P. (1989) Models of Military Expenditure. *Journal of Applied Econometrics* 4: 345–59.

Spindler, Z. A. (1982) The Overstated Economy: Implications of Positive Public Economics for National Accounting. *Public Choice* 38: 181–96.

Steele, Karen Dorn. (1988) Hanford's Bitter Legacy. *Bulletin of the Atomic Scientists* (January/February): 17–23.

Stenehjem, Michele. (1990) Indecent Exposure. *Natural History* (September): 6–22.

Stubbing, Richard A. (1986) *The Defense Game.* New York: Harper and Row.

Twight, Charlotte. (1990) Department of Defense Attempts to Close Military Bases: The Political Economy of Congressional Resistance. In *Arms, Politics, and the Economy: Historical and Contemporary Perspectives,* edited by Robert Higgs. New York: Homes & Meier for The Independent Institute, pp. 236–80.

U.S. Bureau of the Census. (1975) *Historical Statistics of the United States, Colonial Times to 1970.* Washington, D.C.: Government Printing Office.

U.S. Council of Economic Advisers. (1991) *Annual Report, 1991.* Washington, D.C.: Government Printing Office.

U.S. Senate, Staff of the Committee on Armed Services. (1985) *Defense Organization: The Need for Change.* Washington, D.C.: Government Printing Office.

Weida, William J., and Frank L. Gertcher. (1987) *The Political Economy of National Defense.* Boulder, Colo.: Westview Press.

Weidenbaum, Murray. (1992) *Small Wars, Big Defense: Paying for the Military After the Cold War.* New York: Oxford University Press.

Weinberger, Caspar W. (1987) *Annual Report of the Secretary of Defense to the Congress, Fiscal Year 1988.* Washington, D.C.: Government Printing Office.

Weiner, Tim. (1990) *Blank Check: The Pentagon's Black Budget.* New York: Warner Books.

Ziemer, Richard C., and Karl D. Galbraith. (1983) Deflation of Defense Purchases. In *The U.S. National Income and Product Accounts: Selected Topics,* edited by Murray F. Foss. Chicago: University of Chicago Press, pp. 147–99.

Acknowledgment For comments on previous drafts and presentations, I am grateful to Lee Alston, Ted Carpenter, Price Fishback, Chris Grandy, Stan Lebergott, Dwight Lee, Dennis Mueller, Hugh Rockoff, Murray Rothbard, Bruce Russett, Andy Rutten, Gordon Tullock, and especially Charlotte Twight. I also thank the participants in a Peace Studies Program seminar at Cornell University, economic history workshops at Northwestern University and the University of Illinois, and a session at the meetings of the Public Choice Society.

7

Hard Coals Make Bad Law

*Congressional Parochialism
versus National Defense*

THE U.S. NATIONAL DEFENSE PROGRAM is very expensive and notoriously plagued by waste, fraud, and mismanagement. Members of Congress, whose duty it is to oversee the program, often complain about it and take various actions, ostensibly to repair its flaws. Unfortunately, as Representative James Courter (R-N.J.) has said, "Congress is not the answer to waste. Congress is the problem." Economist Herbert Stein, a member of the Packard Commission, has observed that major defense problems "are compounded when the decisions move to Congress." The root of congressional misfeasance, says Stein, is that "hardly anyone [in Congress] feels a primary responsibility for the defense program as the safeguard of our national security. Too many are able to look upon the defense budget as a big pot of money from which they can serve their special interests."[1]

Analysts often dismiss this aspect of defense budget waste as "small potatoes." But is it? In the 1980s, Assistant Defense Secretary Lawrence Korb estimated that the congressional pork barrel cost "at least $10 billion a year [for] things we don't want, things we don't need," but which are put into the budget "to protect vested interest." Richard Stubbing, a longtime defense specialist at the Office of Management and Budget, considers Korb's estimate probably too low.[2] The defense pork barrel looks small only in relation to the gargantuan total defense budget. In any other context, it looks like "real money."

After presenting some facts and arguments pertaining to Congress in general, I shall tell the story of a congressional boondoggle involving the use

197

of anthracite coal. It is one of the many "small potatoes" measures embedded in the defense program. Viewed in isolation, it lacks earth-shattering importance. Yet, it is instructive. Its elements, so visible and so utterly inexcusable from the standpoint of genuine concern for national security, show how and why in other, often more costly ways the members of Congress treat the defense program as a means to serve their own selfish, parochial, and wasteful ends.

Congress: Incentives, Structures, and Strategies

The first thing to notice about members of Congress is that they have a job. They have worked hard to get it and, with few exceptions, they want to keep it. Congress, as political scientists have shown, has become a career for many of its members. Because in modern times some 90 percent of members stand for reelection and about 90 percent of those who do are reelected, Congress consists mainly of people who have spent a long time in the job and who expect to spend many more years in it. Between 1969 and 1986, incumbents averaged about 11 years of service (Davidson and Oleszek, 1985, pp. 37–40; Fiorina, 1977, pp. 39–40, 60, and passim; Mayhew, 1974, pp. 5–6, 16,49, and passim). They may be interested in contributing to good public policy—no doubt some are so interested, always according to their own ideological predilections, of course—but reelection must be their proximate goal. To achieve their policy goals, they must remain in the job. As a former congressman wrote, "All members of Congress have a primary interest in getting reelected. Some members have no other interest"[3]

Accordingly, they strive ceaselessly to gain the approval of a majority of those who will cast ballots in their districts at the next election. Representatives, in particular, are "always running." But senators, whose longer terms give them more breathing room, cannot afford to grow complacent, because their probability of reelection is substantially lower than that of House members: 75 percent versus 91 percent for elections between 1946 and 1984; 75 percent versus 98 percent in 1986 (Davidson and Oleszek, 1985, p. 62; Jackson, 1988). Incumbents need not worry much about conditions or opinions elsewhere in the nation or the world. Retention of the job turns on satisfying a majority of voters in *one's electoral district.*

In this quest, they might support measures that promote the public good at minimum cost to the taxpayers at large. Unfortunately, such behavior fails to win many votes. Voters recognize that a single vote in Congress rarely decides an issue. Even if it should, benefits that flow to others are heavily discounted. In assigning responsibility for laws and policies of national application, voters typically view the actions of a single legislator as inconsequential.

Most voters are realistic and self-interested: they are always asking, in Alben Barkley's immortal words, "What have you done for me lately?" Public opinion surveys confirm that voters want their political representatives to "bring home the bacon." In political scientist Morris Fiorina's words, "Each of us wishes to receive a maximum of benefits from government for the minimum cost. This goal suggests maximum government efficiency, on the one hand, but it also suggests mutual exploitation, on the other. Each of us favors an arrangement in which our fellow citizens pay for our benefits."[4]

Understanding voters' wishes, members of Congress promote themselves by establishing plausible claims to have channeled benefits toward and costs away from their constituents. They and their staffs spend much time on "casework," helping individual citizens cope with the terrors of government bureaucracy. Beyond casework, members of Congress strive to claim credit for "particularized benefits" that enhance the well-being of their constituents and are not available to everyone. Constituents especially value federal contracts and subsidies to local businesses; grants to local governments, schools, training programs, and sanitation facilities; federally funded dams and irrigation works; targeted loans and loan guarantees; military bases; and interstate highways and other construction projects in the district. Representatives and senators can make more politically valuable claims when they are able to point to apparently ad hoc federal largess. Political scientists disagree about the precise effect of particularized benefits on elections. But incumbents have no doubts. "The lore is that they count—furthermore, given home expectations, that they must be supplied in regular quantities for a member to stay electorally even with the board."[5]

Some members bring home more bacon than others. Much of the real action in Congress happens in committees and subcommittees, "small-group settings in which individual congressmen can make things happen and be perceived to make things happen."[6] So members need to belong to the committees that have jurisdiction over the sorts of particularized benefits that they wish to channel to their constituents. When a member seeks a minor favor, "the bureaucracy considers his accommodations a small price to pay for the goodwill its cooperation will produce, particularly if he has any connection to the substantive committee or the appropriations subcommittee to which it reports."[7]

One's influence on committees expands with seniority. Despite the reforms of the 1970s and 1980s, seniority remains the most important qualification for advancement to committee and subcommittee chairmanship. In such commanding positions, one possesses a variety of ways to shape legislation. Lacking a chairmanship, ranking minority members frequently wield extraordinary clout (Davidson and Oleszek, 1985, pp. 39, 219, 222–3; Mayhew, 1974, pp. 104–5).

Besides the elevation of rank and influence that comes with seniority, members of long tenure gain the advantage of "knowing the ropes." Congressional norms, precedents, and procedures are Byzantine. Newcomers must be utterly baffled, while "members who know the rules and precedents have an advantage over procedural novices in affecting policy outcomes." Often, timing is crucial, and only those conversant with the intricacies of congressional procedure know when the most propitious moment occurs and how to seize a momentary opportunity.[8]

Notwithstanding the considerable advantages of committee membership, chairmanship, seniority, and knowing the ropes, no member can get much done without support from others. Members spend much of their time constructing and maintaining alliances. The president can be either a fine friend or formidable foe. Accordingly, one must strive to enter into mutually beneficial political exchanges with the administration. In particular, one tries to obtain favorable treatment from the president and his cabinet in the assignment of particularized benefits to one's district. The administration has much discretion in such assignments, so potential trades can often be arranged.[9] In such dealings, members often find it advantageous to join forces with other members from their states, frequently without regard to party membership. As House Majority Leader Jim Wright (D-Tex.) said, "When a member has his chips on the line for something that affects his district, the others pretty much fall into line and help him."[10] Increasingly, informal alliances—many of them bipartisan—have emerged along issue, regional, or commodity lines. In the mid-1980s, there were, for example, a 55-member Congressional Coal Group in the House and a 39-member Coal Caucus in the Senate (Davidson and Oleszek, 1985, pp. 364–5; Lindsay, 1987; U.S. Senate, 1985, p. 579).

Given the members, structure, and alliances, there remains the strategy. The basic problem is that members want to channel benefits toward and costs away from their own constituents. This situation would appear to be the setting for a war of each against all, in a legislative Hobbesian jungle, where nothing but mutually exploitative behavior could be expected. But that is not how Congress works. Indeed, its actual workings are normally just the opposite. Despite their apparent conflicts of interest, members understand that what matters most for their electoral prospects are visible particularistic benefits and costs clearly associated with the actions of individual senators or representatives. If benefits and costs are not noticed or are ignored because they are small or are not clearly linked to the actions of the representatives for whom one votes, then for political purposes, they do not exist. Members of Congress, therefore, must devise legislative strategies that enhance the visibility of particularistic benefits, but that hide, obscure, or displace responsibility for the costs borne by constituents. Over the centuries, members have perfected several such strategies.

The most important strategy is logrolling, a form of vote trading that entails a tendency toward universalism: Vote for my boondoggle, and I'll vote for yours (maybe now, maybe later). Each of us will then have something to take plausible credit for; and even though, in the aggregate, the costs may vastly exceed the benefits, the voters of any given district will perceive themselves to have received net gains, to have gotten their "fair share." After all, the perceived alternative is to have borne a pro rata share of the costs of all of the other boondoggles nationwide, without any off-setting benefits whatever in one's own district—clearly, a bad deal. Once members have positioned themselves on the committees of greatest serviceability for their reelection strategy, "observance of reciprocity is not very costly in terms of lost opportunities, and it is very profitable in terms of unfettered influence in an area vital to their continued reelection."[11] Representative Ronald V. Dellums (D-Calif.), chairman of the House Armed Services Subcommittee on Military Facilities and Installations, gave voice to the prevailing practice when he said that "as long as 'powerful' members can get their projects through it would be discriminatory to vote against anyone else."[12] Another important legislative strategy for facilitating the members' diverse objectives is improvising a package deal. By attaching riders (that is, substantively unrelated provisions) to a comprehensive bill, such as the appropriation bill for an entire federal department, legislators are able "to execute a hidden ball play. The broader the scope of the measure, the more chance there is of its carrying along to enactment provisions that would otherwise stand no chance of being enacted into law." Within omnibus bills—examples include appropriations measures covering funding for several departments, bills that may run to hundreds of pages and allocate hundreds of billions of dollars—riders occupying a few lines easily gain enactment with little effort by their sponsors. Nor do the sponsors of such riders need to worry about a presidential veto."[13]

An especially innocent-looking variant is the "limitation rider," which restricts the use to which an agency may put appropriated funds. As political scientists Roger Davidson and Walter Oleszek note, however, such riders actually "make policy" under the guise of restricting expenditures.[14] Recent defense appropriations acts, for example, contain dozens, sometimes scores, of limitation riders. Behind each of them, there is a story, usually a story of particularistic benefits conveyed to a special interest group by an individual member or a small group of members of Congress.

"The most pervasive attribute of electoral processes," write Davidson and Oleszek, "is their local character. . . . The candidates, the voters, and often the issues and styles, are deeply rooted in states and districts." And yet, "the aggregate of all these contests is a legislative body charged with addressing national problems and issues" (Davidson and Oleszek, 1985, p. 101).

The residents of the United States need, inter alia, national defense—not defense of merely the Second District of California or the state of Idaho, but *national* defense. Yet, no one in Congress has much incentive to promote the national defense. In fact, all members face incentives and constraints that push them toward support of measures that weaken the national defense by depleting the defense budget to finance particularistic benefits that do nothing to produce genuine national security. Worst of all, selling out the national defense apparently violates no political norm, at least no congressional norm. As a British writer has observed, somewhat aghast, "It would not be thought unusual or wrong for either senators or congressmen to argue for the interests of their state or district even if those interests appeared to the majority to be *contrary* to the national interest."[15]

Except when acting ideologically or seeking electoral gains from public position-taking, an individual member of Congress tends to regard national security and other essential collective goods as conditions beyond control, like acts of God, even though they are the result of the aggregate of actions taken by members of Congress. "It makes much more sense," writes political scientist David Mayhew, "to devote resources to things over which they think they can have some control," and for which they can claim individual credit during the next campaign (Mayhew, 1974, p. 32). Given the structure of our legislative institutions and the strategies of the legislators," the general, long-term welfare of the United States is no more than an incidental by-product of the system" (Fiorina, 1977, p. 49).

On the basis of analysis like that just presented, several political scientists have argued that the growth of the federal government, especially the expansion of the scope of federal activities, has led to a change in the mix of congressional activities: less attention to setting basic policies, more attention to casework and pork barreling. As one congressman put it, "The federal government has projected itself into every aspect of life, from cradle to grave; so people naturally go to Washington to solve their problems." Because so many more people are now likely to have troubles with the federal bureaucracy and so many more opportunities exist to procure particularistic benefits from the federal government, the payoffs have been shifted for legislators. There are now more opportunities for them to take the sorts of actions that best promote their reelection, and they have responded accordingly.[16]

The analysis may be applied to the defense program in particular. Throughout the post-World War II era, the United States has maintained an enormous military establishment, requiring thousands of bases and other facilities, millions of workers, and a multitude of contracts for research, goods, and services supplied by private firms. The governmental allocation of these bases, jobs, and contracts involves great discretion. Members of Congress have recognized that post offices and rivers and harbors projects, the traditional pork barrel measures, are now small potatoes. As Representative Patricia Schroeder (D-Colo.) complained in the early 1980s, no doubt exaggerating somewhat, "If you want anything for your district . . . the only place there is any money at all is in the Armed Services Committee bill."[17] Since World War II, the U.S. Treasury has laid out more than $6,600 billion (in 1982 dollars) for national defense. The potential for pork barreling has become stupendous, and members of Congress have been alert to seize the opportunities, often in ingenious ways.

The Hard-Coal Constituency and Its Congressional Salvation

Anthracite is the hard, shiny coal that burns hot, clean, and almost without flame. In the United States, it is found almost entirely in a small region of northeastern Pennsylvania. (For present purposes, it suffices to say that we are dealing with no more than four congressional districts.) The anthracite industry grew rapidly in the late nineteenth and early twentieth centuries, but after World War I, it began to decline. By 1960, the industry was a shadow of its former self, with output at 18 million tons (down 72 percent since World War I), employment at 20,000 workers (down almost 90 percent since 1914) (Miller and Sharpless, 1985; Pennsylvania Department of Environmental Resources, n.d., pp. 41–3; Powell, 1980; *Congressional District Data Book,* 1963, pp. 428–9). The hard-coal region became a classic economic backwater. But despite the unemployment, outmigration, and despair, not all was lost. The region still had congressmen.

The congressmen had influence with the administration, and they perceived that its management of the defense program might be turned to the advantage of the shriveling anthracite coal industry. The United States had hundreds of thousands of troops stationed in Europe, giving rise to a demand for a million metric tons of solid fuels annually to heat the barracks. Those fuels, bituminous coal and coke, were being purchased from European suppliers. Someone got the idea that substituting Pennsylvania anthracite for German coke could add substantially to the withering market for hard coal. Industry leaders Harry W. Bradbury of the Glen Alden Coal Company and James J. Tedesco of the Pagnotti Coal Company took the initiative in "creating a market where none had existed before." They invested "large measures of tenacity, travel and tact and after six months of effort they prevailed." Their Herculean efforts were not directed at producing or marketing coal; they were aimed at lobbying the state's congressional delegation and the administration ("Impact of the Army Tonnage," 1961, p. 2; "Defense Seeks U.S. Coal for Troops in Germany," 1961, p. 45).

In May 1961, a meeting in Washington of all of the interested parties was arranged by the congressmen with constituents in the hard-coal region. In attendance were Pennsylvania's Senators Joseph S. Clark and Hugh Scott and Representatives Ivor D. Fenton, Daniel J. Flood, William W. Scranton, and Francis E. Walter. Representing the Pentagon were Deputy Assistant Secretary of Defense Edward J. Sheridan, Director of Military Construction General J. B. Lampert, and other high officials of the Department of Defense (DoD) and the army. Representatives of the United Mine Workers and the anthracite producers rounded out the group. On the agenda were two items: (1) opposition to conversions from anthracite to alternate fuels by the army anywhere; and (2) a proposal that the army switch from German coke to Pennsylvania anthracite at its European posts. At stake was the potential opportunity to supply some 700,000 tons of solid fuel. The immediate outcome of the meeting was that Paul A.

Mulcey, a consulting engineer connected with the Pennsylvania Coal Research Board, was dispatched to West Germany "to inspect and investigate the plants in question to ascertain whether there is any valid reason why Pennsylvania anthracite cannot be used as economically and efficiently as German coke." As the summer passed, the people of the hard-coal region looked forward eagerly to an arrangement that might entail 318,700 man-days of work, $6,700,000 in wages, $7,700,000 in sales, and all of the multiplier benefits to "bolster the economy of the distressed anthracite producing region." In anticipation of these benefits, the *Bulletin* of the Anthracite Institute gratefully recognized the congressmen's "effective work in bringing about a new appraisal of anthracite" by the army and DoD; it expressed its great appreciation and extended "the industry's sincere thanks" ("Army Tonnage," 1961, p. 1).

The scheme was nonpartisan. Senator Clark was a Democrat, Senator Scott, a Republican. Representatives Flood and Walter were Democrats; Scranton and Fenton were Republicans. They had but one thing in common: Each represented a voting district consisting in part of voters in the hard-coal region. Flood's Eleventh District was Luzerne County; Walter's Fifteenth District included Carbon County; Scranton's Tenth District included Lackawanna County; Fenton's Twelfth District included Northumberland and Schuylkill counties. Together, they covered virtually all of the hard-coal fields still being worked *(Congressional Directory,* 1962, pp. 139–41). Together, they packed considerable clout—and got results.

In October, the Pentagon announced that its forces in West Germany would purchase more than 485,000 net tons of Pennsylvania anthracite in the next eight months. The announcement was, according to the *Bulletin* of the Anthracite Institute, "the most exhilarating news that the industry and the producing region have received in a long time." The new sales represented an amount equal to about 20 percent of the total production of stove coal and larger sizes. Beyond the benefits to the mining industry, the program promised substantial stimulus to the railroad and supplying industries. Some 8,660 extra carloads would be required to carry the European-bound shipments to tidewater piers, giving rise to some $118,000 in wages for railroad employees per anthracite working day. The beneficiaries were encouraged by getting the program going even though the army had already contracted for a portion of its fuel supplies in Germany earlier in the fiscal year. It seemed "not unreasonable to anticipate" that the Pennsylvanians would be in a "much more favorable position to obtain an even greater tonnage in the year beginning July 1, 1962" ("Impact of the Army Tonnage," 1961, p. 2; "Ten Solid Trainloads of Anthracite Per Day," 1961, p. 1).

Indeed, they would be, because a government program is an easy thing to start, but a hard thing to stop. Besides, this particular program could be clothed in a variety of plausible public interest rhetoric. It was said to express President John F. Kennedy's interest in improving the nation's balance of payments, raising the gross national product, aiding economically distressed regions, and decreasing unemployment. The only losers seemed to be the German coke suppliers, "who need no help at this point." In April 1962, the *Bulletin* concluded: "This government business has done so much to further the President's stated national objectives and coincidentally bolster the local economy, that it is clearly in the best interests of all parties that it not only be continued, but expanded for the year starting July 1st" ("Renewal of the Army Export Contract," 1962, p. 1).

And so it was. In July 1962, the DoD announced that it would award contracts to anthracite firms for about 500,000 net tons for shipment to West Germany. This time, ten firms shared the business and, with the benefits more widely spread, a deeper entrenchment of the program was ensured. Jobs, of course, would appear to be created. The contracts represented about 21 percent of annual production of stove coal and larger sizes and would require a minimum of two and a quarter weeks of union production. In addition, supply, service, and transport firms and their workers would gain. Some 120 more railroad workers would be needed to get the coal to ocean ports, where U.S. flag vessels and their crews would begin to get their share.[18] Everybody seemed to be better off. Not a word was spoken about the additional government outlays needed to conduct the program. Thereafter, it was extended year after year as a matter of course.

By the late 1960s, however, the Pentagon had wearied of this coals-to-Newcastle scheme. Military authorities proposed conversions of the aging, inefficient, and labor-intensive anthracite furnaces in Europe to more modern designs using alternate fuels, usually oil. They expected thereby to save more than $20 million a year. But the DoD's requests for budget authority to convert the furnaces got nowhere in Congress. The proposal repeatedly failed to clear the Defense Appropriations Subcommittee of the House. Year after year, the mighty Pentagon met defeat at the hands of a single congressman. The defense officials should not be faulted too much, however, because their opponent was "the best congressman"(Stubbing, 1986, p. 100; Crile, 1975, p. 63).

The Best Congressman: Dan Flood

Everyone agreed that Daniel J. Flood, the Democratic representative of the Eleventh District of Pennsylvania, was the best congressman. Most important, his constituents agreed. They elected him to Congress first in 1944 and—except in 1946 and 1952, when the Republicans enjoyed nationwide triumphs—reelected him at every election through 1978. Once, running unopposed in 1970, he received 97 percent of the vote. After he had entrenched himself, in the 1960s and 1970s, Flood routinely won by a large margin even when opposed. For 16 terms, he served as the "guardian angel" of the people of his district. He was an ombudsman, a father, a priest, an employment bureau, an entertainer, a fixer, and occasionally a savior. He was, in the words of one adoring constituent, "the next closest thing to God" (Crile, 1975, p. 61; "Flood, Daniel J[ohn]," 1979, p. 134).

Flood had what political scientists call a consummate "home style." He understood the people of his district, and he knew what they wanted from him. His constituents—predominately members of white ethnic groups descended from hard-pressed immigrant miners, long isolated by occupation, ethnicity, and geographical remoteness from the mainstream of national political life—had little interest in matters beyond their Appalachian province. "Local, not national or international, issues mattered most to people. Voters wanted to know what a candidate could do for them—for their family, for their town, for their region of the country. The politician who did not understand this concern simply did not get elected."[19] Flood understood.

Fundamental to the power of this congressman, who "wield[ed] his power ruthlessly to channel untold millions of federal dollars into his district," were seniority, advantageous subcommittee memberships, and rank. By the 1960s, he had become the second-ranking Democrat on the Defense Appropriations Subcommittee. In 1967, he became chairman of the Labor and Health, Education, and Welfare Appropriations Subcommittee. In these two positions, he boasted, he was "identified with three-fourths of the whole federal budget. You can imagine what that means." Spelling out his strategic advantages for reporter George Crile in 1974, Flood explained: "You get to be known, and while you don't threaten anyone—they are very understanding people and very human. . . . It's very technical and I use all of these opportunities, advantages, seniority, and all of this stuff for the purpose of helping whatever is left of the goddamn anthracite coal industry." With his subcommittee positions and rank, Flood had a lot to trade. His congressional colleagues appreciated the potential for gains from trade. Said House Speaker Carl Albert (D-Okla.), "Flood's in a position to accommodate a lot of members."[20]

And accommodate he did. Flood was as popular with his fellow members of Congress as he was with his constituents in the Eleventh District. As Representative Joe Waggonner of Louisiana put it, Flood was "a Congressman's Congressman." Representative Tom Steed of Oklahoma echoed Waggonner's appraisal: "It's true that I do more for Dan Flood than I do for other members of Congress. It's because Dan Flood can do more for me than other members of Congress." Flood became a horse trader supreme. His IOUs were distributed "throughout the power structure of the House, hitting every region and committee, and extending to both parties." He viewed a plea for help from a colleague as "an opportunity rather than a burden." If he needed to be paid back, as when in 1972 the Susquehanna River flooded much of Wilkes-Barre and other places in his district, he could say to his colleagues, "Now look, goddamn it, I've taken care of you before, now you get in line."[21] And they did.

When the Army proposed conversion of its European furnaces from anthracite to oil in the late 1960s, Flood used his strategic position on the Defense Appropriations Subcommittee to block the budget authority required for the conversion. "Hell, yes, I stopped it," he bragged to Crile. "I did it by twisting arms and hammering heads. I'd break a few arms if I had to." The former boxer was hyperbolic, as usual. In truth, he possessed far more effective means of getting his way than physical prowess. In 1972, he gave the anthracite industry's captive military market even stronger protection by adding to the Defense Appropriation Act for fiscal year 1973 the following limitation rider: "None of the funds available to the Department of Defense shall be utilized for the conversion of heating plants from coal to oil at defense facilities in Europe."[22] Thereafter, the same provision—two-and-a-half innocuous-looking lines tucked obscurely into a bill with hundreds of complex sections—reappeared year after year. The U.S. Army, therefore, was stuck with its anthracite furnaces and had to continue buying, transporting, storing, and handling the hard coal to fuel them.

Over time, the anthracite program was costing the DoD—which is to say, the taxpayers—hundreds of millions of dollars in excessive heating costs. Why, a writer asked Flood, did the defense authorities let him get away with his costly obstruction? "They can't be blamed," he answered. "After all, here's Flood, a nice fellow, and he's got a great reputation for being for defense appropriations—bang, bang, bang, and all that. Jesus Christ, suppose you were one of those goddamn generals or secretaries or deputy secretaries. What are you going to do? Jeopardize the Army materiel command with a son of a bitch like that for a couple of million dollars, for a couple of tons of coal? Bullshit."[23] Obviously, the congressman had the military authorities over a barrel. Having more important projects to promote and fund, they did not consider it worthwhile to antagonize a powerful member of the Defense Appropriations Subcommittee in order to save a few hundred million dollars consumed by his favorite boondoggle. Flood eventually met defeat, not at the hands of his constituents, who loved him to the end, but in federal court, where he was charged in the late 1970s with a variety of offenses, including perjury, conspiracy, and acceptance of bribes. In a plea bargain struck in February 1980, he was found guilty of conspiracy to violate federal campaign laws. In consideration of his old age and ill health, he was given a suspended sentence and placed on a year's probation. He resigned his congressional seat on January 31, 1980 (Orlofsky, 1979, pp. 239–40, 500, 685; "Flood, Daniel J[ohn]," 1979, p. 134; Orlofsky, 1981, p. 190).

The Second-Best Congressman: Joe McDade

Joseph M. McDade is a dull man, in appearance, speech, and behavior the very opposite of Dapper Dan Flood. But politically, McDade has much in common with Flood, who represented an adjacent congressional district and with whom he worked amiably for almost two decades in the service of the anthracite region in general and the hard-coal industry in particular. Serving in his thirteenth term, McDade was the senior member of the Pennsylvania delegation. Though a Republican, he enjoyed the support of organized labor. His appeal was to members of both parties. Avoiding strong partisan and ideological positions, he had never received less than 60 percent of the vote since 1966. He was "a model casework congressman, the kind who sometimes seems to function as little more than an ambassador for his district" (Naughton, 1987, pp. C1–C2; Barone and Ujifusa, 1985, pp. 1167–8; Barone and Ujifusa, 1987, pp. 1031–2; Ehrenhalt, 1981, pp. 1043–5).

Given his seniority, what was most conspicuous about McDade was his inconspicuousness. But lack of publicity had not kept him from cultivating influence with congressional colleagues. "He is one of those guys who is very effective by learning the ropes and being a nice guy," said Representative Morris Udall of Arizona. "I don't know anybody who doesn't like him." According to Representative Don Young of Alaska, "He has the ability to put together packages that are acceptable to every man." Unknown to the public outside the anthracite region, he made a deeper impression on his colleagues. Representative Jack Murtha of Pennsylvania said that "it would be difficult to have much more influence" than McDade had.[24] Like Flood, McDade built his congressional career on seniority, committee membership, and rank—all employed in the cause of ample casework and generous infusions of particularistic benefits for the homefolks. He was, as one political guidebook puts it, "a creature of the Appropriations Committee" (Ehrenhalt, 1981, p. 1043). In 1985, he gave up his position as ranking minority member of the Interior Appropriations Subcommittee, where he "always fought for the interests of coal," to become the ranking Republican on the Defense Appropriations Subcommittee. Like Flood, he "[wasn't] bashful about funneling funds to General Dynamics and other Pentagon contractors with plants in his district"; nor was he "shy about shovelling federal money into the anthracite country or protecting the interests of coal."[25] So, even after Flood had left the scene, that same limitation rider, forbidding conversions of European base furnaces from coal to oil, kept appearing in the defense appropriations bill, year after year. After all, the Eleventh District, like all the others, "[wanted] a piece of the military-industrial complex to call its own."[26]

With 25 years of experience in pork barrel politics, McDade expressed no shame about his sponsorship of the anthracite boondoggle. "I guarantee you," he proudly told the *New York Times*, "that if we weren't burning [anthracite] coal in Europe we wouldn't be burning it anywhere. This is a way to keep the industry alive." To clothe this domestic welfare program in a thin garment of military rationality, some supporters alleged that, in its absence, the German bases would be vulnerable to energy blackmail because of European dependence on Soviet natural gas or Persian Gulf oil and the possibility of terrorist attacks on the pipeline system. The argument is pathetic, and can be exploded by a moment's reflection. U.S. Army officials rejected it, maintaining that district heat or oil-fired systems presented no greater security risk than coal-fired plants. Still, McDade was happy to trot out the discredited security argument. "I'll be doggoned if I'll tell the people that they're going to heat their bases with Russian gas," said the mock-patriotic congressman. "It's not unseemly to ask that United States coal be burned on a United States base."[27]

In late December 1982, McDade and other congressional friends of coal added to the Defense Appropriation Act for fiscal year 1983 the following rider: "None of the funds available to the Department of Defense during the current fiscal year shall be used by the Secretary of the military department to purchase coal or coke from foreign nations for use at United States defense facilities in Europe when coal from the United States is available" (96 Stat. 1833 [1982] at 1863). The provision gave added assurance that the hard-coal industry would retain its captive military market.

Diplomacy and Economy Versus the Pork Barrel

While Congress played games with taxpayers' money, a diplomatic confrontation was steadily building in Germany. At its root were the old anthracite furnaces on U.S. bases. The furnaces caused a lot of air pollution in a heavily industrialized area that was already subject to severe air pollution. Damage to German forests accelerated rapidly in the early 1980s; by 1985, nearly half of the trees had been affected. The Germans reacted by imposing stringent antipollution standards, including requirements that existing boilers be retrofitted with scrubbers and, in some areas, that no coal be burned, regardless of the equipment. According to the DoD's 1985 energy management plan, "German officials at all levels are unalterably opposed to the use of coal (any kind, from any country) where connection to a local district heating system is an available alternative. . . . The Department of Defense is becoming increasingly unable to comply with congressional direction on U.S. coal use in Europe and German law." The Pentagon found itself, in the words of Jeffrey Jones, Acting Director for Energy Policy, "pinned between U.S. law and German law."[28]

In a letter surveying the problem, General Scott B. Smith, the Deputy Chief of Staff, Engineer, for the U.S. Army in Europe, cited a study that estimated that the army could save about $500 million over a 25-year life cycle of its heating equipment if congressional restrictions on conversions were removed. Further, removal of the restrictions "would greatly enhance the image of the U.S. Army in the eyes of the German government and its citizens." Smith noted that "good relations with Host Nations are our greatest assurance of gaining their support for the fielding of new weapons systems, the construction of new facilities, and the needed cooperation in realizing other common aims." High-level diplomatic communications underscored the seriousness of the irritation of German-American relations. The German Minister of Finance wrote Secretary of State George Shultz to point out "the importance of the heating issue for maintaining the good relations between the forces and the local population." And the German ambassador, Gunther van Well, wrote Senator Barry M. Goldwater, chairman of the Senate Armed Services Committee, seeking support for legislation to drop congressional restrictions on conversion of European furnaces.[29]

Faced with the excessive costs of continuing to operate the anthracite furnaces, including the prospect of some $385 million of additional defense budget outlays just to bring them into compliance with German environmental regulations, and the growing diplomatic flap with German authorities, Congress took action—and made the problem even worse.

The Defense Appropriations Act for fiscal year 1985, passed by Congress in October 1984, included the standard restriction on conversions of European furnaces from coal to oil; it also carried forward the requirement, first enacted in 1982, that all coal used on European bases be U.S. coal. Still open, however, was the alternative being pressed by the Germans that the bases switch to district heating, tapping into networks of surplus heat produced by nearby factories, mills, and utilities. Ever vigilant, Representative McDade slammed shut that door, too. Just before the defense appropriations bill left the House Appropriations Committee in September 1984, McDade attached an amendment providing that "none of the funds available for Defense installations in Europe shall be used for the consolidation or conversion of heating facilities to district heating distribution systems in Europe."

The DoD, already engaged in negotiations with several local authorities in Germany for just such conversions, protested the committee's action. In response, the Senate Appropriations Committee conceded "that those facilities identified by the Department of the Army as of September 24, 1984, as being in advanced stages of negotiations shall be exempt from such provision upon written notification to the Committees on Appropriations of the House of Representatives and the Senate from the Department justifying the conversion for each facility." Offsetting its slight concession, however, the Senate committee directed the Army to purchase an additional 520,000 metric tons of U.S. coal to build a one-year "strategic reserve" in Europe. These reserves, according to General Smith, were "not needed." The Senate provision, subsequently enacted by Congress, would simply add to existing, already sufficient reserves at a cost of $63 million to $75 million, with a cost of more than $17 million for transport alone. But the sponsor, Pennsylvania's Republican Senator Arlen Specter, was delighted to announce the action and to characterize it as "good news for the anthracite coal fields."[30]

Every Pentagon protest, every diplomatic difficulty, every additional extraction from the taxpayer's pocketbooks seemed only to whet the congressmen's appetite for more pork. McDade, as always, had "worked closely with the anthracite industry." Specter, facing a close race in 1986, began to play a more prominent role in the diversion of defense funds to the anthracite region. In appreciation, the National Coal Association and its political action committee (Coalpac) designated him a priority candidate and contributed $2,000 to his campaign, out of a total of $15,750 given to all Senate candidates between January 1985 and June 1986 ("Coals to Newcastle," 1985, p. 12; "Coalpac Supports Candidates in Four Key Senate Races," 1986, p. 13). Political action committees sponsored by individual coal companies and the United Mine Workers made additional contributions. McDade, as expected, and Specter, with relief, easily won reelection in 1986.

A cynic might well have viewed the campaign contributions from the coal interests as a naked payoff for actions taken in Congress in 1985, when the boondoggle reached its height. That year, seeking to escape from the untenable position in which conflicting German and American laws had placed it, the DoD proposed a "Solomonic compromise." In a letter dated August 30, 1985, the Assistant Secretary of Defense for Acquisition and Logistics proposed to the Senate Defense Appropriations Subcommittee that in exchange for a lifting of the restrictions on furnace conversions in Europe, the department would increase the use of coal for heating its bases in the continental United States. Coal purchases would be increased—indeed, more than doubled—by 1.6 million short tons (including at least 300,000 tons of anthracite) by fiscal year 1994 (Gruson, 1986, p. 26; "Defense Department Wants to Stop Buying U.S. Coal" 1986, p. 17; Copulos, 1986, pp. 1, 4; *Congressional Record* 132 [8 August 1986] p. S10844). When the conferees finished their reconciliations and the Defense Appropriations Act for fiscal year 1986 finally became law on December 19, 1985, it was the best Christmas present ever for the coal interests. It continued all of the previous restrictions on DoD energy use in Europe: no coal-to-oil conversions, no use of foreign coal, and no conversions to district heating, except at those bases the army had identified as of April 11, 1985, as being in advanced stages of negotiation and at Bad Kissingen (99 Stat. 1185 [1985] at 1205, 1207, 1210, 1214). So the DoD's proposed deal had fallen through. But Congress did accept part of the proposal, the pork barrel part: It mandated increased use of coal on bases in the continental United States. To implement an amendment sponsored by Senator Robert C. Byrd of West Virginia, funds were provided to pay for conversion of furnaces on domestic bases from gas or oil to coal. Section 8110 of the act reads:

> Of the funds available in the Army Industrial Fund, $25,000,000 shall be available to be used to implement immediately, or to transfer to another appropriation account in this Act to be used to implement immediately, the program proposed by the Department in its letter of August 30, 1985, from the Assistant Secretary of Defense for Acquisition and Logistics, to rehabilitate and convert current steam generating plants at defense facilities in the United States to coal burning facilities in order to achieve a coal consumption target of 1,600,000 short tons of coal per year above current consumption levels at Department of Defense facilities in the United States by fiscal year 1994; *Provided,* That anthracite or bituminous coal shall be the source of energy at such installations; *Provided further,* That during the implementation of this proposal, the amount of anthracite coal purchased by the Department shall remain at least at the current annual purchase level, 302,000 short tons. (99 Stat. 1185 [1985] at 1222)

For the first time, a statute had actually prescribed a minimum tonnage of hard coal that the Pentagon must buy—it was micromanagement with a vengeance.

This legislation anticipated the conversion of heating systems to use coal at 37 installations in the continental United States. Estimates of the costs of the conversion varied widely, from about $1.4 billion, according to the DoD, to as much as $5 billion, according to analyst Milton R. Copulos, director of energy studies at the Heritage Foundation (Copulos, 1986, p. 6). Copulos placed the congressional coal scheme "among the most astounding examples of parochialism," but he noted, with reference to the military authorities, that "no one wants to get the people [in Congress] who write your budget mad." Congressman William E. Dannemeyer of California's Thirty-Ninth District—an Orange County district conspicuously short of coal mines—expressed outrage at the program. "It's a joke," he declared, "a terrible, sad example of porkbarrel politics"; but it exemplified "how our political process works."[31]

It was either too good (for coal-state members of Congress and their privileged constituents) or too bad (for everyone else) to last. With the Pentagon still caught in the middle and with gas-state representatives in Congress bringing pressure to preserve gas sales to military bases in the continental United States, the scheme had to be altered; and in 1986, it was.[32] Along the way, a revealing debate took place in the Senate.

In early August, as the senators were laboring through days of lengthy sessions to consider scores of proposed amendments to the defense authorization bill, Specter offered an amendment cosponsored by fellow Pennsylvania Republican John Heinz, Byrd and John D. Rockefeller of West Virginia, and Paul S. Trible of Virginia. The amendment called essentially for reenactment of the provision passed in 1985, requiring the DoD to implement the plan to increase its coal consumption by 1.6 million tons, including at least 300,000 tons of anthracite, in the continental United States by fiscal year 1994, by converting furnaces. Speaking in support of the measure, Specter, who faced an uncertain election just three months away, underscored the supposed lessons of the 1973 Arab oil embargo and the dangers of dependence on foreign energy materials. He stressed the importance of supporting domestic energy sources. By adopting his amendment, the Senate could continue its "commitment to the American coal industry" and ensure that "the U.S. coal producers, railroads, maritime industry, and our Nation's security will not be jeopardized."

Heinz then spoke in support of the amendment, noting that it was "the result of years of discussions and planning by the Defense Authorizing and Appropriations Committees in both Chambers." He expressed "deep reservations" about letting the DoD off the hook in Europe and worried that the military authorities might manage their energy use to the detriment of the coal industry. "The amendment," he declared, "would guarantee a livelihood to some 2,000 to 3,000 coal miners in Pennsylvania" and, by the by, avoid grave repercussions for national security "that can not be underestimated." Byrd spoke briefly in support of the amendment, explaining that it would ensure that "there will be no misunderstanding or faltering by the Defense Department in the pursuit of this program in fiscal year 1987" (*Congressional Record* 132 [8 August 1986], pp. S10842-S10843).

Senator Strom Thurmond of South Carolina, the floor manager of the bill under debate, explained that Specter's amendment should be viewed in the context of other provisions of the bill approved by his subcommittee. At long last, the Armed Services Committee had approved conversion of heating plants at defense facilities in Europe "from coal to district heat or gas or oil whenever it is cost effective or required by the host nation." This would allow savings of $20 million to $40 million in operating costs and preclude the necessity of installing antipollution devices, at a cost of $385 million, to comply with German environmental regulations. Acknowledging the political swap being made, Thurmond characterized Specter's amendment as part of "an orderly transition from using coal in Europe to using coal in the United States." His committee, having considered the new coal requirements, was "willing to make that concession in order to get the big plan approved."[33]

At that point, Senator Phil Gramm of Texas interjected some sour notes. He did not intend to oppose Specter's amendment, he said, because it was "a step in the right direction." But he reminded his colleagues that "in the name of domestic politics, we have literally been carrying coals to Newcastle . . . . It is absolutely absurd policy which cheats the taxpayer and creates tremendous problems with our allies." The compromise being proposed "may be an improvement, but it is plain wrong as far as foreign policy and defense are concerned." He called it "an absolute outrage" that ought to be stopped, and he promised that in the future he would not compromise on the issue. Senator Ted Stevens of Alaska agreed. He noted the opportunity cost of the coal program: "We are now buying more coal than we need," and such purchases divert dollars from buying airplanes, research, and other things required for national defense. "This is an entitlement," he concluded. "Let us make sure everyone understands" (*Congressional Record* 132 [8 August 1986], p. S10843). No doubt everyone did. Specter's amendment was adopted by a voice vote (*Congressional Record* 132 [8 August 1986], p. S10846).

Later that day, when the Senate was debating another defense boondoggle—to use strategic stockpiling to create a de facto domestic subsidy—Senator Gramm reflected on what the Senate had done earlier with respect to coal:

> Why did we do that? We did it because of the logrolling buddy system that somebody wanted to do something to help their region. It was only the taxpayer paying for it, so we all looked the other way. We created international problems with the Germans by forcing the burning of high-sulfur coal when they had low-sulfur coal. We created the absurdity of paying a higher price for coal, then paying huge transportation costs and coming over and burning it on the very site that we could have bought cheaper coal with no transportation cost and lower sulfur. And we did that because the Congress was micromanaging resources and we had political logrolling going on. (*Congressional Record* 132 [8 August 1986], p. S10865)

No one denied the charge.

Ultimately, Specter's amendment was enacted as section 9099 of the 1987 Defense Appropriation Act, passed in October 1986. The section called for the 1.6 million tons (including at least 300,000 tons of anthracite) to be added to DoD purchases by fiscal year 1994, but provided that the fuel used in any new or converted heating system be the most cost-effective. Again, to make certain that anthracite kept its captive market during the transition, the law stipulated that the DoD buy at least 300,000 short tons of anthracite during fiscal year 1987 (100 Stat. 3341–83 [1986] at 3341–117 and 3341–118).

The 1987 Defense Authorization Act, passed in November 1986, consolidated the existing statutes regarding coal requirements on military bases and revised the U.S. Code (10 U.S.C., sec. 2690). The act stipulated that new heating systems use the most cost-effective fuel. Further, military departments were forbidden to convert heating sources unless they determined that the conversion is either required by the host country or is cost-effective over the life cycle of the equipment. Departments must submit notification of conversions to Congress and wait 30 days before proceeding. Older, conflicting provisions were repealed (100 Stat. 3816 [1986] at 3971–72).

Still Not the End

Late in 1986, press reports indicated that the Pentagon would stop shipping U.S. coal to Europe in 1987 ("U.S. Bases in Europe to Stop Using Pa. Coal," 1986; "Pentagon Stops Shipping Coal to Overseas Bases" 1986). The reports were incorrect. At the end of 1987, the DoD was still buying U.S. coal, including anthracite, for shipment to its European facilities. Several hundred conversions to district heat had been made—with large savings expected in life cycle costs—but American forces in Europe maintained hundreds of installations where such conversions were, for various technical and economic reasons, not feasible. The air force, in particular, because of the remoteness of its bases from cities, had few opportunities to connect to district heating systems. European stockpiles of coal were being drawn down, and shipments from the United States were being reduced. But projections made by the General Accounting Office in August 1987 showed that, in 1991, U.S. coal, including some anthracite, would still be used to heat U.S. bases in Europe.[34] Congress had not repealed the requirement that all coal used by U.S. forces in Europe be U.S. coal, nor was it likely to do so.

In fact, section 8038 of the 1988 Defense Appropriations Act, wrapped into the omnibus Continuing Appropriations Resolution passed in December 1987, reenacted the requirement that the DoD use only U.S. coal "when available"(101 Stat. 1329–44 [1987] at 1329–69). The act also prohibited conversion of the DoD's European heating plants from coal to oil, natural gas, or district heating, except as provided in 10 U.S.C. 2690 (101 Stat. 1329–44 at 1329–63, 1329–65, and 1329–85). (As indicated earlier, this section allows a conversion when it is either required by the host country or is shown to be cost-effective over the life cycle of the equipment, provided that Congress receives a 30-day notice.) These sections of the latest defense appropriations act, along with the reports of insiders, show that industry and congressional supporters of the boondoggle remained active.[35]

So when the *Wall Street Journal* reported on April 5, 1988, that, this year, for the first time since the early 1960s, the Pentagon would ship no anthracite to Germany, one had reason to be suspicious (Wessel, 1988). The report, of course, was not quite accurate. According to Jeffrey Jones, the DoD's director of energy policies, some anthracite might be, or might already have been, shipped to Europe in 1988. The Pentagon was attempting to minimize the shipments and planned to feed its European anthracite furnaces from stockpiles already built up in Germany in amounts sufficient to last more than four years.[36] But with or without the shipments, the DoD's anthracite problem would continue.

The source of the problem should come as no surprise. Tucked into the DoD's 1988 appropriations act, the one folded into the massive omnibus spending bill passed in a mad rush just before Christmas 1987, situated comfortably within a long list of limitation riders, is section 8113, which directs the DoD to achieve a rate of domestic coal consumption of 1.6 million tons by fiscal year 1994, including 300,000 tons of anthracite, and to purchase during fiscal year 1988 at least 300,000 tons of anthracite (101 Stat. 1329–44 at 1329–82). This provision was not in the House version of the bill.

It appeared when Senator Stevens, the subcommittee chairman, as part of a deal with Pennsylvania's Heinz and Specter, added it to the Senate's bill as it passed through the Defense Appropriations Subcommittee. Once that deal was made, the big deed itself was effectively done, because the whole Senate never voted on the DoD Appropriations Act as such. There were no floor amendments. The whole Senate approved the measure only as part of the gigantic "Christmas tree" spending resolution of December 22.[37] One would be hard pressed to find a better example of the "hidden ball trick."

So the Pentagon was again purchasing anthracite coal it did not need and did not want, at a cost of more than $20 million per year, for the plain purpose of buying a few votes for a few members of Congress. The Pentagon planned to store the hard coal as close to its source as possible, to save at least some transportation costs, building a pile 20 feet deep over 45 acres in northeastern Pennsylvania, a place already blighted by slag heaps and other scars of its mining past. Senator Gramm said that the whole thing was "plain wrong," but he did not represent the hard-coal constituency. Senator Specter made no apologies. "It is true that this coal is being stockpiled," he admitted, "but it will be used."[38] Politically speaking, it already had been, and so had the American taxpayers.

Notes

1. Courter, as quoted in Fossedal (1985). See Stein (1986).
2. Korb, as quoted in Stubbing (1986, p. 101). Stubbing's own observation appears on the same page.
3. Frank E. Smith (D-Miss.), as quoted in Mayhew (1974, p. 16). See also Representative Carl Vinson's advice to a new congressman, as quoted in Reed (1984, pp. 234). For a clever test of the influence of ideology on defense voting in the Senate, see Nelson and Silberberg (1987). On the question of self-interest versus ideology and most other matters discussed in this section, I am indebted to James Lindsay (1987, 1988, and 1990).
4. Fiorina (1977, p. 40). See also Davidson and Oleszek (1985, pp. 37, 101, 435).
5. Mayhew (1974, p. 57). See also Davidson and Oleszek (1985, pp. 412–14, 419–20) and Jackson (1988, pp. 1, 29). For a counterargument, see Maass (1983, pp. 71, 261). On the electoral efficacy of casework, narrowly construed, see, Johannes (1984, pp. 187–211).
6. Mayhew (1974, p. 92). See also Lindsay (1987) and U.S. Senate (1985, p. 580).

7. Fiorina (1977, p. 43); see also U.S. Senate (1985, pp. 570–80, 603–5); Reed (1984, pp. 240–41); and Lindsay (1987) for details on committee jurisdictions and power struggles in relation to defense.

8. Davidson and Oleszek (1985, pp. 267, 285). For a superb example, see Apcar (1983).

9. Davidson and Oleszek (1985, pp. 302–5) and Weida and Gertcher (1987, pp. 22–5). On the scope for executive discretion and legislative deal-seeking in relation to defense, important contrasting cases are base closures or realignments (see Twight, 1990) and placement of subcontracts (see Mayer, 1990).

10. Wright, as quoted in Davidson and Oleszek (1985, p. 362).

11. Fiorina (1977, p. 67). See also Mayhew (1974, pp. 88, 105, 114–16, 119) and Davidson and Oleszek (1985, pp. 116–17, 193, 223, 398–401).

12. Dellums, as quoted in Weida and Gertcher (1987, p. 83).

13. Gross (1953, p. 209). See also Mayhew (1974, p. 114), U.S. Senate (1985, pp. 588–89), and Weida and Gertcher (1987, p. 25). The omnibus spending bill for fiscal year 1988 was signed by President Reagan on December 22, 1987. It included the defense appropriation, had more than 2,000 pages, and appropriated more than $600 billion. Senator Daniel Evans (R-Wash.) recently wrote that on the evening of December 22, 1987, "I was speaking in the Senate about the impossibility of even knowing what we were about to vote on when the doors opened and a messenger from the House entered carrying a large cardboard box containing the 2,100-page bill. As he approached the presiding officer, the shouts of 'Vote! Vote!' forced me to end my remarks, and in less than half an hour the Senate had adopted a $604 billion budget that not one senator had fully read. Weeks later, we were still discovering special little provisos that members of the Appropriations Committee had inserted into the bill" (Evans 1988, p. 50; see also p. 91). One of those "little provisos" had to do with anthracite coal; see my concluding section below.

14. Davidson and Oleszek (1985, p. 328). See also Maass (1983, pp. 136–38).

15. Hobkirk (1983, p. 54), emphasis added. See also Weapons Industry Lobby (1982, pp. 87–92), Feld and Wildgen (1985, pp. 41–3), Russett (1970, pp. 186–87), and Aspin (1981).

16. Congressman, as quoted in Johannes (1984, p. 37). See also pp. 36, 55, and Fiorina (1977, pp. 46–49, 87–93).

17. Schroeder, as quoted in Lindsay (1988, p. 65). See also Weida and Gertcher (1987, pp. 22–25, 82–83); see also Bacon (1978) and Mossberg (1983).

18. "Export Tonnage for U.S. Army to Be Continued" (1962, p. 1). See also "Anthracite Shipments to Army Continue" (1962, p. 43).

19. Miller and Sharpless (1985, p. 331). On home style, see Mayhew (1974, p. 51).

20. Quotations from Crile (1975, pp. 64–65) and Flood (1979, p. 133).

21. Waggonner, Steed, and Flood, as quoted in Crile (1975, p. 65).

22. Flood, as quoted in Crile (1975, p. 63); 86 Stat. 1184 (1972) at 1203.

23. Flood, as quoted in Crile (1975, p. 63).

24. Udall, Young, and Murtha, as quoted in Naughton (1987, pp. C1–C2).

25. Barone and Ujifusa (1985, p. 1167) and Barone and Ujifusa (1987, p. 1031). One wonders whether McDade's 1985 move to the Defense Appropriations Subcommittee had

anything to do with his receipt of $26,700 from the political action committees of the 20 top defense firms in support of his 1984 campaign. See Parry (1985). Announcing his intention to seek a 14th term, McDade boasted that his current term "may have been his most successful in bringing jobs and economic growth" to his district ("McDade Announces Bid for 14th Term," 1988).

26. See, for example, 95 Stat. 1565 (1981) at 1585 and 96 Stat. 1833 (1982) at 1857; see also Naughton (1987, p. C2).

27. McDade, as quoted in Gruson (1986). For a presentation of the security risk argument for coal-fired plants, see the remarks of David G. Wigg inserted into the record by Senator Heinz, *Congressional Record* 132 (8 August 1986, pp. S10845–S10846). For the Army's refutation of the arguments, see *Military Facilities: Conversion to District Heat in Germany* (1987, pp. 3, 24–5).

28. Major General Scott B. Smith to Major General Richard K. Kenyon, 19 May 1986, as printed in *Congressional Record* 132 (8 August 1986, pp. S10844–S10845); DoD energy management plan, as quoted in Copulos (1986, p. 5) and Jones, as quoted in Gruson (1986, p. 26). See also "Defense Department Wants to Stop Buying U.S. Coal" (1986, p. 17).

29. For the letters, see *Congressional Record* 132 (8 August 1986, pp. S10844–S10845).

30. Smith to Kenyon, *Congressional Record* 132 (8 August 1986, p. S10844); 98 Stat. 1904 (1984) at 1926, 1928, 1934, 1941; Copulos (1986, p. 4); Specter, as quoted in "Coals to Newcastle" (1985, p. 12).

31. Copulos and Dannemeyer, as quoted in Gruson (1986, p. 26). See also "Defense Department Wants to Stop Buying U.S. Coal" (1986, p. 17).

32. "U.S. Bases in Europe to Stop Using Pa. Coal" (1986). Michael Baly, vice president of the American Gas Association, reported that, "We raised a lot of hell on Capitol Hill and talked with some of our friends" (Wessel, 1988).

33. *Congressional Record* 132 (8 August 1986, p. S10843). It has become increasingly popular for members of Congress to introduce floor amendments to defense authorization bills; by 1985, more than 100 were introduced in each chamber. See U.S. Senate (1985, pp. 589, 601, 610). As the Senate report (p. 601) points out, "This poses a dilemma for the floor managers. Fighting superfluous amendments would prolong the debate and add to its contentiousness. It is much easier to modify amendments to make them relatively benign and accept them on the floor, rather than fight them. This establishes a pattern, however, of yielding to almost any member's wishes for the sake of expediency in securing adoption of the bill." See also Lindsay (1988, p. 64).

34. Author's interview of Jeffrey Jones, 17 November 1987; U.S. General Accounting Office (1987).

35. Author's interviews of Jeffrey Jones, 17 November 1987 and 18 April 1988; author's interview of a member of Representative McDade's staff, 17 November 1987.

36. Author's interview of Jeffrey Jones, 18 April 1988; Wessel (1988).

37. Author's interview of Bill Morley, legislative assistant to Senator Specter, 25 April 1988.

38. Wessel (1988); author's interview of Jeffrey Jones, 18 April 1988.

References

Anthracite Shipments to Army Continue. (1962) *Coal Age* (September).

Apcar, Leonard M. (1983) Big Spender. Rep. Whitten Pushes Money Bills Through by Baffling Opponents. He Mumbles Foes to Death, Aids Mississippi District With Much Federal Help. Safeguarding a Canal & Land. *Wall Street Journal* (4 October).

Arms, Politics, and the Economy: Historical and Contemporary Perspectives, edited by Robert Higgs. (1990) New York: Holmes & Meier for The Independent Institute.

Army Tonnage. (1961) *Anthracite Institute Bulletin* (25 May).

Aspin, Les. (1981) Congress versus the Defense Department. In *The Tethered Presidency: Congressional Restraints on Executive Power,* edited by Thomas M. Franck. New York: New York University Press, pp. 245–63.

Bacon, Kenneth H. (1978) The Congressional-Industrial Complex. *Wall Street Journal* (14 February).

Barone, Michael, and Ujifusa, Grant. (1985) *The Almanac of American Politics 1986.* Washington, D.C.: National Journal.

Barone, Michael, and Ujifusa, Grant. (1987) *The Almanac of American Politics 1988.* Washington, D.C.: National Journal.

Coalpac Supports Candidates in Four Key Senate Races. (1986) *Coal Age* (October).

Coals to Newcastle. (1985) *Common Cause Magazine* (March/April).

Congressional Directory, 87th Congress, Second Session. (1962) Washington, D.C.: Government Printing Office.

Congressional District Data Book. (1963) Washington, D.C.: Government Printing Office.

Copulos, Milton R. (1986) Congressionally Mandated Energy Waste at the Department of Defense. National Defense Council Foundation. *Issue Alert* (24 February).

Crile, George. (1975) The Best Congressman. *Harper's* 250 (January): 60–66.

Davidson, Roger H., and Oleszek, Walter J. (1985) *Congress and Its Members,* second edition. Washington D.C.: Congressional Quarterly.

Defense Department Wants to Stop Buying U.S. Coal. (1986) *Coal Age* (July).

Defense Seeks U.S. Coal for Troops in Germany. (1961) *Coal Age* (October).

Evans, Daniel J. (1988) Why I'm Quitting the Senate. *New York Times Magazine* (17 April): 48, 50, 90–91.

Export Tonnage for U.S. Army to Be Continued. (1962) *Anthracite Institute Bulletin* (5 April).

Facts on File Yearbook 1978, edited by Stephen Orlofsky. (1979) New York: Facts on File.

Facts on File Yearbook 1980, edited by Stephen Orlofsky. (1981) New York: Facts on File.

Feld, Werner J., and Wildgen, John K. (1985) *Congress and National Defense: The Politics of the Unthinkable.* New York: Praeger.

Fiorina, Morris P. (1977) *Congress: Keystone of the Washington Establishment.* New Haven: Yale University Press.

Flood, Daniel J(ohn). (1979) In *Current Biography Yearbook 1978,* Edited by Charles Moritz. New York: H. W. Wilson Co., pp. 131–4.

Fossedal, Gregory. (1985) The Military-Congressional Complex. *Wall Street Journal* (8 August).

Gross, Bertram M. (1953) *The Legislative Struggle.* New York: McGraw-Hill.

Gruson, Lindsey. (1986) Pentagon Is Seeking to Halt Coal Shipments to Germany. *New York Times* (8 June).

Hobkirk, Michael D. (1983) *The Politics of Defence Budgeting: A Study of Organization and Resource Allocation in the United Kingdom and the United States.* Washington D.C.: National Defense University Press.

Impact of the Army Tonnage. (1961) *Anthracite Institute Bulletin* (19 October).

Jackson, Brooks. (1988) Constant Congress. Incumbent Lawmakers Use the Perks of Office to Clobber Opponents. *Wall Street Journal* (22 March).

Johannes, John R. (1984) *To Serve the People: Congress and Constituency Service.* Lincoln: University of Nebraska Press.

Lindsay, James M. (1987) Congress and Defense Policy, 1961–1986. *Armed Forces & Society* (Spring): 371–401.

Lindsay, James M. (1988) Congress and the Defense Budget. *Washington Quarterly* (Winter): 57–74.

Lindsay, James M. (1990) Congress and the Defense Budget: Parochialism or Policy? In *Arms, Politics, and the Economy: Historical and Contemporary Perspectives,* edited by Robert Higgs. New York: Holmes and Meier for The Independent Institute, pp. 174–201.

Maass, Arthur. (1983) *Congress and the Common Good.* New York: Basic Books.

Mayer, Kenneth R. (1990) Patterns of Congressional Influence in Defense Contracting. In *Arms, Politics, and the Economy: Historical and Contemporary Perspectives,* edited by Robert Higgs. New York: Holmes and Meier for The Independent Institute, pp. 202–35.

Mayhew, David R. (1974) *Congress: The Electoral Connection.* New Haven: Yale University Press.

McDade Announces Bid for 14th Term. (1988) *Easton (Pa.) Express* (16 February).

Military Facilities: Conversion to District Heat in Germany. (1987) U.S. General Accounting Office. GAO/NSIAD-87-172. August

Miller, Donald L., and Sharpless, Richard E. (1985) *The Kingdom of Coal.* Philadelphia: University of Pennsylvania Press.

Mossberg, Walter. (1983) Some Congressmen Treat Military Budget as a Source for Patronage. *Wall Street Journal* (15 April).

Naughton, Jim. (1987) The Consensus on Rep. Joe McDade. *Washington Post* (6 August).

Nelson, Donald, and Silberberg, Eugene. 1987. Ideology and Legislator Shirking. *Economic Inquiry* 25 (January): 15–25.

Parry, Robert. (1985) Defense Corporations' Contributions Doubled. *Easton (Pa.) Express* (1 April).

Pennsylvania Department of Environmental Resources. (1970) *Annual Report.* Anthracite, Bituminous Coal and Oil and Gas Divisions, n.p., n.d.

Pentagon Stops Shipping Coal to Overseas Bases. (1986) *Coal Age* (December).

Politics in America: Members of Congress in Washington and at Home, edited by Alan Ehrenhalt. (1981) Washington, D.C.: Congressional Quarterly.

Powell, H. Benjamin. (1980) The Pennsylvania Anthracite Industry, 1769–1976. *Pennyslvania History* 46 (January): 3–17.

Reed, James W. (1984) Congress and the Politics of Defense Reform. In *The Defense Reform Debate: Issues and Analysis,* edited by Asa A. Clark IV, Peter W. Chiarelli, Jeffrey S. McKitrick, and James W. Reed. Baltimore: Johns Hopkins University Press, pp. 230–9.

Renewal of the Army Export Contract. (1962) *Anthracite Institute Bulletin* (5 April).

Russett, Bruce M. (1970) *What Price Vigilance? The Burdens of National Defense.* New Haven: Yale University Press.

Stein, Herbert. (1986) On Pentagon Reform. *Wall Street Journal* (14 March).

Stubbing, Richard A. (1986) *The Defense Game.* New York: Harper & Row.

Ten Solid Trainloads of Anthracite Per Day. (1961) *Anthracite Institute Bulletin* (9 November).

Twight, Charlotte. (1990) Department of Defense Attempts to Close Military Bases: The Political Economy of Congressional Resistance. In *Arms, Politics, and the Economy: Historical and Contemporary Perspectives,* edited by Robert Higgs. New York: Holmes and Meier for The Independent Institute, pp. 236–80.

U.S. Bases in Europe to Stop Using Pa. Coal. (1986) *Allentown (Pa.) Morning Call* (1 November).

U.S. Senate. (1985) Staff of the Committee on Armed Services. *Defense Organization: The Need for Change.* Committee Print. S. Prt. 99–86, 99th Congress, First Session, 16 October.

Weapons Industry Lobby. (1982) In *The Washington Lobby,* edited by Nancy Lammers. Washington, D.C.: Congressional Quarterly, pp. 87–92.

Weida, William J., and Gertcher, Frank L. (1987) *The Political Economy of National Defense.* Boulder, Colo.: Westview.

Wessel, David. (1988) Pentagon's Anthracite Mound Will Be Monument to Congress and Coal Lobby. *Wall Street Journal* (5 April).

Acknowledgments   The author acknowledges financial support of this project by the Earhart Foundation and the Bradley Foundation. Dick Everett, Edward Crane, David Boaz, Jeffrey Jones, and Milton Copulos called valuable sources to the author's attention. Richard Welch made helpful suggestions for revision of an earlier draft.

8

Airplanes the Pentagon Didn't Want, but Congress Did

WITH REGARD TO SPENDING for national defense, we are accustomed to regarding some people as "hawks" and others as "doves." These birds disagree sharply in their answers to the question, "How much defense spending is enough?" In the 1980s, a new bird, the "cheap hawk," began to be sighted with growing frequency. This one wants a strong defense, may or may not want more spending for the military, but definitely wants more bang for the buck. He worries about weapons that don't work as they are supposed to and about spending for purposes that deliver less military punch than other programs that are sacrificed in the budget process.

The advent of the cheap hawk pushed the defense budget debate beyond the old question of how much is enough and brought to the forefront the more important question of how we should spend whatever amount is available. Obviously, the nation's security is not promoted simply by spending money under the heading of defense.

Unfortunately, a great deal of the budget is eaten up by items that masquerade as defense but actually make little or no contribution to national security. Many of these spending programs are, in effect, welfare programs—not for inner-city dwellers, homeless people, or other unfortunates, but welfare nonetheless.

In contriving and delivering this pseudo-defense largesse, another common defense bird enters the picture. Though informed bird watchers all know about this one, it has yet to receive an accepted name. I propose to call it the "pork-hawk."

In Congress, the pork-hawk may appear to be a hawk, a dove, or a cheap hawk. You can't tell by the plumage or the call. You have to check its nesting habits. You can generally identify it by its tendency to lie down very close to constituents and political action committees and by its constant twittering about reelection. If you observe its behavior in the defense field, you'll find it pecking away at the tiniest details. The pork-hawk thrives on micromanaging the defense program, stipulating not only how much will be spent for certain broad defense purposes, but also how much will be spent for each of the several thousand line items in the annual defense budget and exactly how the Pentagon must manage that spending.

The A-7 Stretch-Out

The habits of the pork-hawk can be observed, for example, in the history of the A-7. This subsonic attack plane, produced by the Vought Corporation and first used in the late 1960s by both the navy and the air force for close air support, was an effective weapon in its day. By the mid-1970s, however, Pentagon planners considered it obsolescent. The navy wanted to start acquiring the F/A-18, and the air force, the F-16. In the late 1970s and early 1980s, the air national guard was the only military service that wanted any more A-7s, and even the guard wanted only the two-seat trainer.

Nevertheless, Congress continued to fund the program for years. Why? Because Dallas-based Vought, the air national guard, and the powerful Texas congressional delegation demanded it. Such a three-sided coalition is aptly described by political scientists as an "iron triangle." The Texas delegation is one of the largest and most cohesive in Congress. At the time, it included the venerable George Mahon, a Democrat, who chaired the House Defense Appropriations Subcommittee for three decades, before retiring in 1979, and Republican Senator John Tower, a senior member of the Armed Services Committee and its chairman in the early 1980s. Whereas some senators are known to favor one weapon or another, one service or another, Tower was said simply to "favor Texas" (Liske and Rundquist,

1974, pp. 39–47, 76, 87). Of course, the Texans always claimed that the A-7 still had substantial military value.

The purity of the coalition's motives was put to a test in the House of Representatives in July 1981. Representative Toby Moffett (D-Conn.) offered an amendment to the authorization bill that would switch funds from A-7s to more modern F-16s for the air national guard. The beauty of the proposal was that the guard would get its planes, better ones at that; it would get more planes, because thirteen F-16s, coming from a big production run, could be purchased for the same price as twelve A-7s from a small production run; and to top it off, the F-16 was also manufactured in Texas.

It was a deal that no one could refuse—unless, of course, the real issue was the fortunes of Vought and its congressional allies. Sure enough, the Texas delegation opposed the amendment, concerned that keeping Vought going had more political value than giving a bit more business to General Dynamics, which produced the F-16 at a Texas plant. Vought's friends in Congress were joined by the guard, which was intent on fulfilling its plans for acquiring the A-7K two-seat trainer. (Several sources, including Defense Secretary Harold Brown, alleged that the guard wanted the A-7Ks because its commanders were too old to fly high-performance aircraft by themselves [U.S. House of Representatives, Defense Appropriations Subcommittee, 1980, p. 585]). Moffett's amendment went down on a vote of 148–268.

Without doubt, the A-7s that were funded in fiscal years 1978–81 resulted from congressional micromanagement. (Arguably, many of the planes bought earlier also sprang from this source.) Altogether, the Pentagon got fifty-six aircraft that it did not want—twenty-four A-7Es for the navy and thirty-two A-7Ks for the air national guard (Keller, 1981, pp. 1280–1).

Many defense commentators tend to dismiss such congressional micromanagement as "small potatoes." They admit that many members of Congress, especially the chairmen and the senior members of key defense and appropriations committees, make their little grabs and carry the loot back to the home folks to buy votes. These experts believe, however, that the real action, the truly massive waste and mismanagement in the defense budget, lies elsewhere—in the millions that Litton Industries overcharged the Pentagon for military electronics products, for example, or in the several billion dollars required to fix the poorly performing B-1 bomber.

Yet, the A-7s procured by the pork-hawks cost the taxpayers hundreds of millions of dollars. Although it is difficult to identify the costs specifically attributable to adding the fifty-six unwanted planes to the inventory, it appears, from scattered information presented by the services to congressional committees, that the total cost was approximately *$575* million—equivalent to nearly three times that much in 2006 dollars. Because those aircraft crowded out more effective weapons, their net contribution to the nation's military might was actually *negative*. One can hardly say that such waste is small potatoes.

The Rise of Congressional Defense Micromanagement

Congressional micromanagement of the defense program, on the increase since the early 1970s, burgeoned in the 1980s. Within Congress, its sources included growing committee rivalries, fragmented power, and proliferating staff. The momentous shifts of the political landscape associated with the Vietnam War and the Watergate scandal added impetus to the growth of micromanagement. By diminishing the prestige of the military establishment and the executive office of the president, those forces gave rise to a more assertive and resourceful legislative branch. In the new environment, the pork-hawk soared.

Congressional micromanagement reveals itself in various forms. One is the requirement that the Pentagon take specific actions. Once, for example, Congress ordered the Department of Defense (DoD) to double its purchases from minority suppliers during the next year. On another occasion, Congress dictated how many European-made subsystems to include in the U.S. version of the Roland missile—not less than 350. At various times, Congress prohibited the Pentagon from developing a second source for M-1 tank engines, ordered the air force to maintain air transport that it didn't want at McChord Air Force Base, and banned the army's proposed relocation of helicopter maintenance from Pennsylvania to Texas. In several different years, it directed the DoD to purchase 300,000 tons of expensive anthracite coal—produced in Pennsylvania—for shipment to bases in Europe (Higgs, 1988, pp. 79–106). The variety of such actions makes them impossible to summarize, but without doubt, they increased tremendously. In 1970, Congress required eighty-two specific actions; in 1976, 304; and in 1987, 807.[1]

An even more important development than specific mandates was Congress's mounting compulsion to adjust the line items of the defense budget—such as appropriating funds for the fifty-six A-7s that the Pentagon didn't want. Again, 1970 provides a base year for comparison. In that year, Congress made 830 adds or cuts to line items in authorization and appropriations acts. By 1976, the number had climbed to 1,254, and in 1987, Congress micromanaged 3,422 line items.[2]

This form of congressional involvement in the details of the defense budget doesn't just add to spending. It can also undermine effective management at the DoD, the armed forces, and the contractors. Interconnected parts of the budget are thrown out of proper relation to one another. For example, Congress directs the Pentagon to buy additional M-1 tanks, but not more of the support vehicles that are needed to operate them; or additional aircraft carriers, but not more of the naval aircraft that use them. It slashes the ammunition budget in order to buy more guns. It stretches out the planned purchases of F-14s, and therefore Grumman's production lines are no longer used at an optimal rate. Such juggling of the budget makes effective planning nearly impossible.

Although most of the micromanagement takes place in the armed services committees and the defense appropriations subcommittees, activity on the floor of the House and the Senate also escalated. Before 1969, the House usually considered only a handful of amendments to the authorization bill, and the Senate, none at all. By 1985, each house was considering more than a hundred amendments and spending more than a week debating the bill. Many of the amendments were position-taking actions on broad policy matters, such as nuclear weapons or arms control, but a look at the legislative history of the authorization bill for any recent year reveals that many of the amendments amount to pure micromanagement.

The pork-hawk flies over the entire defense field, including research and development and the procurement of major weapons systems. However, even if we look only at pork barreling in the "soft underbelly"—the construction, operations, and maintenance accounts—huge amounts of spending are at stake and up for congressional grabs.

Former Senator Barry Goldwater (R-Ariz.), one of the few recent members of Congress to speak frankly, was not afraid to take aim at the pork-hawk. He was uncommonly well informed about the military, and shortly after his retirement from the Senate in 1987, he wrote an article for *Armed Forces Journal International* blasting Congress for promoting "instability, inefficiency, delay, and confusion." He pointed to "the increasing number of legislators who want to play 'pork barrel' politics with the defense budget," and he warned that "their patronage appetites continue to grow" ("Overdose of Oversight and Lawless Legislating," 1987, pp. 54, 56).

Even Senator Goldwater, however, had an ambiguous record. His role in another pork-hawk case illustrates that ambiguity.

The A-10 Stretch-Out

The story of the A-10, another subsonic attack plane, resembles the story of the A-7 in important respects. After buying some 700 A-10s in the late 1970s and early 1980s, the air force decided that acquiring more of them was less important than purchasing other weapons, especially F-16s, which were adaptable to the same close air support mission, but capable of effective battlefield air interdiction as well. Of course, people with a stake in continued production of the A-10 fought to keep it going. The large New York delegation and its powerful committee heads—Democrat Joseph Addabbo, Chairman of the House Defense Appropriations Subcommittee from 1979 to 1986, and Democrat Samuel Stratton, Chairman of the House Armed Services Committee's Subcommittee on Procurement—intervened to stretch out the procurement program. It was, observed journalist Hedrick Smith, "a case study in protecting pork for the home folks" (Smith, 1988, p. 178).

Addabbo, who represented a Queens district, was certainly no hawk, but he was manifestly a pork-hawk. Although he opposed many programs pushed by the Pentagon, he invariably promoted military installations and contractors, especially Grumman and Fairchild, located in or near his district. A *New York Times* reporter described him as "a champion of Long Island military projects" and fellow congressman George J. Hochbrueckner, also a Democrat, praised Addabbo as "the big savior of Long Island" (Markoff, 1988). When Hedrick Smith questioned Addabbo about the apparent inconsistency of his dovishness and his support for military pork-barrel projects, he shrugged and responded, "Why not build them in your own area, the same as everyone else does?"[3]

For a while, Goldwater, a senior member of the Armed Services Committee, gave the A-10 strong support, but in 1982, he abruptly turned against further acquisitions. Addressing air force witnesses at a hearing, he made an extraordinary statement. "I know what you are up against," he told the generals. "You have the parochial problem of Massachusetts, New York, Pennsylvania, and Maryland, all wanting to keep that A-10 going just like they bought A-7s to keep Texas happy." Goldwater, however, now thought that the time had come to just say no. "I know most of you [in the air force] think you don't need them, but you come over here to tell us you do need them just to keep some people [in Congress] happy" (U.S. Senate, Armed Services Committee, 1982, pp. 2594–6).

Ultimately, Goldwater did use his influence to shut down the A-10 line, which received no procurement funding after 1982, despite the determined efforts of the New Yorkers and their allies, but the A-10 program staggered to its demise in a way that reflected credit on no one.

Through 1980, the program was defensible. It allocated resources to an important and neglected military mission. It was, in defense analyst Richard Stubbing's words, "a rare managerial success—coming in close to cost and performing as well as promised" (Stubbing, 1986, p. 142).

The trouble arose when the plane approached the end of its planned production run. Members of Congress and contractors tried to prolong its life, and the stretch-out began. Unit costs soared. In 1980, the air force procured 144 planes for about $6.3 million each. The next year, when procurement fell to sixty planes, the cost jumped to $8.7 million per plane. By 1982, the Pentagon was down to twenty planes, each one costing $10.5 million. Only a modest fraction of the cost escalation reflected inflation. Had the friends of the A-10 succeeded in spending the $357 million appropriated, but, owing in large part to Goldwater's opposition, not authorized in fiscal 1983, the unit cost would have been almost $18 million—for an airplane that a committee of military men believed could be replaced with a better attack plane that could be produced for less than $3 million.

Although the administration's budgetary shifts and the gamesmanship of the air force contributed to the debacle, certain members of Congress deserve much of the blame. Addabbo, Republican Senator Alfonse D'Amato, and others in the New York coalition hardly bothered to conceal their attempt to turn the A-10 into a pure make-work program, but Goldwater's actions also raise questions. In 1982, he was remarkably frank about the parochialism involved in prolonging acquisitions, but his own behavior had been erratic, swinging from emphatic support in 1981 to ridicule in 1983—a switch that lacked a compelling military rationale and seemed capricious.

The T-46 Debacle

Whatever else one might say about the A-7 and A-10 programs, the planes did have some military utility. The same could not be said about the T-46 trainer aircraft program, which consumed several hundred million dollars and then sank in an ignominious denouement that featured contractor incompetence and congressional parochialism. After the T-46's supporters had taken extraordinary measures to salvage the program even though it was manifestly not worth saving, a congressional compromise finally terminated it. Altogether, the T-46 line had brought forth only two prototypes and a single production-model aircraft.

Did the termination signify that lawmakers had spared the taxpayers some wasteful military spending? Not exactly, because the fix was itself a monument to congressional parochialism. The cure was only a little better than the disease.

The air force awarded the T-46 development contract to Fairchild in 1982, but the program never really got going. In 1985, air force examiners found that approximately 40 percent of the hardware was defective, and company inspectors were passing 24 percent of the defective items. Fairchild's costs were running 80 percent above budget, and the project had fallen behind schedule. The examiners rated the company unsatisfactory in all eight areas of management and contract compliance that they checked *(Congressional Record* 132 [October 17, 1986], pp. S16589, S16597; "Fairchild Tightens Procedures Following Air Force Review," 1985, pp. 18–19).

The air force expressed its displeasure by halving its progress payments to Fairchild and by asking Cessna how much the company would charge to upgrade the existing trainer fleet of T-37s. Under increasing pressure to restrain spending, the air force recommended that the T-46 be dropped from the service's five-year budget plan or, alternatively, that the program be switched to another contractor. Congressional friends of the T-46 swung into action.

Not surprisingly, its chief proponents were the New Yorkers, especially Representative Thomas Downey, a Democrat, whose district included Fairchild's plant on Long Island, where various military projects were winding down and thereby threatening to wipe out "the vast majority of the 3600 jobs"—and a corresponding number of votes? *(Congressional Record* 132 [October 17, 1986], p. S16602; Smith, 1988, p. 178; "New York Legislators Ask for Fairchild Reprieve," 1985, p. 18; *Power in Congress,* 1987, p. 71). Production of the T-46 would provide continued employment.

Downey exemplified the dove as pork-hawk. Like his colleague Addabbo, he often opposed the Pentagon's favored projects, but he never failed to support military programs promising jobs and income for his constituents. A paradigmatic "casework congressman," Downey was willing to ignore the national interest and to forget his ideology when it clashed with the demands of politically active constituents. Although the T-46 eventually went down, it went down with Downey fighting for it all the way.

On October 16, 1986, congressional conflict over the T-46 program came to a remarkable climax in the Senate. The coalition there included the two New York senators, the two Maryland senators (Fairchild had a facility at Hagerstown, Maryland), and Democratic Senator Dennis DeConcini of Arizona, where the Garrett Corporation was to build T-46 engines. Besides these five, each of whom had a transparent parochial interest in preserving the troubled trainer, only a handful of senators supported keeping the program alive. A few can often prevail, however, especially in the Senate, where the rules allow even a single member to perform miracles of obstruction that induce others to fall into line. Leading the opposition to the T-46 were Senator Goldwater and Senator Robert Dole, acting on this occasion as the senator from (Wichita-based) Cessna.

Goldwater fired the first shot, offering an amendment to prohibit spending money for the T-46 either from funds previously appropriated but withheld by the air force or from funds under debate for 1987. Opponents let loose a procedural barrage. The amendment also faced the impatience of senators who had no particular interest in it but just wanted to pass a spending resolution. The latest of four stopgap funding resolutions that had carried the government into the 1987 fiscal year would expire at midnight, and unless new appropriations were made, the government would have to shut down all nonessential activities and send its employees home.

In a last-ditch effort to save the T-46, Senator D'Amato, New York Democratic Senator Patrick Moynihan, and Senator DeConcini waged a filibuster lasting almost twenty-four hours, and the government did shut down. Federal workers were sent home on October 17 (Wehr, 1986, pp. 2584–5). It was estimated, at the time, that such shutdowns cost the government—that is, the taxpayers—some $60 million a day.

Finally, the staffs in the cloakroom arrived at a compromise. It provided that no 1987 money be spent on the T-46 and that the previously appropriated funds could be drawn on to pay for a "fly-off" in which the T-46, the T-37, and any other suitable trainers would compete for the air force's contract (*Congressional Record* 132 [October 17, 1986], p. S16603). This gave the T-46 a faint hope of survival.

The air force subsequently appealed to Congress to release it from the fly-off requirement. Staging such a competition made no sense when the service no longer planned to procure a new generation of trainers in the next five years. In March 1987, the air force and Fairchild announced that they had reached an agreement whereby the service would cap its payments to the company at $159 million, approximately what had been paid already, and Fairchild would terminate its T-46 line. To cut its losses, Fairchild would close the Long Island plant. "A very black day for Long Island" lamented Downey, "a human tragedy of the first order" (Carrington, 1986; Goodman 1987, p. 56; May 1987, pp. 1, 39).

In the spring of 1987, the Senate did release the air force from the obligation to conduct the fly-off, and this action survived in the final defense bill for 1988–89. The pork-hawks had extracted a price for their agreement, however: A total of $300 million, previously appropriated but not spent, for the T-46 was reallocated to navy aircraft programs—the EA-6B, the A-6, and the E-2C—all the business of the Grumman Corporation on Long Island. As a House source told *Armed Forces Journal International,* "The New York delegation is not concerned about the competition. What they were concerned about is what happened to the [T-46] money" (Ganley, 1987, p. 8).

What should we make of the T-46 story? The program was stopped, a lot of money was saved, and the air force was rescued from acquiring an airplane that it did not want. Still, several hundred million dollars went down the drain, including the costs of the government shutdown when the T-46 coalition's filibuster held up passage of a funding act for the entire federal government. In the end, $300 million was reallocated from air force to navy aircraft in a fashion that, from a military standpoint, can only be called arbitrary and capricious.

Of course, the reallocation made perfect political sense, which is precisely the point. The whole story illustrates how different and conflicting are the dictates of congressional politics and the dictates of a sensible, economical national defense program.

It's Treachery, but Nobody Minds

Wise men say that complaining about Congress is as futile as complaining about the weather. For as long as anyone can remember, members of Congress have been plundering the public to finance the largesse that they trade for reelection. By now, they have nearly perfected their system, as almost all incumbents who seek reelection are reelected, especially in the House. We are talking about a ruling class that approximates a self-perpetuating group about as closely as one can imagine in a democracy. So, perhaps nothing can be done about the mismanagement and waste that attend congressional micromanagement of the defense program.

Some commentators have gone so far as to argue that we should be happy with the system as it is. After all, the guns do shoot some of the time. We do enjoy some national security. Moreover, given the institutional realities, it is impossible to imagine a reform that would improve on the existing system, because the reformers would face the same incentives and constraints that got us where we are now. Reforms could only make the situation worse (Lee, 1990, pp. 22–36). Maybe the pessimists are right. Their arguments are certainly weighty. My hunch, however, is that a slight chance exists to alleviate the ills associated with congressional micromanagement of defense.

A necessary condition for pork-barrel defense procurement is acceptance—by members of Congress and by the informed public—of what amounts to treachery. Members of Congress, with only a few exceptions, routinely betray the public's trust. In pursuit of their very private interest in reelection, they sell out the national defense of the United States. They know that they are doing it; their colleagues know that they are doing it; and the public, if it pays any attention at all, knows that they are doing it. Yet, everyone accepts it.

When opinion leaders, and hence the public, start to view these acts of treachery as acts of treachery rather than as politics as usual, the incentives will change for members of Congress. They are sensitive to public opinion;

they will not continue to act as they do when people view their actions as intolerably reprehensible and treat the guilty parties accordingly.

What I am contemplating would amount to ideological change on a fairly wide scale, so it is hardly likely, but ideological changes have occurred in the past, and they may occur again. Until they do, however, Congress will go on micromanaging the defense program for parochial purposes, and the resulting waste will continue. Doves and hawks will coo and shriek, while the pork-hawks bring home the bacon at taxpayer expense.

Notes

1. Figures for 1970 and 1976 from U.S. General Accounting Office (1986); figures for 1987 from James M. Lindsay (1988, p. 61).
2. Figures from Department of Defense, Office of the Controller, as printed in Lindsay (1988, p. 61).
3. Addabbo, as quoted in Smith, Hedrick (1988), p. 179.

References

Carrington, Tim. (1986) Air Force Renews Campaign to Scrap Fairchild Industries' T-46 Trainer Jet. *Wall Street Journal* December 10.

Congressional Record (1986) 132 (October 17).

Fairchild Tightens Procedures Following Air Force Review. (1985) *Aviation Week and Space Technology* (September 9): 18–19.

Ganley, Michael. (1987) Congress Appears Close to Reversing Its Call for a USAF Trainer Competition. *Armed Forces Journal International* (July): 8.

Goldwater, Barry. (1987) Overdose of Oversight and Lawless Legislating. *Armed Forces Journal International* (February): 54, 56.

Goodman, Glenn W., Jr. (1987) Wide Open USAF Trainer Competition Likely if Service Recalcitrance Blunted. *Armed Forces Journal International* (January): 56.

Higgs, Robert. (1988) Hard Coals Make Bad Law: Congressional Parochialism versus National Defense. *Cato Journal* 8 (Spring/Summer): 79–106.

Keller, Bill. Reagan, Like Previous Presidents, Fails To Cut Guard's A-7 Jet Fighter. (1981) *Congressional Quarterly Weekly Report* 39 (July 18): 1280–1.

Lee, Dwight R. (1990) Public Goods, Politics, and Two Cheers for the Military-Industrial Complex. In *Arms, Politics, and the Economy: Historical and Contemporary Perspectives,* edited by Robert Higgs. New York: Holmes & Meier, pp. 22–36.

Lindsay, James M. (1988) Congress and the Defense Budget. *Washington Quarterly* (Winter): 57–74.

Liske, Craig, and Barry Rundquist. (1974) *The Politics of Weapons Procurement.* Denver: University of Denver.

Markoff, John. (1988) Long Island Inquiry Widens in Arms Purchases. *New York Times* July 17.

May, Clifford D. (1987) 2,500 to Lose Jobs in L.I. Plant as U.S. Ends Jet Contract. Fairchild Republic to Shut by End of Year After Halt in Air Force T-46 Work. *New York Times* March 14, pp. 1, 39.

New York Legislators Ask for Fairchild Reprieve. (1985) *Aviation Week and Space Technology* September 9, p. 18.

Power in Congress, edited by Tracy White. (1987) Washington, D.C.: Congressional Quarterly.

Smith, Hedrick. (1988) *The Power Game: How Washington Works.* New York: Random House.

Stubbing, Richard A. with Richard A. Mendel. (1986) *The Defense Game: An Insider Explores the Astonishing Realities of America's Defense Establishment.* New York: Harper & Row.

U.S. General Accounting Office. (1986) Legislative Oversight: Congressional Requests for Information on Defense Activities. GAO/NSIAD-86–65BR, February, Appendix III.

U.S. House of Representatives, Defense Appropriations Subcommittee. (1980) *Hearings on Department of Defense Appropriations for Fiscal Year 1981,* Pt. 1.

U.S. Senate, Armed Services Committee. (1982) *Hearings on Authorization for Department of Defense Appropriations for Fiscal Year 1983,* Pt. 4.

Wehr, Elizabeth. (1986) Congress Clears $576 Billion Spending Measure. *Congressional Quarterly Weekly Report* 44 (October 18): 2584–5.

9

Profits of U.S. Defense Contractors
Ruben Trevino & Robert Higgs

DO BIG DEFENSE CONTRACTORS earn greater returns than other companies? The question has long been controversial, and despite numerous studies, the issue has remained unsettled (Gansler, 1989, pp. 253–4; Rogerson, 1989, pp. 1290–1). Most of the studies have been made by interested parties—the armed services or the Department of Defense. Some of the studies fail to meet professional standards; others are patently tendentious.[1] But even the studies published in professional journals disagree widely.[2]

The disagreement is hardly surprising, because the various studies are not comparable. They have considered different groups of firms and different periods, and they have employed different measures of profitability.

There are two basic types of profitability measure: accounting rate of return and stock market rate of return. Most previous studies have examined some variant of the accounting rate of return. In this case, one calculates net income (annual revenues minus annual costs) as a percentage of a book value of capital invested. Return on investment (ROI) and return on assets (ROA), which we define later, are the most common measures of this type, although reports of return on equity or some other accounting measure are not uncommon.

Unfortunately, various problems associated with accounting data, such as differences between book values and market values, render accounting measures of profitability highly suspect. In the view of some analysts (Fisher and McGowan, 1983), accounting rates of return are virtually worthless as indexes of economic profitability, in any event. Studies comparing returns for the defense business and the commercial business *within* firms have had to contend with additional intractable accounting problems: attribution of common costs to the different portions of a firm's operations, as noted by Willis Greer and Shu Liao (1986, p. 1261), and "certain [intrafirm] external-ities of defense business," as noted by Douglas Bohi (1973, pp. 722–3).

One study, by George Stigler and Claire Friedland (1971), sidestepped these accounting complications and considered a large group of leading defense contractors over an extended period. Stigler and Friedland's approach was to compute the total market rate of return (MRET) to investors owning stock in the firms (that is, annual dividends paid to shareholders plus stock price appreciation, the sum being divided by the initial value of the stock and the quotient expressed as a percentage). Note that whereas accounting rates of return, such as ROI and ROA, are measures of the prof-itability of the firm, MRET is a measure of profitability to the shareholder of the firm. There is no necessary relation between the accounting returns and the market returns in a particular year. Consider, for example, a firm that had an extraordinarily large ROI in 1980. If investors in 1979 had ex-pected that impending profitability, they would have bid up the price of the stock in anticipation, and as a result, the MRET of shareholders would have increased for 1979, but not for 1980.

Stigler and Friedland calculated shareholders' MRET for a set of top defense contracting companies and compared this return over two pe-riods, 1948–61 and 1958–68, with the comparable return to investors in all companies listed on the New York Stock Exchange. They found that during the first period, the defense firms outperformed the market by a large margin, and during the second period, the difference was negative or positive, depending on whether the investor held stock in the defense firms that were ranked high in defense contracting as of the beginning of the period or in the defense firms that were ranked high in defense contracting as of the end of the period.

Controversy over the profitability of defense contractors has continued to flare from time to time, but no one has updated the Stigler-Friedland study for the 1970s and 1980s. To do so is our principal objective in this chapter. For completeness, we also present findings for two accounting measures of firm profitability, ROI and ROA, which are often discussed, notwithstanding their potential flaws, in the literature of business and defense economics. Like Stigler and Friedland, however, we focused our analysis on the stock market rates of return. We also evaluated whether relatively greater firm dependence on defense was associated with greater stock market returns to investors and whether the risks borne by defense investors differed from those borne by investors in other companies. Finally, we computed the cumulative market return to investors in leading defense firms over a long period and compared it with the cumulative return to investors in the overall stock market.

Companies Analyzed and Data

For each fiscal year, the Department of Defense publishes a list of the 100 companies receiving the largest dollar volume of prime contract awards. Our procedure for selecting the "top" defense contractors was to accept the rankings on this list. It should be noted that prime contract awards are not the same as income from defense sales in the same year. Prime contract awards often give rise to sales revenues stretching over a period of years. Also, many prime defense contractors receive defense dollars indirectly, by acting as subcontractors, and some defense sales are concealed in a secret "black budget." Despite these qualifications, it is not unreasonable to use the published list of prime contractors to identify the firms that tend to do the most business with the Department of Defense. Stigler and Friedland, as well as many other investigators, used this approach. Besides, no alternative ranking exists, because many companies do not ordinarily report their defense and nondefense sales separately.

To gauge the financial performance of the leading defense contractors, we employed data provided to us by Standard & Poor's Compustat for the period 1970–89. We have adjusted the data so that each company's performance is shown on a calendar-year basis, even though its fiscal year may be different. The Compustat data have some gaps, usually because firms disappeared in mergers. If gaps existed in the data for a period that we were analyzing, we reported the arithmetic average performance for the firms that remained in the specified group. Also, our analysis included only publicly traded U.S. corporations. The few top contractors that are foreign, are not publicly traded, or are not-for-profit institutions were excluded.

Findings on Financial Performance

To assess the average financial performance of the top defense companies, we present in table 9-1 our findings for companies ranked among the top fifty and the top ten prime contractors. The figures are arithmetic averages of annual values for the periods indicated. Findings for the 1970s, the 1980s, and the two decades combined, are given separately. Findings are presented for three different measures of financial performance: return on investment (ROI), return on assets (ROA), and total market return (MRET). Return on investment is defined as net after-tax income, as a percentage of the sum of long-term debt, preferred and common stock, and minority interest, all as evaluated by the accountants. Return on assets is defined as net after-tax income as a percentage of total assets, again as evaluated by the accountants. Note that, by accounting conventions, assets are valued at book values rather than market values, and any government-owned equipment or buildings used by the firm (not uncommon in the defense industry) are not counted among the firm's assets. Total market return is defined as the sum of the year's capital gain or loss (the December closing price of a company's shares minus the previous year's December closing price) and the year's dividends per share, divided by the previous year's December closing price of the shares, with the quotient being multiplied by 100 to express a percentage rate of return. MRET is the annual percentage increase of the wealth of a shareholder who holds the stock for the duration of the year. We use the Standard & Poor's 500 stocks as our comparative standard, which we call the overall market, or simply, "the market."

Table 9-1. Average financial performance of top defense
contracting companies, 1970–1989

Performance period and firm group	Performance Measure (% per year)		
	ROI	ROA	MRET
1970–1979			
1969 top 50 contractors	7.71	4.99	12.56
1969 top 10 contractors	8.27	4.72	16.42
1979 top 50 contractors	8.50	5.43	14.55
1979 top 10 contractors	7.49	3.97	19.24
Standard & Poor's 500	8.23	3.93	7.33
1980–1989			
1979 top 50 contractors	9.19	4.93	17.94
1979 top 10 contractors	12.13	5.85	15.97
1989 top 50 contractors	10.20	5.45	16.27
1989 top 10 contractors	12.88	6.18	16.33
Standard & Poor's 500	7.68	3.19	17.69
1970–1989			
1979 top 50 contractors	8.85	5.18	16.24
1979 top 50 contractors (D/S > 5%)*	9.51	5.33	16.72
1979 top 10 contractors	9.81	4.91	17.60
1979 top 10 contractors (D/S > 5%)*	10.14	5.07	17.46
Standard & Poor's 500	7.96	3.56	12.51

*(D/S > 5%) denotes firms for which prime defense contract awards (average for 1981–1983)
divided by sales in 1983 exceeds 5%.

Note: ROI is the firm's average return on investment; ROA is the firm's average return on
assets; MRET is average stock market return to stockholders of the firms. For full accounting descriptions of how these rates of return are measured, see text.

Source: Computed from basic financial data supplied by Standard & Poor's Compustat, Inc.

Like Stigler and Friedland, we present two sets of findings for each
decade. Thus, one can see whether an investor, knowing only which
companies rank high in defense business at the beginning of the decade,
would have done better or worse than an investor with the foresight to

248 | *Depression, War, and Cold War*

predict which companies would rank high in defense business at the end of the decade.

In the bottom third of the table, we present comparisons for the entire period 1970–89 between the 1979 top fifty contractors as a whole and the top fifty contractors minus the firms for which prime defense contracts (1981–83 average) equaled less than 5 percent of total sales in 1983. The dates used for this division of the firms reflect the availability of data compiled for these dates by Linda Shaw, Jeffrey Knopf, and Kenneth Bertsch (1985, pp. 198–9), but the partition would surely be similar for other dates near the middle of the period, because the relative dependence of the top contractors on defense business normally changes little from year to year.

For the 1970s, the top defense contractors performed about the same as the market in terms of ROI, somewhat better than the market in terms of ROA, and much better than the market in term of MRET. On the last measure, the poorest performing contractor group in the table had 1.71 times the average annual MRET of the market, and the best performing group had 2.62 times the average annual MRET of the market. The top ten firms showed mixed results relative to the top fifty firms on ROI and ROA, but performed substantially better in terms of MRET, the difference being about 31 to 32 percent.

For the 1980s, the top defense contractors performed substantially better than the market in terms of ROI and ROA, and about equal to the market in terms of MRET. The top ten firms consistently outperformed the top fifty firms on ROI and ROA, although the differences were not great, while the two groups differed little in terms of MRET.

As the bottom third of table 9-1 shows, for the two decades combined, the top defense contractors outperformed the market substantially, by all three measures. The 1979 top fifty firms surpassed the Standard & Poor's 500 by 11 percent on ROI, 46 percent on ROA, and 30 percent on MRET. For the whole period 1970–89, the top ten firms did slightly better than the top fifty on ROI and MRET and slightly worse on ROA, but in no case was the difference greater than 11 percent. Firms with a relatively high reliance on defense business performed slightly better than the others on five of the six comparisons and slightly worse on the remaining comparison.

Stigler and Friedland reported a significant correlation (r^2 = 0.295) between MRET and the ratio of defense to total sales for top contractors in the 1950s, but no such correlation for the 1960s (r^2 = 0.00008). Our comparisons from the table for the top fifty contractors show little difference between the average annual MRET in the group with relatively high reliance on defense business (16.72) and the average annual MRET of the entire group (16.24) during the period 1970–89.

As a further, and more exacting, test of this relation, we regressed the average annual MRET (1970–89) on the ratio of defense awards (1981–83 average) to total sales (1983) for the cross-section of the 1979 top fifty contractors. Gaps in the Compustat data reduced the set of companies in this test to 40. The slope coefficient of the regression is 4.08, with a t statistic of 0.82. Thus, the data display a positive relation, but one having virtually no statistical significance (r^2 = 0.018).

Inspection of the data shows, however, that a single firm, Ling-Temco-Vought (LTV), was an extreme outlier from the estimated relation and that the empirical relation was nonlinear. If LTV is deleted from the data set and a second-degree polynomial is fitted, the result is:

$$\text{MRET} = 13.04 + 34.63 \text{ D/S} - 40.65 \text{ (D/S)}^2$$
$$(11.79) \qquad (14.78)$$
$$R^2 = 0.19, \text{ SEE} = 5.40, \text{ N} = 39$$

where D/S denotes the ratio of defense awards to sales, and the standard errors are shown in parentheses. The equation shows that there was a statistically significant nonlinear relation between the top firms' relative dependence on defense business and their total market return during the period 1970–89.

Setting the first derivative of the regression equation equal to zero and solving for D/S, one finds a maximum at 0.426. Only seven firms had D/S values of greater than 0.426, namely, Grumman (0.873), General

Dynamics (0.816), Todd Shipyards (0.676), McDonnell Douglas (0.665), Lockheed (0.522), Martin Marietta (0.476), and Sanders Associates (0.471). For the shareholders of these firms, the firms' heavy specialization in the defense sector seems to have been too much of a good thing.

Findings on Relative Risk

The finding that over a period of twenty years, investors in the top defense contractors received a far better total market return than investors in the overall market raises the suspicion that the market returns of the defense firms might have been riskier. Stigler and Friedland assessed the riskiness of the defense contractors in their study by correlating the variability of total sales over time and the defense share of sales. Finding coefficients of determination of 0.337 for 1950–57 and 0.245 for 1958–63, they concluded tentatively that investment in defense contracting companies was riskier. Stigler and Friedland did not compare the riskiness of the contractors as a group with a set of comparable nondefense firms.

To access the relative riskiness of investment in the defense contractors, we follow the now-standard approach of computing the beta coefficients of the Capital Asset Pricing Model. In this model, β, which is a measure of systematic risk (i.e., risk that cannot be diminished by diversification), is defined as the slope coefficient in a time-series regression of a firm's rate of return on the market rate of return. If a firm's returns are more (less) variable than market returns, β is greater (less) than one.

We have computed the β values of MRET for the period 1970–89. For the 1979 top fifty contractors, β is 1.25; for the 1979 top fifty firms with relatively high dependence on defense business, it is 1.27; and for the 1979 top ten contractors, it is 1.22. Although the β values all exceed unity, which may have some importance in the eyes of investors, none differs significantly from unity (the market β value, by definition) at any conventional test level: No estimate of β differs from unity by more than 1.314 times the standard error of estimate. Hence, we conclude that investors in the group of defense contractors analyzed here were not subject to significantly greater risk than investors in the overall market. No risk adjustment is necessary or justifiable in making the comparisons of MRET that we made earlier.

Differences in Cumulative Returns

For total market return, the difference between defense investments and the overall market after 1970 arose entirely from the difference during the 1970s; there was virtually no difference during the 1980s alone. From 1970 to 1989, however, an investor who maintained a portfolio of the 1979 top fifty defense firms would have increased the value of his holdings by a multiple of 14.78, versus a market multiple of 8.19 for the Standard & Poor's 500. By holding only the 1979 top fifty firms with a relatively high dependence on defense business, the investor would have done even better (16.18), and by holding only the 1979 top ten contractors with a relatively high dependence on defense business, better still (19.22).[3]

By linking the two periods studied by Stigler and Friedland, one can determine the cumulative market return to stockholders of the top defense companies over the period 1948–69. (We extended Stigler and Friedland's results one year beyond the terminal year of their study, 1968.) We linked the cumulative MRET for their 1950–57 top fifty-four defense contractors over the period 1948–61 (12.573-fold) with the cumulative MRET for their 1969 top forty-eight defense contractors over the period 1961–69 (1.981-fold). For the whole period 1948–69, the cumulative MRET equals 24.9 times the original investment for the defense investors, compared with 16.1 times the original investment for investors in the overall market as proxied (following Stigler and Friedland) by the New York Stock Exchange.

Linking the cumulative returns for Stigler and Friedland's top contractors during the period 1948–69 with the cumulative returns we have computed for the period 1970–89, one arrives at an overall cumulative multiple of defense MRET for the period 1948–89 of about 331, compared with a cumulative multiple for the overall market, which we proxy by linking the Standard & Poor's 500, of about 137. Thus, an investor who stubbornly insisted on holding a portfolio of top defense firms over this period of more than four decades would have had at the end a sum about 2.4 times larger than that of an investor of an equal initial amount who held a diversified market portfolio.

Conclusions

For the period 1970–89 as a whole, by every measure, the top defense firms outperformed the market by a huge margin. On average, the difference ranged from 11 to 27 percent for ROI, from 38 to 50 percent for ROA, and from 30 to 41 percent for MRET, depending on the specific contractor group considered. Given the potential frailties of the accounting rates of return, we have elected not to inquire deeply into the reasons for their apparent excessiveness, although the defense firms' subsidized use of government-owned capital is an obvious possible explanation, especially for the defense firms' extraordinarily high ROA (Gansler, 1980, pp. 88–9; Weida and Gertcher, 1987, pp. 140–2). The elevated MRET of defense investors, however, cannot be denied, and it cries out for an explanation.

The claim that investment in defense companies was riskier than investment in the overall market is not compelling. For the 1950s and 1960s, Stigler and Friedland found only weak evidence of risk differences among the defense contractors themselves and presented no evidence that an investor in the defense contractors as a group bore greater risk than an investor in the overall market. We found that the systematic risk, as measured by β, borne by an investor in the top contractors as a group did not differ significantly from the risk borne by an investor in the overall market during the 1970s and 1980s.

These findings establish that the financial performance of the leading defense contracting companies was, on the average, much better than that of comparable large corporations during the period 1948–89. The findings do not justify a normative conclusion that the profits of defense contractors were "too high," particularly in the case of the accounting rates of return (Fisher and McGowan, 1983). By themselves, the findings tell us nothing about why the difference existed, and our efforts (not reported here) to explain the time-series variation of differential MRET during the period 1970–89 have met with limited success. The huge discrepancy in total market return does establish, however, that defense investors, over the long term, were receiving rates of return that were far greater than those of investors in comparably risky nondefense companies. Either (a) the Capital Asset Pricing Model does not capture some relevant risk perceived by investors in defense firms or (b) investors persistently guessed wrong, leaving defense stocks undervalued over very long periods.

Notes

1. For devastating criticism of the major study by the Department of Defense, see U.S. General Accounting Office (1986).
2. See D. E. Kaun (1988, pp. 2–7) for a survey of the literature.
3. Performance of the 1989 top firms over the same long period, not reported here, was virtually identical; that of the 1969 top firms was somewhat poorer, but still much better than that of the overall market.

References

Bohi, D. R. (1973) Profit Performance in the Defense Industry. *Journal of Political Economy* 81 (3): 721–8.

Fisher, F. M., and J. J. McGowan. (1983) On the Misuse of Accounting Rates of Return to Infer Monopoly Profits. *American Economic Review* 73 (1): 82–97.

Gansler, J. S. (1980) *The Defense Industry*. Cambridge, Mass.: MIT Press.

Gansler, J. D. (1989) *Affording Defense*. Cambridge, Mass.: MIT Press.

Greer, W. R., Jr., and S. S. Liao. (1986) An Analysis of Risk and Return in the Defense Market: Its Impact on Weapon System Competition. *Management Science* 32 (10): 1259–73.

Kaun, D. E. (1988) Where Have All the Profits Gone? An Analysis of the Major U.S. Defense Contractors: 1950–1985. *Research Paper No. 4*. University of California Institute on Global Conflict and Cooperation.

Rogerson, W. P. (1989) Profit Regulation of Defense Contractors and Prizes for Innovation. *Journal of Political Economy* 97 (6): 1284–1305.

Shaw, L. S., J. W. Knopf, and K. A. Bertsch. (1985) *Stocking the Arsenal: A Guide to the Nation's Top Military Contractors.* Washington, D.C.: Investor Responsibility Research Center.

Stigler, G. J., and Friedland, C. (1971) Profits of defense contractors. *American Economic Review* 61 (4): 692–4.

U.S. Department of Defense. (1969, 1979, 1989) *100 Companies: Companies Receiving the Largest Dollar Volume of Military Prime Contract Awards.* Washington, D.C.: Directorate for Information Operations and Reports.

U.S. General Accounting Office. (1986) *Government Contracting: Assessment of the Study of Defense Contractor Profitability.* Washington, D.C.: GAO/NSIAD-87-50.

Weida, W. J., and F. L. Gertcher. (1987) *The Political Economy of National Defense.* Boulder, Colo.: Westview Press.

Acknowledgments   We thank George Stigler and Claire Friedland for sharing their data with us, and Jerry Viscione, participants in a Seattle University seminar, and the referees for comments on a previous draft.

10

Public Opinion

A Powerful Predictor of U.S. Defense Spending
Robert Higgs & Anthony Kilduff

MANY ANALYSTS HAVE TRIED to explain variations in U.S. defense spending. In a survey article, Robert E. Looney and Stephen L. Mehay (1990) listed nine types of variables believed to have had an influence. They also noted (p. 13) that "single theories have not been particularly accurate in . . . accounting for past spending patterns." Their own econometric contribution, like those of many other analysts, proceeded on the assumption that domestic economic conditions and the Soviet threat were the important variables explaining changes in military spending. They remarked (p. 33) that several other possible causal factors, including public opinion, are not subject to empirical testing because of deficiencies in the data.

Notwithstanding Looney and Mehay's observations, many empirical studies in political science have assessed the connection between public opinion and defense spending.[1] Although the political scientists who have studied public opinion have usually concluded that it has played a part in determining the size of the defense budget, they have not defined the public opinion variable operationally in a manner that exploits all of the information contained in the responses to public opinion surveys. Some analysts have used as an operational variable *either* the percentage of poll respondents favoring increased defense spending or the percentage favoring decreased defense spending (Kriesberg and Klein, 1980; Russett, 1989; Russett, 1990). Others have lost much of the information contained in the survey responses by transforming them into dichotomous variables (Ostrom, 1978; Ostrom and Marra, 1986).

The research findings that we report here show that with a simple statistical model, one can explain a high proportion of the variance of the annual rate of change of U.S. defense outlays from the mid-1960s through the 1980s. Public opinion can be measured in a way that exploits all of the genuine information in the polls, and a single public opinion variable, with several lags and a proper control, is the only one required for an accurate prediction of annual changes in defense outlays. When this statistical explanation is considered in light of information about how the defense budget process operates, it suggests that defense spending was influenced by the effect of public opinion on both the executive branch and Congress. Notwithstanding the close relationship between public opinion and defense budget decision-making, however, we argue that it would be unwarranted to conclude—à la simple democratic theory—that defense spending policy was simply a case in which "the public got what it wanted."

Measuring Public Opinion

Political scientists and political sociologists have long employed public opinion survey data with sophistication to analyze attitudes, opinions, and ideologies (Bennett, 1980; McClosky and Zaller, 1984; Page and Shapiro, 1992). Defense economists occasionally cite such data (Stubbing, 1986, p. 13; Weida and Gertcher, 1987, p. 78), and one economist has attempted to use the data in estimating demand functions for defense (Hewitt, 1986, p. 480). We shall exploit public opinion data in a new way.

From various published sources and from data supplied to us by the Roper Center for Public Opinion Research and by researchers Thomas Graham and Thomas Hartley at Yale University, we have compiled a total of 193 comparable national surveys, taken from 1949 to 1989, regarding opinion about defense spending.[2] We have used the survey information only if the question put to the respondents allowed them the alternatives "spend more" and "spend less" and was specifically about spending, not about whether the armed forces should be enlarged, whether the nation's defense is adequate, or other matters not *explicitly* about spending. Although the questions vary slightly in wording, we have used only those that seem identical in substance and devoid of cues that might bias the response (e.g., introductory statements referring to "the president's plan" or calling attention to the federal deficit). Typical wording is: "There is much discussion as to the amount of money the government in Washington should spend for national defense and military purposes. How do you feel about this? Do you think we are spending too little, too much, or about the right amount?" (Gallup poll, July 1969).

Altogether, 24 different polling organizations generated the evidence that we analyzed, although most of the data came from the large, well-known polling organizations (Gallup, Harris, Roper, NBC, CBS, ABC, and the National Opinion Research Center). All of the polling organizations appear to use similar methods and to produce results with similar degrees of sampling reliability, typically with standard deviations of about 2 percent. Between 1953 and 1965, there were several years without a survey asking a comparable question about defense spending. Because our statistical methods required a continuous series of data, we did not analyze the pre-1965 data. From 1965 onward, there was at least one usable survey each year; after 1970, there were at least three per year, and often ten or more. When multiple surveys were available, we collapsed the results into a single number by simply averaging. Altogether, the time series on public opinion analyzed here contains information from 181 national surveys.

From the surveys, we have constructed a variable that compresses two responses into one. Our procedure creates an "opinion balance" variable (OPBAL) by subtracting the percentage of respondents favoring less defense spending from the percentage favoring more. For example, if 30 percent of the respondents favor more and 20 percent favor less, the opinion balance has a value of plus 10. In this way, we compress into a single variable all of the survey response information related to the public's preferences for a *change* in defense spending.

Notice, however, that the opinion balance variable alone does not capture all of the information in the surveys that is potentially of interest to policymakers. Obviously, particular values of opinion balance can arise in many different ways (e.g., 20 − 10 = 10; 33 − 23 = 10; 51 − 41 = 10). Given a particular level of opinion balance, the "residuum" (OPRES), which contains all those who either favor the existing level of spending or express no opinion, can be a greater or smaller percentage of all respondents. We do not think it serves any purpose to distinguish the two components of the residuum. Many of those who express a preference for the existing level of spending surely do so because they have little information about, or interest in, the matter; hence, in reality, they do not differ from those who explicitly respond with "no opinion."[3] In any event, whether a respondent actively prefers the existing level of spending or has no opinion, the effect on policy decisions (if any) is the same—preservation of the status quo. However, the effect (if any) of a particular opinion balance can be presumed to vary with the size of the associated residuum: The greater the residuum, the smaller the effect of a given opinion (im)balance on spending decisions, because the residuum encourages policymakers to maintain the status quo.

In statistical models, one can deal with the problem of the residuum simply by including it as a variable, along with the opinion balance variable, in the regression equations. OPRES then serves as a control variable that allows one to interpret the effect of variations of OPBAL in a straightforward manner. OPRES itself has no a priori relation to the rate of change of defense spending; hence, we advise against attempts to interpret the sign or statistical significance of its estimated regression coefficient.

What Happened?

Figure 10-1 shows how the opinion balance (OPBAL) moved from 1965 to 1989. During the first three years of the Vietnam War, the opinion balance remained positive, although it declined by 18 points between 1966 and 1967. The year 1968 witnessed the peak of U.S. engagement in the war as well as the Tet offensive, which occurred early in the year and transformed many former supporters of the war into opponents (Russett and Graham, 1989, p. 252; Matusow, 1984, p. 391; Page and Shapiro, 1992, pp. 56–7, 232–4).[4] In 1968, the opinion balance plummeted 38 points, to reach minus 33. During the next two years, it fell to even lower levels,

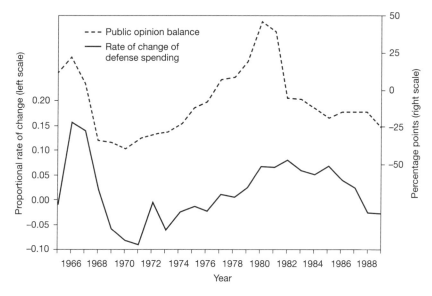

Figure 10-1. Rate of change of real defense spending (left scale)
and public opinion balance, in percent (right scale).

with a trough of minus 39 in 1970. (Of course, given the sampling variance, changes of a few points cannot bear much weight.) After 1970, the
opinion balance began to increase monotonically, slowly at first, and then
more rapidly during the late 1970s. It first achieved a positive value (+7.5) in
1977. At its peak, in 1980, the opinion balance stood at 46.7. It then fell for
five years, with a huge drop of more than 45 percentage points in a single
year, 1982—surely no statistical artifact.[5] From 1986 to 1988, the balance remained virtually unchanged at about minus 15, roughly where it had been
back in 1975, before falling another 10 points in 1989. Scanning the series,
one gathers the distinct impression of cyclical change, with a peak in 1966,
a trough around 1970, steady increase toward another peak in 1980, and
then a quick decline to a low plateau in the second half of the 1980s.[6]

Our defense spending variable is real national defense purchases of
goods and services, as measured in the national income and product accounts (U.S. Council of Economic Advisers, 1991, p. 287). This standard
measure of defense spending, which is calculated on a calendar-year basis, does not include military pensions, purchases of previously produced

assets, or other transfer payments. Because the deflator constructed by the Commerce Department for defense expenditures is problematic in several respects (Weida and Gertcher, 1987, p. 63; Smith, 1989, pp. 350–1), we used the gross national product deflator to reduce the nominal spending figures to constant 1982 dollars (U.S. Council of Economic Advisers, 1991, p. 290). This deflator is actually more appropriate, in any event, if one thinks of defense spending in terms of its societal opportunity costs, that is, as necessarily entailing sacrifices of generalized national product.

In part because the *level* of real defense spending was highly autocorrelated during the years under investigation ($r = 0.91$ for the one-year lag; $r = 0.76$ for the two-year lag), for statistical modeling we employ a transformation, namely, the annual proportional rate of change (OUTLAY GROWTH). Employing this transformation also makes sense theoretically, because it allows us to examine empirically the exact relation at issue, that is, the relation between the *intensity of the public's preference for change* in defense spending and the *actual rate of change*.

The OUTLAY GROWTH series, shown in figure 10-1, also gives one an impression of cyclical movement, although the pattern is not quite as smooth as that of the opinion balance. After reaching the Vietnam War peak in calendar year 1968, real military outlays began to fall. During the next eight years, the annual rate of change varied but remained negative in every year. (Note that the small local growth-rate peak in 1972 was at least partly spurious, reflecting the stringent price controls in effect throughout the year, which caused the reported gross national product deflator to rise by less than the actual rate of inflation, much of which was concealed in 1972 and then revealed in 1973. Correction of the data for this mismeasurement, which is beyond the scope of this chapter, would produce a smoother change of our series between 1971 and 1974.) Between 1973 and 1982, OUTLAY GROWTH rose haltingly but substantially, reaching a peak of 8.4 percent in 1982. It then diminished, finally becoming negative in 1988 and 1989.

Scanning figure 10-1, one suspects that the two series might have some relation. During the period 1969–76, the opinion balance was always negative, as was the annual change of real defense spending. In 1977, when the opinion balance first became positive again, real defense spending increased for the first time since 1968. In 1979 and 1980, both series increased, and in the latter year, the opinion balance reached a maximum. After 1981, however, the opinion balance plummeted, becoming negative again in 1982. The rate of change of defense outlays did not begin its descent until after 1982, and did not become negative until 1988. All in all, there seems to be a connection here, but without a more systematic analysis, one has no way to know whether a causal relation existed and, if so, in which direction it ran.

Predictive Antecedence

An obvious statistical technique for examining these questions is Granger causality testing (Freeman, 1983; Kinsella, 1990). Although econometricians have concluded that this technique alone cannot establish the presence of causality in the substantive sense—that is, exogeneity in a structural model[7]—it can be used to *refute* claims of exogeneity. To apply a formula stated by Thomas Sargent to the present case, there will exist an equation expressing OUTLAY GROWTH as a one-sided distributed lag of OPBAL, with OPBAL strictly exogenous if, and only if, OUTLAY GROWTH fails to Granger cause OPBAL.[8] So, the *absence* of Granger causation tells us something, while the *presence* of Granger causation is merely suggestive. Following David Kinsella (1990, p. 300), we employ Granger causality testing only as "an appropriate first step in structural modeling . . . when theoretically derived restrictions are lacking or when equally persuasive but opposing causal arguments need assessing." (John Freeman [1983, p. 329] also views Granger causality testing as only a useful first step in model-building.) If the Granger test indicates predictive antecedence in one direction but not the other, then further testing is appropriate, with the postulated exogeneity as indicated by the Granger causality tests.

Contributors to the literature have considered the possibility that the causal relation between public opinion and defense spending might run in either direction (Russett and Graham, 1989, pp. 241–3; Hartley and

Russett, 1992). To test for Granger causality running from opinion to spending, we estimated the parameters of an equation in which the rate of change of defense outlays (OUTLAY GROWTH) was regressed on itself lagged once, twice, three times, and four times, as well as on correspondingly lagged OPBAL and OPRES.[9] We then tested the hypothesis that the coefficients of lagged OPBAL are jointly zero—that is, there is no Granger causation running from opinion to the growth rate of spending. We also performed a similar test for Granger causality running from the rate of change of defense spending to the public opinion balance. This test differs in the number of lags employed.[10] The estimated equation also includes the contemporaneous value of OUTLAY GROWTH as well as lagged values.[11]

The two tests yielded different results. In the equation estimated to identify Granger causality running from the rate of change of defense spending to the public opinion balance, the null hypothesis—no Granger causality—cannot be rejected at any customary level of type I error ($F[2,15]$ = 2.14; p = 0.151). In contrast, the result of the test for Granger causality running from the opinion balance to the rate of growth of defense spending is consistent with rejection of the null hypothesis at a level of type I error just over 8 percent ($F[4.8]$ = 3.07; p = 0.083).

Employing Sargent's formula again, we conclude from these tests that there probably does exist an equation expressing OUTLAY GROWTH as a one-sided distributed lag of OPBAL with OPBAL strictly exogenous, because the test results indicate that OUTLAY GROWTH probably did not Granger cause OPBAL, but—at a fairly high level of confidence— OPBAL did Granger cause OUTLAY GROWTH. However, Granger causality testing cannot take us beyond this limited conclusion.

The Structure of Causation

Because of the nature of the hypothesis tests associated with the Granger technique (i.e., tests that the coefficients are jointly zero), one cannot identify *which* lagged value of OPBAL might have been associated, and *how much*, with changes in the rate of change of real defense spending.

To answer these questions, we have estimated several variants of equations in which the dependent variable is OUTLAY GROWTH and the explanatory variable is OPBAL with one or more lags (and each OPBAL with its corresponding lagged OPRES). Three of these estimated equations appear in table 10-1.[12]

Table 10-1. Regression estimates of the relation between the rate of change of real defense spending and the public opinion balance, 1965–1989

Variable	Equation 1	Equation 2	Equation 3
Constant	−0.0743	−0.0474	0.0620
	(−1.4285)	(−0.8490)	(0.8042)
OPBAL(−1)	0.0023		0.0011
	(6.1895)		(2.5592)
OPBAL(−2)		0.0018	0.0013
		(4.6229)	(2.1171)
OPBAL(−3)			−0.0002
			(−0.3877)
OPBAL(−4)			0.0003
			(0.6683)
OPRES(−1)	0.0024		0.0008
	(2.0934)		(0.8812)
OPRES(−2)		0.0016	0.0009
		(1.2815)	(1.1234)
OPRES(−3)			0.0010
			(1.1097)
OPRES(−4)			−0.0035
			(−4.4165)
R^2	0.649	0.518	0.889
Adjusted R^2	0.616	0.470	0.815
SEE	0.040	0.042	0.023
D-W	1.204	1.514	1.554
F	19.447	10.471	11.997
Years predicted	66–89	67–89	69–89

Note: For variables OPBAL(i) and OPRES(i), *i* is the number of years the variable is lagged. Parenthetical numbers beneath the regression coefficients are Student's *t* statistics.

The most remarkable aspect of the results is that these simple equations explain a high proportion of the variance of the dependent variable.[13] Using only OPBAL(–1)—that is, one-year-lagged OPBAL (along with the corresponding OPRES)—one accounts for 65 percent of the variance. Using just OPBAL(–2) instead (along with the corresponding OPRES), one obtains a somewhat lower R^2 but still explains more than half of the variance. With four lags of OPBAL entered simultaneously (along with corresponding OPRES variables), one can account for a high proportion of the variance $(R^2 = 0.89)$. To achieve such a high degree of statistical explanation of the *rate of change* of defense spending by using only a single explanatory variable (along with its control) is extraordinary. After all, analysts have attributed changes in defense spending to a large number of variables (Looney and Mehay, 1990; Schneider, 1988). Although our findings, by themselves, do not necessarily refute any claims regarding the causality of other variables, they demonstrate that one can, with considerable precision, account for changes in defense spending from the mid-1960s through the 1980s with reference to public opinion data alone. What are we to make of this remarkable finding?

Interpretation

Defense spending in a particular year is the final outcome of a sequence of actions by various institutionally situated actors, who act with greater or lesser influence at various stages of the budget process. The actual change in defense outlays from calendar year $t-1$ to calendar year t reflects mainly the appropriations legislation enacted by Congress late in calendar year $t-1$, which sets expenditures for fiscal year t. The detailed budget proposals presented to Congress by the president in January of year $t-1$ were composed within the executive branch during the course of year $t-2$. Even earlier, armed forces personnel were making plans, with an eye to the future budgetary requirements of research and development for new weapons systems, procurement of existing weapons, changes in force levels and troop deployments, and many other aspects of managing the military establishment.[14]

Our findings indicate that public opinion in both years $t-1$ and $t-2$ affected, more or less equally, the rate of change of real defense outlays in year t. This finding would seem to show that public opinion influenced both the executive branch, as it composed its future budget requests during year $t-2$, and Congress, as it reacted to the proposals, generally cutting the requested amount of funding, to some extent, during year $t-1$. But one ought to be skeptical of such a simple view of the process. The mere fact of congressional cuts of presidential requests during year $t-1$, for example, is insufficient to establish that the estimated effect of public opinion during that year reflects solely a *congressional* response to public preferences *at that time.* Nor is the existence of a two-year-lagged effect necessarily indicative of simply an *executive branch* response to public preferences *at that time (t − 2)*.

At no time were decisions by one branch of government independent of what was being sought by the other. In reality, the executive branch normally entered into a political arrangement with Congress, whereby each side could better achieve its important aims. The armed forces got the resources they wanted most urgently, and Congress got political credit for slashing a "bloated" defense request. Building "cut insurance" into the president's request was the key to this deal. As described by Richard Stubbing (1986, pp. 96–97), a veteran defense analyst for the Office of Management and Budget, the process worked as follows:

> [E]ach year the executive branch anticipates the congressional need to lower defense spending and therefore includes in its request extra funds for removal by the Congress. . . . [I]n the back rooms DoD and congressional staff are working out mutually acceptable lists of reductions which will cause little or no damage to the program DoD really wants to pursue. These "cut insurance" funds can then be slashed from the defense-budget request by the Congress, permitting members to demonstrate their fiscal toughness to their constituents without harming the defense program. Almost all the

so-called "cuts" are simply deferred to the next year's budget, and the overall total is never cut below the minimum level acceptable to the military leadership.

Similarly, the president's proposal normally omits or underfunds certain items (e.g., equipment for the reserves and national guard). The executive branch makes its proposals with full awareness that Congress will "add on" funding for these items and then take political credit for the supplements with the ostensibly favored constituents.

It would be unwarranted, however, to interpret our findings simply as follows. Indirectly, the mass public decides how the defense budget will be changed, by expressing its preferences to the pollsters. The executive branch, with some preliminary congressional input and provision for "cut insurance," responds to the polls as it crafts the proposals that it will present to Congress the following January. Afterward, both Congress and the executive branch, jointly responding to the more recent polls, make the mutual (and partly spurious) adjustments that immediately precede the autumn enactment of appropriations legislation. This view, though an improvement over the usual depiction, is nonetheless still unacceptable, because it takes the public's opinions themselves to be autonomous or spontaneous.

Such autonomy is implausible. In the extreme opposite case, as described by Russett and Graham (1989, p. 257), "policymakers might first form a new opinion and then persuade opinion leaders in the media, who in turn persuade the mass public so that, finally, the very people in government who initiated the change can then 'respond' to public opinion."[15] In countless ways, the president and other leading political figures, including those in charge at the Pentagon, try to sway public opinion. One may argue about the extent to which, and the conditions under which, they *succeed* in molding public opinion. There is substantial evidence, however, that their efforts often have some effect (Ginsberg, 1986; Page and Shapiro, 1992). Hence, one cannot view public opinion as independent of the desires of the very officials toward whom the public's preferences for governmental actions are directed.

Although surprising at first, the finding that public opinion alone is a powerful predictor of changes in defense spending seems, on reflection, exactly what one ought to have expected. Despite how defense (and other) analysts normally conceive of public opinion—as one element in a long list of commensurable influences (Looney and Mehay, 1990; Schneider, 1988)—public opinion actually stands conceptually on a plane by itself. It is a different kind of variable. Public opinion expresses people's preferences regarding policy action. Other "causes" that are normally advanced by analysts (domestic economic conditions, perceived foreign threats, and so forth) do not *directly* determine changes in defense spending; rather, they determine what decision makers and the public *prefer* with regard to changes in defense spending. Once public opinion has revealed itself in the polls (or in other ways), government officials, especially those immediately concerned with reelection, face a constraint. They must either act in accordance with public opinion or bear the political risk inherent in deviating from it.

There is, however, a way to loosen the constraint. Politicians who, for whatever reason, do not want to act in accordance with public opinion can argue their case. They can try to mold as well as merely react to public opinion. Clearly, a contest for the determination of public opinion goes on ceaselessly, becoming especially active or noticeable from time to time. This contest is at the very heart of the political process. Although certain facts, such as the government deficit or the rate of inflation, cannot be denied, many other "facts," such as the detailed military capabilities and intentions of potential adversaries, are known—if, indeed, they are known at all—only to members of the national security elite.[16] Given their capacity to control access to important information, defense leaders and insiders have disproportionate ability to mold public opinion. They can also exploit their positions of authority to try to change the meaning or weight that the public attaches to known, indisputable facts. Clearly, however, their power is far from absolute, as shown the large fluctuations of public opinion, and particularly its movement, at times, in a direction obviously disfavored by the national security elite.[17]

Once public opinion has been deflected as much as possible by defense policymakers, whether in Congress or the executive branch, they have substantial incentives to match their defense spending decisions more or less closely with the public's ultimate preference—hence, the close association reported here. We emphasize, however, that important aspects of the defense budget process are: (1) the status of public opinion as a single proximate cause, incorporating and expressing a variety of more remote determinants of spending decisions, and (2) the ceaseless contest among rival interests, within as well as outside the government, to move public opinion in a desired direction.

Conclusion

Public opinion survey responses regarding the desirability of changes in defense spending can be compressed into a single variable, the public opinion balance, which, when accompanied by a control variable measuring the proportion of responses in the "residuum" (no opinion or keep the status quo), permits an accurate prediction of subsequent changes in the rate of change of defense outlays from the mid-1960s through the 1980s. In a model with four lags of OPBAL, 89 percent of the variance in OUTLAY GROWTH can be statistically explained. Public opinion lagged one year and public opinion lagged two years had roughly the same influence.

One is not justified, however, in regarding public opinion as entirely autonomous or spontaneous. There occurs a ceaseless contest over the determination of public opinion, and in this contest, defense policymakers, whose preferences may differ from those of the mass public, occupy a powerful position. Hence, even after finding a strong association between OUTLAY GROWTH and lagged OPBAL, we remain uncertain of the extent to which public opinion about defense spending was independent of the desires of government officials and, therefore, may be viewed as an important autonomous determinant of spending decisions.

Future modelers and interpreters of defense spending would do well to take into account this more complex and realistic view of defense budget policymaking.

Notes

1. Ostrom (1978), Ostrom and Marra (1986), Kriesberg and Klein (1980), Russett (1989), Russett (1990), Russett and Graham (1989), Hartley and Russett (1992), Bishop (1987), and other studies cited in these sources.

2. The authors will provide on request a list of the raw data and their sources.

3. Bishop (1987, p. 229) reports that a status quo option "usually attract[s] a substantial number of people who may be ambivalent about the other alternatives presented to them" Hartley and Russett (1992, p. 907) remark that "with the problem conceptualized in terms of change, those with no current interest could either fail to express an opinion or simply support the status quo."

4. Page and Shapiro (1992, p. 233) describe the "Tet-induced drop in the proportion of hawks" as "one of the largest, most abrupt opinion changes" ever measured by opinion surveys.

5. Inspection of the individual surveys shows that the collapse of the opinion balance began well before the end of 1981. Unfortunately, seven of the nine usable polls in 1981 took place during the first four months of the year.

6. The appendix gives the complete series for OPBAL and OPRES.

7. Learner, as quoted in Baek (1991, p. 252).

8. Sargent, as quoted in Freeman (1983, p. 329).

9. For OUTLAY GROWTH, four lags are optimal in that they minimize Akaike's final prediction error (FPE) criterion. Given four lags of OUTLAY GROWTH, Akaike's FPE tends to decline as more lags of OPBAL and OPRES are employed, up to six lags. We cannot use so many lags, however, given our small sample size and the consequent scarcity of degrees of freedom. The use of four lags of OPBAL and OPRES is a reasonable compromise.

10. For OPBAL and OPRES, Akaike's FPE is minimized by the use of two lags. Given two lags of OPBAL and OPRES, the use of one lag of OUTLAY GROWTH minimizes the FPE.

11. Conceivably, the current rate of change of defense outlays could influence current public opinion concerning the desired rate of change of defense outlays. However, it is quite unlikely that the current public opinion balance could affect the current rate of change of defense outlays, because the latter has been largely predetermined by policymakers during previous years.

12. To test the sensitivity of the estimates to the sample period 1965–89, each of the equations in table 10-1 was estimated for a sample period without the first three years (i.e., 1968–89) and for a sample period without the last three years (i.e., 1965–86). The results are essentially the same as those reported in table 10-1.

13. Because the correlogram of autocorrelation and partial autocorrelations suggests the possibility of a first-order autoregressive error, we also made estimates using the Cochran-Orcutt technique. The results are broadly similar to the OLS results in table 10-1.

14. For a description and analysis of the defense budget process, see Stubbing (1986, pp. 55–105) and Weida and Gertcher (1987, pp. 10–14, 56–61).

15. For an extended argument that something akin to this course of events has become the rule rather than the exception in the politics of modern liberal democracies, see Ginsberg (1986).

16. This restriction of knowledge was especially the case during the Cold War era, when the Soviet Union was an isolated, tightly controlled society, with a very secretive government.

17. For example, in 1987, Secretary of Defense Caspar Weinberger complained that "new weapons can be developed by our adversaries . . . much more rapidly because [in the USSR] there are no funding restraints imposed by public opinion" (Weinberger, 1987, p. 16). For extended discussion of the molding of public opinion by the authorities and the limits of such actions, see Page and Shapiro (1992).

References

Baek, E. G. (1991) Defence Spending and Economic Performance in the United States: Some Structural VAR Evidence. *Defence Economics* 2 (3): 251–64.

Bennett, W. L. (1980) *Public Opinion in American Politics.* New York: Harcourt Brace Jovanovich.

Bishop, G. F. (1987) Experiments with the Middle Response Alternative in Survey Questions. *Public Opinion Quarterly* 51 (2): 220–32.

Freeman, J. R. (1983) Granger Causality and the Time Series Analysis of Political Relationships. *American Journal of Political Science* 27 (2): 327–58.

Ginsberg, B. (1986) *The Captive Public: How Mass Opinion Promotes State Power.* New York: Basic Books.

Hartley, T., and B. Russett. (1992) Public Opinion and the Common Defense: Who Governs Military Spending in the United States? *American Political Science Review* 86 (4): 905–15.

Hewitt, D. (1986) Fiscal Illusion from Grants and the Level of State and Federal Expenditures. *National Tax Journal* 39 (4): 471–83.

Kinsella, D. (1990) Defence Spending and Economic Performance in the United States: A Causal Analysis. *Defence Economics* 1 (4): 295–309.

Kriesberg, L., and R. Klein. (1980) Changes in Public Support for U.S. Military Spending. *Journal of Conflict Resolution* 24 (1): 79–111.

Looney, R. E., and S. L. Mehay. (1990) United States Defence Expenditures: Trends and Analysis. In *The Economics of Defence Spending: An International Survey,* edited by K. Hartley and T. Sandier. London: Routledge, pp. 13–40.

Matusow, A. J. (1984) *The Unraveling of America: A History of Liberalism in the 1960s.* New York: Harper & Row.

McClosky, H., and J. Zaller. (1984) *The American Ethos: Public Attitudes toward Capitalism and Democracy.* Cambridge, Mass.: Harvard University Press.

Ostrom, C. W., Jr. (1978) A Reactive Linkage Model of the U.S. Defense Expenditure Policymaking Process. *American Political Science Review* 72 (3): 941–57.

Ostrom, C. W., Jr., and R. F. Marra. (1986) U.S. Defense Spending and the Soviet Estimate. *American Political Science Review* 80 (3): 819–42.

Page, B. I., and R. Y. Shapiro. (1992) *The Rational Public: Fifty Years of Trends in Americans' Policy Preferences.* Chicago: University of Chicago Press.

Russett, B. (1989) Democracy, Public Opinion, and Nuclear Weapons. In *Behavior, Society, and Nuclear War,* edited by P. Tetlock et al. New York: Oxford University Press, pp. 174–208.

Russett, B. (1990) *Controlling the Sword: The Democratic Governance of National Security.* Cambridge, Mass.: Harvard University Press.

Russett, B., and T. W. Graham. (1989) Public Opinion and National Security Policy: Relationships and Impacts. In *Handbook of War Studies,* edited by M. I. Midlarsky. Boston: Unwin Hyman, pp. 239–57.

Schneider, E. (1988) Causal Factors in Variations in US Postwar Defense Spending. *Defense Analysis* 4 (1): 53–79.

Smith, R. P. (1989) Models of Military Expenditure. *Journal of Applied Econometrics* 4 (4): 345–59.

Stubbing, R. A. (1986) *The Defense Game: An Insider Explores the Astonishing Realities of America's Defense Establishment.* New York: Harper & Row.

U.S. Council of Economic Advisers. (1991) *Annual Report.* Washington, D.C.: U.S. Government Printing Office.

Weida, W. J., and F. L. Gertcher. (1987) *The Political Economy of National Defense.* Boulder, Colo.: Westview Press.

Weinberger, C. W. (1987) *Report of the Secretary of Defense Casper W. Weinberger to the Congress.* Washington, D.C.: U.S. Government Printing Office.

Appendix

Indexes of Opinion Balance (OPBAL)
and the Residuum (OPRES)

Year	OPBAL	OPRES
1965	12.00	56.00
1966	23.00	51.00
1967	5.00	51.00
1968	−33.00	27.00
1969	−35.00	44.34
1970	−39.00	41.00
1971	−32.50	44.00
1972	−29.34	50.00
1973	−27.80	48.20
1974	−22.85	48.57
1975	−12.33	46.33
1976	−7.00	47.28
1977	7.50	49.50
1978	8.71	48.43
1979	19.40	40.20
1980	46.69	27.31
1981	40.45	30.89
1982	−5.07	45.89
1983	−5.33	40.93
1984	−11.90	46.30
1985	−18.46	46.20
1986	−14.50	44.22
1987	−15.06	45.94
1988	−14.70	52.50
1989	−25.09	47.27

Sources

GRATEFUL ACKNOWLEDGMENT is made to the following for permission to reprint copyrighted materials, each of which is here in revised form.

"Regime Uncertainty" from the Spring 1997 (Vol. 1, No. 4) issue of *The Independent Review: A Journal of Political Economy*, Copyright © 1997, The Independent Institute.

"Private Profit, Public Risk" from *The Sinews of War: Essays on the Economic History of World War II*, edited by Geofrey T. Mills and Hugh Rockoff. Copyright © 1993, Iowa State University Press.

"Wartime Prosperity?" from the March 1992 (Vol. 52, No. 1) issue of *The Journal of Economic History*, Cambridge University Press. Copyright © 1992, The Economic History Association.

"Wartime Socialization of Investment" from the June 2004 (Vol. 64, No. 2) issue of *The Journal of Economic History*, Cambridge University Press. Copyright © 2004, The Economic History Association.

"From Central Planning to the Market" from the September 1999 (Vol. 59, No. 3) issue of *The Journal of Economic History*, Cambridge University Press. Copyright © 1999, The Economic History Association.

"The Cold War Economy" from the July 1994 issue of *Explorations in Economic History*. Copyright © 1994, Academic Press.

"Hard Coals Make Bad Law" from the Spring/Summer 1988 issue of the *Cato Journal*, Copyright © 1988, Cato Institute, 1000 Massachusetts Avenue, N.W., Washington, D.C., 20001.

"Airplanes the Pentagon Didn't Want, but Congress Did" from the June 1989 (Vol. 21, No. 2) issue of *Reason*. Copyright © 1989, The Reason Foundation.

"Profits of U.S. Defense Contractors" from the 1992 (Vol. 3) issue of *Defence Economics*. Copyright © 1992, Harwood Academic Publishers GmbH.

"Public Opinion" from the 1993 (Vol. 4) issue of *Defence Economics*. Copyright © 1993, Harwood Academic Publishers GmbH.

Index

regime uncertainty and funding for, 41–42,
46–47, 48*t*
relative price since WWII, 155*n*5
Murtha, Jack, 211

N

National Coal Association, 215
National Defense Act (1920), 42
National Defense Advisory Council (NDAC),
44–45, 57–58, 67
national defense expenditures
black budget for, 182
Carter–Reagan buildup, 168, 171–72, 178,
190*n*17
for Cold War buildup, 165–68, 166*f*
consumer opinions of, 184–86, 186*f*, 188*n*2,
192*n*42
decline in, 1968–1976 timespan, 183–85
defense spending variable, 259
deflators for, 189*n*10
for filling "gaps" in American defense
capabilities, 180–81, 187–88
GNP and GNP* considerations, 175–76,
176*f*, 177*f*, 187
as "necessary regrettable," 174–75
overview, 161–62, 188*n*4, 229–30
percentage of GNP, 183–85
public opinion about, xv, 186*f*, 190*n*20,
192*n*43, 255–56, 258–61
purchase of intermediate goods, 85–86
relationship to public opinion, 255–56, 258–61
wartime allocation of resources versus market
prices, 87–88, 112–13, 120, 126*n*5, 153–54,
157*n*21, 172, 174–75
national defense expenditures, congressional
micromanagement of
A-7 subsonic attack plane, 230–31
A-10 subsonic attack plane, 234–36
anthracite purchase requirements, 216, 219
congressional floor amendments to defense
authorization bills, 224*n*33
national security funds for bringing home
the bacon, 198–99
overview, 232–34
pork barrel politics, 198–99, 203–4, 213–20,
229–30, 232–34, 240–41
pork-hawk politics, 229–30, 237–39

T-46 trainer aircraft program, 236–39
See also anthracite mining industry
National Emergencies Act (1999), 168
National Income and Product Accounts (NIPA)
data, xi, 105–15 *passim*, 162–64, 188*n*4, 259–60
National Labor Relations Act, 16
National Product in Wartime (Kuznets), 83, 120
National Resources Planning Board, 16
national security
as political byproduct, 203
pork-hawk masquerade, 229–30
as value from defense, 173–75
National Security Act (1947), 181
National Security Council (NSC), 182
National Survey of Liquid Assets, 156*n*14
NDAC (National Defense Advisory Council),
44–45, 57–58, 67
"necessary regrettable," 174–75
negotiated contracts, 38, 47–49
Nelson, Donald, 44, 48–49, 52
Neutrality Acts, 41–42
New Deal policies
executive branch reorganization and, 16–17
genuine prosperity versus, ix
and Great Depression, ix, 30–31
and labor organizations, 16
versus private property rights, 11–14, 12*t*, 31
pro-business replacement of, 4
Reconstruction Finance Corp., 59
revival of private investment versus, 8
Second New Deal, 8, 28, 30–31, 153–54,
157*n*26
of Truman, 24–25
wartime policies versus, 21–22
New York congressional delegation and
continued funding of a useless planes,
230–31, 237–39
New York Times, 235
NIPA (National Income and Product Accounts)
data, xii, 105–15 *passim*, 162–64, 188*n*4,
259–60
Nixon, Richard M., 165–68, 185–86
Nordhaus, William, 86, 174
Novick, David, 100*n*19
NSC (National Security Council), 182
NSC–68, 165, 189*n*7
nuclear experiments, 182–83

About the Author

ROBERT HIGGS is Senior Fellow in Political Economy for The Independent Institute and Editor of the Institute's quarterly journal *The Independent Review.* He received his Ph.D. in economics from Johns Hopkins University, and he has taught at the University of Washington, Lafayette College, Seattle University, and the University of Economics, Prague. He has been a visiting scholar at Oxford University and Stanford University.

He is the recipient of numerous awards, including the Gary Schlarbaum Award for Lifetime Defense of Liberty, Thomas Szasz Award for Outstanding Contributions to the Cause of Civil Liberties, Friedrich von Wieser Memorial Prize for Excellence in Economic Education, and Templeton Honor Rolls Award on Education in a Free Society.

Dr. Higgs has spoken at more than 100 colleges and universities and at the meetings of such professional organizations as the Economic History Association, Population Association of America, International Economic History Congress, Public Choice Society, International Studies Association, Allied Social Sciences Association, American Political Science Association, American Historical Association, and others. A contributor to numerous scholarly volumes, he is the author of more than 100 articles and reviews in academic journals and hundreds of articles in newspapers and on the web.

Dr. Higgs is the author of:

Against Leviathan: Government Power and a Free Society
Competition and Coercion: Blacks in the American Economy, 1865–1914
Crisis and Leviathan: Critical Episodes in the Growth of American Government
Neither Liberty Nor Safety: Fear, Ideology, and the Growth of Government
Politická ekonomie strachu (*The Political Economy of Fear*, in Czech)
Resurgence of the Warfare State: The Crisis Since 9/11
Transformation of the American Economy 1865–1914

Dr. Higgs is the editor of:

Arms, Politics, and the Economy: Historical and Contemporary Perspectives
Emergence of the Modern Political Economy
Hazardous to Our Health?: FDA Regulations of Health Care Products
Opposing the Crusader State: Alternatives to Global Interventionism (with Carl Close)
Re-Thinking Green: Alternatives to Environmental Bureaucracy (with Carl Close)
The Challenge of Liberty: Classical Liberalism Today (with Carl Close)

INDEPENDENT STUDIES IN POLITICAL ECONOMY

THE ACADEMY IN CRISIS: The Political Economy of Higher Education | *Ed. by John W. Sommer*

AGAINST LEVIATHAN: Government Power and a Free Society | *Robert Higgs*

ALIENATION AND THE SOVIET ECONOMY: The Collapse of the Socialist Era | *Paul Craig Roberts*

AMERICAN HEALTH CARE: Government, Market Processes and the Public Interest | *Ed. by Roger Feldman*

ANARCHY AND THE LAW: The Political Economy of Choice | *Ed. by Edward P. Stringham*

ANTITRUST AND MONOPOLY: Anatomy of a Policy Failure | *D. T. Armentano*

ARMS, POLITICS, AND THE ECONOMY: Historical and Contemporary Perspectives | *Ed. by Robert Higgs*

BEYOND POLITICS: Markets, Welfare, and the Failure of Bureaucracy | *William Mitchell & Randy Simmons*

THE CAPITALIST REVOLUTION IN LATIN AMERICA | *Paul Craig Roberts & Karen Araujo*

THE CHALLENGE OF LIBERTY: Classical Liberalism Today | *Ed. by Robert Higgs & Carl P. Close*

CHANGING THE GUARD: Private Prisons and the Control of Crime | *Ed. by Alexander Tabarrok*

THE CHE GUEVARA MYTH AND THE FUTURE OF LIBERTY | *Alvaro Vargas Llosa*

CUTTING GREEN TAPE: Toxic Pollutants, Environmental Regulation and the Law | *Ed. by Richard Stroup & Roger E. Meiners*

THE DECLINE OF AMERICAN LIBERALISM | *Arthur A. Ekrich, Jr.*

DEPRESSION, WAR, AND COLD WAR: Challenging the Myths of Conflict and Prosperity | *Robert Higgs*

THE DIVERSITY MYTH: Multiculturalism and Political Intolerance on Campus | *David O. Sacks & Peter A. Thiel*

DRUG WAR CRIMES: The Consequences of Prohibition | *Jeffrey A. Miron*

ELECTRIC CHOICES: Deregulation and the Future of Electric Power | *Ed. by Andrew Kleit*

THE EMPIRE HAS NO CLOTHES: U.S. Foreign Policy Exposed | *Ivan Eland*

ENTREPRENEURIAL ECONOMICS: Bright Ideas from the Dismal Science | *Ed. by Alexander Tabarrok*

FAULTY TOWERS: Tenure and the Structure of Higher Education | *Ryan Amacher & Roger Meiners*

THE FOUNDERS' SECOND AMENDMENT: Origins of the Right to Bear Arms | *Stephen P. Halbrook*

FREEDOM, FEMINISM, AND THE STATE | *Ed. by Wendy McElroy*

GOOD MONEY: Private Enterprise and the Foundation of Modern Coinage | *George Selgin*

HAZARDOUS TO OUR HEALTH?: FDA Regulation of Health Care Products | *Ed. by Robert Higgs*

HOT TALK, COLD SCIENCE: Global Warming's Unfinished Debate | *S. Fred Singer*

JUDGE AND JURY: American Tort Law on Trial | *Eric Helland & Alex Tabarrok*

LESSONS FROM THE POOR: Triumph of the Entrepreneurial Spirit | *Ed. by Alvaro Vargas Llosa*

LIBERTY FOR LATIN AMERICA: How to Undo Five Hundred Years of State Oppression | *Alvaro Vargas Llosa*

LIBERTY FOR WOMEN: Freedom and Feminism in the Twenty-first Century | *Ed. by Wendy McElroy*

MAKING POOR NATIONS RICH: Entrepreneurship and the Process of Economic Development | *Ed. by Benjamin Powell*

MARKET FAILURE OR SUCCESS: The New Debate | *Ed. by Tyler Cowen & Eric Crampton*

MONEY AND THE NATION STATE: The Financial Revolution, Government, and the World Monetary System | *Ed. by Kevin Dowd & Richard H. Timberlake, Jr.*

NEITHER LIBERTY NOR SAFETY: Fear, Ideology, and the Growth of Government | *Robert Higgs & Carl P. Close*

OPPOSING THE CRUSADER STATE: Alternatives to Global Interventionism | *Ed. by Robert Higg & Carl P. Close*

OUT OF WORK: Unemployment and Government in Twentieth-Century America | *Richard K. Vedder & Lowell E. Gallaway*

PARTITIONING FOR PEACE: An Exit Strategy for Iraq | *Ivan Eland*

PLOWSHARES AND PORK BARRELS: The Political Economy of Agriculture | *E. C. Pasour, Jr. & Randal R. Rucker*

A POVERTY OF REASON: Sustainable Development and Economic Growth | *Wilfred Beckerman*

PRIVATE RIGHTS & PUBLIC ILLUSIONS | *Tibor R. Machan*

RACE & LIBERTY IN AMERICA: The Essential Reader | *Ed. by Jonathan Bean*

RECARVING RUSHMORE: Ranking the Presidents on Peace, Prosperity, and Liberty | *Ivan Eland*

RECLAIMING THE AMERICAN REVOLUTION: The Kentucky & Virginia Resolutions and Their Legacy | *William J. Watkins, Jr.*

REGULATION AND THE REAGAN ERA: Politics, Bureaucracy and the Public Interest | *Ed. by Roger Meiners & Bruce Yandle*

RESTORING FREE SPEECH AND LIBERTY ON CAMPUS | *Donald A. Downs*

RESURGENCE OF THE WARFARE STATE: The Crisis Since 9/11 | *Robert Higgs*

RE-THINKING GREEN: Alternatives to Environmental Bureaucracy | *Ed. by Robert Higgs & Carl P. Close*

SCHOOL CHOICES: True and False | *John Merrifield*

STRANGE BREW: Alcohol and Government Monopoly | *Douglas Glen Whitman*

STREET SMART: Competition, Entrepreneurship, and the Future of Roads | *Ed. by Gabriel Roth*

TAXING CHOICE: The Predatory Politics of Fiscal Discrimination | *Ed. by William F. Shughart, II*

TAXING ENERGY: Oil Severance Taxation and the Economy | *Robert Deacon, Stephen DeCanio, H. E. Frech, III, & M. Bruce Johnson*

THAT EVERY MAN BE ARMED: The Evolution of a Constitutional Right | *Stephen P. Halbrook*

TO SERVE AND PROTECT: Privatization and Community in Criminal Justice | *Bruce L. Benson*

THE VOLUNTARY CITY: Choice, Community, and Civil Society | *Ed. by David T. Beito, Peter Gordon & Alexander Tabarrok*

TWILIGHT WAR: The Folly of U.S. Space Dominance | *Mike Moore*

VIETNAM RISING: Culture and Change in Asia's Tiger Cub | *William Ratliff*

WINNERS, LOSERS & MICROSOFT: Competition and Antitrust in High Technology | *Stan J. Liebowitz & Stephen E. Margolis*

WRITING OFF IDEAS: Taxation, Foundations, and Philanthropy in America | *Randall G. Holcombe*